Contemporary Psychoanalytic Approaches to Early Childhood Education

Critical Childhood & Youth Studies: Theoretical Explorations and Practices in Clinical, Educational, Social, and Cultural Settings

Series Editors: Awad Ibrahim, Gabrielle Ivinson, Michael O'Loughlin, and Marek Tesar

Mission Statement

Critical Childhood & Youth Studies is a scholarly series that is concerned with understanding the lived experiences of children and youth in economic, social, cultural, political and historical contexts, and addresses complex experiences only knowable through multidisciplinary lenses. The series seeks to address the following core questions: How do notions of childhood & youth differ across time and space? What new theories and methodologies can we employ to enhance our understanding and wellbeing of young people? What position and meaning is attributed to children and childhoods in/across different societies, and what are the public and political discussions concerning children's general position in society? Is agency possible, or must children live in states of exception? What can it mean to theorize the conditions and processes through which children and young people embody a meaningful existence in light of the histories they inherit?

Advisory Board

Jennifer Adair, Sonja Arndt, Marianne (Mimi) Bloch, Gail Boldt, Steven Bruhm, Erica Burman, Hannah Dyer, Giorgia Dona, Lisa Farley, Joanne Faulkner, Peggy Froerer, Lise Paulsen Galal, Madeleine Grumet, Janette Habashi, Lucia Hodgson, Richard Johnson, Julie Kaomea, Helen May, Zsuzsanna Millei, Leigh O'Brien, Carol Owens, Lacey Peters, Valerie Polakow, Elizabeth Quintero, Jenny Ritchie, Richard Ruth, Paula Salvio, Shilpi Sinha, Margaret Somerville, Kathryn Bond Stockton, Joseph Tobin, Mathias Urban, Honey Oberoi Vahali, Joseph Valente, Dan Woodman, and Handel Wright.

Books in Series

Contemporary Psychoanalytic Approaches to Early Childhood Education Edited by
   Alex Collopy
Refusing the Limits of Contemporary Childhood: Beyond Innocence Edited by
   Julie C. Garlen & Neil T. Ramjewan
*Precarities of 21st Century Childhoods: Critical Explorations of Time(s), Place(s), and
   Identities* Edited by Michael O'Loughlin, Carol Owens, and Louis Rothschild
Critiquing Social and Emotional Learning: Psychodynamic and Cultural Perspectives by
   Clio Stearns

Contemporary Psychoanalytic Approaches to Early Childhood Education

Edited by Alex Collopy

LEXINGTON BOOKS

Lanham • Boulder • New York • London

Lexington Books
Bloomsbury Publishing Inc, 1385 Broadway, New York, NY 10018, USA
Bloomsbury Publishing Plc, 50 Bedford Square, London, WC1B 3DP, UK
Bloomsbury Publishing Ireland, 29 Earlsfort Terrace, Dublin 2, D02 AY28, Ireland
www.rowman.com

British Library Cataloguing in Publication information available

Library of Congress Cataloging-in-Publication Data

Names: Collopy, Alex, 1992- editor.
Title: Contemporary psychoanalytic approaches to early childhood education / edited by
    Alex Collopy.
Description: Lanham : Lexington Books, [2025] | Series: Critical childhood
    & youth studies: theoretical explorations and practices in clinical,
    educational, social, and cultural settings | Includes bibliographical
    references and index.
Identifiers: LCCN 2024045937 (print) | LCCN 2024045938 (ebook) |
    ISBN 9781666964646 (cloth) | ISBN 9781666964653 (epub)
Subjects: LCSH: Early childhood education—Psychological aspects.
Classification: LCC LB1139.23 .C6585 2025 (print) | LCC LB1139.23 (ebook)
    | DDC 372.2101/9—dc23/eng/20241106
LC record available at https://lccn.loc.gov/2024045937
LC ebook record available at https://lccn.loc.gov/2024045938

For product safety related questions contact productsafety@bloomsbury.com.

∞™ The paper used in this publication meets the minimum requirements of American
National Standard for Information Sciences—Permanence of Paper for Printed Library
Materials, ANSI/NISO Z39.48-1992.

Contents

Introduction   1
Alex Collopy

PART I: PSYCHOANALYTIC APPROACHES TO
UNDERSTANDING CHILDREN AND CHILDHOOD   21

1   Psychoanalytic Temporality: From Chronology to Duration in
    the Making of Childhood History   23
    Lisa Farley

2   Contemporary Gender(s): Reconsidering Freudian,
    Postfoundational, and Psychoanalytic Perspectives for
    Educators and Practitioners   45
    Janice Kroeger, Christopher Konieczko, Dana Oleskiewicz,
    Alexandra C. Gunn, and Andrea Sanchez

3   "Reading Is Cheating!": Children with Learning Disabilities
    and Their Need to Communicate   73
    Ionas Sapountzis

4   Projective Identification at Work in the Psychological
    Assessment of Children   89
    Greta Carlson

PART II: PSYCHOANALYTIC APPROACHES TO EARLY
CHILDHOOD EDUCATION SETTINGS   107

5   Is There a Place for Psychoanalytic Theory in the Classroom?   109
    Michael Trout

6 Winnicott Comes to School: Using Transitional Objects in
Classroom Life   127
Lesley Koplow

7 The Narcissism of Curriculum: The Importance of Listening to
Children   141
Eileen Johnson

8 Psychotherapeutic Practices Are for Everyone   159
Alex Collopy

9 The Essential Role of Play in Early Childhood Education   173
Joanna Fortune

**PART III: PSYCHOANALYTIC APPROACHES TO EARLY
CHILDHOOD TEACHER EDUCATION**   **189**

10 A Case for Early Childhood Teacher Education Informed by
Psychic Genera   191
Clio Stearns

11 Work Group Discussions in Teacher Education: Evoking
Associative Objects   209
H. James Garrett

12 Our First Foray into Work Discussion Groups with a
University Laboratory School   223
Alex Collopy, Kailey Price, Lydia Bingham, and Carley Rader

Appendix: Trauma-Informed Healing-Centered Practice: Teddy
Bears in Traumatic Times (Fall 2021): The Center for Emotionally
Responsive Practice at Bank Street   245
Lesley Koplow

Index   249

About the Editor and Contributors   255

Introduction

Alex Collopy

You need not look far in popular news articles, academic scholarship, university classrooms, or public discourse for the question "Is Psychoanalysis Dead?" and no further for an answer "Yes."

As an early student of psychoanalysis, this didn't bother me. I understand its value. It is immediately, comically clear to me when people I encounter in academia and schools who are resistant to psychoanalytic thinking have little if any knowledge of the primary sources founding any school of psychoanalysis, let alone the ways contemporary advocates of psychoanalysis creatively interpret those theories, or the richness it may bring to our ways of experiencing the world with others necessary to implement those theories with integrity. Many have been told, accept, and regurgitate unfounded claims of any number of ways that psychoanalysis is outdated, that it's always about sex, that psychoanalysis is only about diagnosing problems in childhood, or that the success of psychoanalytic psychotherapy lacks evidence. Though one cannot be an expert in every theory or applied practice, one must know enough to provide any worthwhile, progressive critique, and all of us, me included, can strive with greater responsibility to avoid bastardized, second- or third-hand interpretations of any field, theory, or method. It is blatantly foolish to claim that something is outdated or lacks evidence without reading the scholarship published that very year; it is imprudent to pass on such uninformed positions to others. Great news! Psychoanalysis, it turns out, helps us to explore what we do not know, what we refuse to know, and what we cannot bear to know: as individuals, as professional fields, as cultures.

That (admittedly elitist) comic relief is quickly suffocated when I think about why psychoanalysis so seriously matters for education. What has bothered, frightened, and fueled me, as with other contributors to this volume, is seeing first-hand the ways in which policymakers, scholars, teacher

1

educators, administrators, in-service and pre-service teachers dismiss the tremendous potential of applied psychoanalysis in favor of prescriptive approaches that *strategically* neglect the depth of inner lives already and always forcefully present in the classroom. As an educator, I've needed to interpret the literature of which I am intimately familiar to those who will not *but really need not be*; to develop more accessible, practical ways of explaining "why psychoanalysis?" and "what does it look like in education?" This has been an equally frustrating and rewarding process that has expanded my own emotional experiences, thinking, and teaching, and on some glistening occasions, colleagues' and students'.

Analysis affords unique tools for observation and interpretation of one's earliest and ongoing self-formation with the potential to free clients of recurring symptoms and patterns of relating, changing (what is always) the work of living in the world with others. Psychoanalysis continues to be a clinical method, which I refer to here as Analysis, but also an interpretive lens applied by anthropologists, social workers, neuroscientists, historians, visual artists, and cultural, political, literary, gender, and disability theorists, among others. The popularity of psychoanalysis in each of these spaces has risen and waned for over a century, and it will rise and wane again. "Is Psychoanalysis Dead?" may be great internet clickbait, but it's certainly the wrong question, neglecting how psychoanalysis has already and may continue to evolve. Instead of answering whether psychoanalysis is dead, we might instead turn our curiosity toward the reasons why folks keep asking and answering that question at all, and the ways in which professionals across disciplines are responding. This volume strives to do both.

In some ways, psychoanalysis remains a clinical method and applied intellectual occupation for those with the education, money, and social capital to access it, despite a long tradition of analysts who have provided pro-bono services to children, families, and professionals in residential, school, judicial, and other public settings. Sigmund Freud believed in mental health care as a fundamental right and imagined a "psychotherapy for the people." Following World War I, Sándor Ferenczi, Anton von Freund, Max Eitingon, Ernst Simmel, Eduard Hitschmann, Wilhelm Reich, Karen Horney, and Ernest Jones, among others, hoped to advance psychoanalysis as public health through free outpatient treatment with adaptations to the duration and technique of analysis to best serve those settings (Danto 2005; Gaztambide 2012). Between 1920 and 1938, twelve clinics offering free psychoanalytic therapy to those in need were established across seven countries with the support of psychoanalytic societies (Danto 2005). In 1919, Anna Freud began volunteering in a shelter for Jewish war orphans before founding in 1937, with the support of Dorothy Burlingham, a nursery school for poor children in Vienna ("Our History" n.d.; Young-Bruehl 2008). After fleeing World War II to London,

Anna Freud and Dorothy Burlingham founded the Hampstead War Nurseries serving children separated from their parents or left homeless (Freud and Burlingham 1942; Young-Bruehl 2008). With Anna Freud's background as a teacher, they later offered psychoanalytically oriented preschool education ("Our History" n.d., Young-Bruehl 2008). In addition to this history, several authors in this book also engage with the theories and practices of another Object Relations pioneer in London, Donald Winnicott, who with his oft-uncredited wife Clare treated children displaced by World War II but was also dedicated to public education, working to support mothers through nearly two decades of BBC radio broadcasts (Phillips 2007; Kanter 2018; Trout 2020). You will also learn in this volume of more contemporary examples, such as analysts from the Washington-Baltimore Center for Psychoanalysis, who provide pro-bono services to a local preschool that serves children from low-income families, many of whom can attend for free. For this partnership, those analysts received the American Psychoanalytic Association's (APsA) Anna Freud Educational Achievement Award in 2017. It is worth noting, in contrast, that the 2019 recipient of that same APsA award is charging $55,500 for one year of tuition for children aged from three to five, and $47,900 for children below age three. The extension of psychoanalysis to community and school settings does not always, as Freud hoped, "sharpen in all directions the sense of social justice" (Freud 1955, 267).

There are many analysts and psychoanalytic institutions today deeply concerned about structural inequality and engaged in ongoing discussions about expanding not only clinical services but also professional training. For those educators less aware, psychoanalytic institutes and practitioners often distinguish psychoanalysis from psychoanalytically-oriented psychotherapy, which may share many features, by the qualifications of the clinician, including not only advanced degrees and clinical hours but long-term psychoanalytic supervision, and by the number of sessions expected of each client. Analysis typically requires four to five sessions per week, though some contemporary practitioners more flexibly consider fewer sessions per week on an individual basis. Some psychoanalysts maintain that analysis requires that a client lie reclined on the couch for the entirety of those sessions, while more analysts I know have never used a physical couch at all. An analyst may allow for clients' seating preferences, which have also necessarily changed with the increase of teletherapy during the COVID-19 pandemic. Teletherapy has also expanded access to psychoanalysis for clients living in geographic areas with few, if any, analysts, who are often concentrated in cities—a great, even if incidental step toward more equitable access to psychoanalysis. Still, in its requirement of multiple sessions per week, often at high rates not covered by insurance, analysis in this form has always been inaccessible to most people in need of mental health care. Today, even those individuals and families of middle-class and lower socio-economic status fortunate to have steady paid work are facing cost-of-living increases at often far higher rates than their employers' pay adjustments. Though many analysts around the world offer services on a sliding scale, analysts' own costs of living are too increasing, as are their years of professional experience, both grounds for increased hourly rates. This is not the fault of psychoanalytic institutes or individual psycho-analysts, who are working very hard within a broader crisis of healthcare and education systems in the United States that have not been designed to serve all those in need of care. For example, organizations today such as the Anna Freud Foundation and the Association for Child Psychoanalysis provide grants to analysts subsidizing their treatment of low-income clients or their engagement in community outreach.

Most institutes offer need-based scholarships for tuition and supervision, some specifically for populations underrepresented in the field. Still, psy-choanalytic training remains inaccessible to many clinicians and educators interested in becoming analysts who fall outside of a determined financial "need." Psychoanalytic institutions offer free fellowships which provide an introduction to psychoanalysis, but those fellowships openly serve as a recruitment tool for their costly training programs. Many clinicians and educators who will never become analysts still choose to pursue continuing education hours at psychoanalytic institutes, as I have. I highly recommend these opportunities to anyone who can afford them, though I know very few of my late millennial peers, and fewer in Gen Z interested in human service work, who will ever have such disposable income, even if they look beyond the clickbait. Graduate students and professors of education may be able to attend psychoanalytic conferences and training only because of travel fund-ing provided by universities to supplement salaries too low to accommodate continuing education. These supplemental funds are typically minimally or not at all available to non-tenure-track faculty, staff, or students. My college students in education and in early childhood mental health cannot afford psy-choanalytic training now, nor are they likely to in the future. Many students and graduates struggle to afford health insurance premiums and specialist co-pays for occasional mental health care, let alone multiple sessions per week with often out-of-network psychoanalysts. Many graduates already struggle to pay off federal student loans that may not be used for tuition at psychoana-lytic institutes. Though some psychoanalytic institutes have begun offering interest-free loans themselves, such private loans will not be eligible for (the yet under threat) Public Service Loan Forgiveness (PSLF), on which many college graduates depend as they launch and sustain their careers.

It is no surprise, among several other reasons, that some psychoanalytic institutions have needed to increase dues, limit programming, or even still struggle to stay afloat, unable to carry out their ever-important missions. In the last two years, we have seen the indefinite "pause" of reputable training hubs such as the Salt Lake City branch of the International Psychotherapy Institute, and the permanent shuttering of the Washington School of Psychiatry, one of the largest post-graduate psychoanalytic training programs in the United States, founded in 1936 by Harry Stack Sullivan, whose interpersonal approach was groundbreaking in both psychiatry and anthropology. I learned and grew as a preschool teacher, researcher, and professional educator through case presentations and seminars I attended at the Washington School of Psychiatry and at IPI SLC. I first had the opportunity to hear one of the contributors to this volume, Ionas Sapountzis, speak at an IPI seminar. I met another contributor, Michael Trout, through a short course on the Winnicott's offered by Joel Kanter, which I joined after attending a talk Joel delivered years earlier at the Washington School of Psychiatry (WSP). WSP was also known for its use of an approach to Infant Observation founded by Esther Bick at the Tavistock Clinic. After learning about this method through WSP faculty, Jim Garrett and I each adapted it for use in teacher education; our respective work is included in this volume. WSP and IPI SLC have directly shaped contemporary psychoanalytic approaches to early childhood education. I am heartbroken knowing that other educators may not have those opportunities, for themselves and for the children and families with whom they work.

Psychoanalysts and those non-clinical practitioners and researchers borrowing ideas from psychoanalysis presumably share a belief in the value of psychoanalysis as both a process and an interpretive lens, and, I hope, share a commitment to improving the lives of others. We are likely to agree, given shared reverence for the transformative potential of psychoanalysis, that increased access to psychoanalytic ideas, implicitly and explicitly, applied in critical, reflexive, and ethical ways, is a general good. Given financial and time constraints, psychoanalysis must continue to extend beyond the bounds of Analysis through research, classroom practices, and other interdisciplinary community settings. We can do this only by collaborating across fields. This book, therefore, features the work of professors, social workers, psychologists, Infant Mental Health experts, school directors, and preschool teachers—each understanding and applying psychoanalysis in education today. It is a call to active thinking and practice for faculty, clinicians, and the educators they prepare, as an act of advocacy for young children.

The consideration of psychoanalysis in/as education spans back over a century to Freud's initial insistence that education carries psychic potentials, yet psychoanalytic perspectives on early childhood education remain drastically underrepresented in undergraduate programs, including teacher education licensure programs. O'Loughlin (2013) pointed to a widespread neglect of emotional discourse in teacher preparation programs, arguing that "too often pedagogy is presented as being instrumental teachers acting instrumentally on students" (38). In favor of a more "emotionally focused, human, person-centered pedagogy," he argues for a consideration of both teachers' and students' psychic experiences (O'Loughlin 2013, 37). An earnest attempt at early childhood education (especially if we are claiming to be "inclusive," "social and emotional," or "emotionally responsive") may *require* professionals to be prepared to think with a psychoanalytic lens insofar as classroom relationships are filled with the desires, anxieties, and drives of both teacher and student, uniquely attended to by psychoanalysis. Despite increased (though controversial) presence of Social and Emotional Learning and Trauma-informed practice in professional competencies, early learning standards, and classrooms, these approaches generally do not tap the proverbial goldmine that is psychoanalysis—typically neither discussing nor implicitly demonstrating attention to the psyche at all. Clio Stearns, author of chapter 10 in this volume, previously argued that this absence limits teachers' ability to tolerate and make space for children's and their own related "negative" emotions, in turn, inhibiting children's own abilities to tolerate, explore, and show us those parts of themselves (e.g., Stearns 2019; Pyscher and Crampton 2020). Moreover, while "attention to trauma as a guiding force in children's lives can be helpful in pulling professional attention to the significance of relationships," Clio adds here, "trauma sometimes becomes an umbrella term for anything getting in the way of pedagogical efficiency and standardization."

Psychoanalytic perspectives also remain sparse in master's and doctoral programs meant to prepare students for academic careers where they will both produce research that shapes the field and educate future generations of teachers. This makes sense, as most academics teaching graduate courses have not been exposed themselves to psychoanalysis beyond Freud's psychosexual and Erikson's psychosocial stages presented in introductory child development and psychology textbooks. In chapter 2 of this volume, Janice Kroeger, Christopher Konieczko, Dana Oleskiewicz, Alexandra C. Gunn, and Andrea Sanchez describe mainstream textbooks' continued neglect of critical perspectives on gender, sexuality, and bodies long represented in anthropology, feminist, and queer scholarship, instead perpetuating the pathologization of differences for which developmental theories have been very understandably implicated. Freud's theories, they argue, have been central to the construction of still-pervasive heteronormativity, which through education and other professions carries psychological and emotional, indeed life-threatening consequences, for gender-diverse children. Janice and her co-authors explain, with fervor and care, teachers' and parents' responsibility for helping children understand themselves and those around them: a task that requires adults to deconstruct their own binary conceptions of gender while left without the necessary ideological and social support to do so. Tools from clinical psychoanalytic therapy, together with knowledge of cognitive schemas (Piaget's and Kohlberg's theories), they suggest, may support adults in listening to and empowering gender-diverse children to express themselves, if we remain open to what of these theories may be worth salvaging. Yet with limited understanding of such tools, and well aware of our present conservative political landscape, why in the world would progressive teacher educators seek further study or teach psychoanalytic theories in their own courses? How would they be aware of and curious about what psychoanalytic theories might inform not only *what*, but *how* they teach emerging educators?

In graduate school during the 2010s, classmates and professors in curriculum and instruction, art education, philosophy, English, and Disability Studies lightheartedly referred to "sexy theories": the most captivating and trendy theories to talk and write about at that time. Though Félix Guattari's critique of Freudian analysis remained hot, psychoanalysis was otherwise terribly unsexy, left untouched by all but a few of us. Poststructural, Critical Race, and Postcolonial theories held sway, but most of all, New Materialism: now *that* was sexy. That was your "in" at the "cool kids' tables" on campus and at conferences worldwide. If you wanted or now want to study psychoanalysis in early childhood education specifically, your best bet is to find professors whose courses are grounded in psychoanalysis but may or may not be titled and advertised as such, or to seek their supervision of independent studies. Those professors include authors in this volume and the professors whose publications we each cite. Through mostly independent studies, I encountered several profound texts on psychoanalysis and early childhood education, such as O'Loughlin's (2013), that retain great value today, but it is time for a complementary update. That generation of scholars' own thinking has evolved, as have their students' (i.e., my peers and I), who now have our own students, the next generation engaging with psychoanalysis (i.e., my co-authors of chapter 12). This volume is unique not only in its representation of multiple disciplines but of scholars across multiple generations of psychoanalytic thinking and practice, illustrating how each has informed the other. There exists a forty-year age gap between some of our youngest and eldest authors in this volume. Some are highly published field experts transitioning to retirement; others include first year master's students dipping their toes into psychoanalysis, and others of us in between. After "sitting with" their chapters separately and together, I'm inclined to think that this is the way it should be, and I suspect that readers will too. Texts and ideas live through particular social, cultural, and political contexts. By understanding the ways in which specific fields, generations, and individuals use psychoanalysis separately and together at any given time, we gain greater, multiplicious insight into the meaning of those theories, freeing us to think and feel in new ways. Though most higher education programs, preschools, and elementary schools, and the policymakers and accrediting bodies by which each is governed are not presently hospitable to psychoanalysis, I want to believe they might be, through greater knowledge of its use. This volume therefore seeks to address: *Who is thinking psychoanalytically; why, where, and how? What may psychoanalytic theories afford us in twenty-first-century research and practice that approach, actively engage with, and represent the dynamic lived experiences of the children with whom we study and work?*

Beyond WSP and IPI connections, the rest of our contributors and series editors have been connected through the Association for the Psychoanalysis of Culture and Society Conference and/or the Reconceptualizing Early Childhood Education conference, which have inspired and made this work possible. Reconceptualizing Early Childhood Education (RECE) scholarship has traditionally challenged positivist research methods as well as policies, schools, and classroom practices that proliferate deficit perspectives of diverse children and childhoods. In response to these concerns, RECE scholars have taken up critical, post-structural, feminist, postcolonial, and psychoanalytic theories to reimagine research and school and classroom practices (Bloch 2013). This work encourages us to consider children and other marginalized populations as experts and meaning-makers in their own lives, and to consider the inequitable relationships between researcher and researched, adults and children, and between racial, gender, cultural, linguistic, and socioeconomic groups. In chapter one, RECE scholar Lisa Farley acknowledges these critiques of psychoanalysis while considering the oft-conflated concepts "development" and "developmentalism" (Burman 2024). "Development," psychoanalytically defined, may be precisely that meaning-making process long understood by interdisciplinary advocates of its value; this orientation may, in fact, not only allow but be necessary for us to confront the ways in which it is instead "developmentalism" that emerges in early childhood education as the problematic construct limiting our ways of understanding development. Developmentalism demands conformity to a specific linear (even if fluid, bidirectional) trajectory, one Lisa demonstrates is inherently shaped by related constructs of chronology and of dis/ability. As a Disability Studies in Education scholar, I believe this distinction between development and developmentalism, and Lisa's incisive, new exploration of analytic time, may make "the space between social and clinical psychoanalysis" not only more palatable but also quite useful, in ways that surprise those in Disability Studies. Lisa's argument is supported through exploration of a clinical case of Donald Winnicott's "Squiggle Game" that, as a creative encounter, already suggests a different orientation to time. This makes quite a lot of sense. It is not only inner conflicts that may provide insight into development and historically defined neuroses (or through which we can claim to understand identified developmental differences), but the ways in which one struggles to make meaning of those conflicts, within and "latching onto" environments and relationships as they continue to be lived and relived. Such reliving, which Lisa understands as "creative labor," might only be understood through a psychoanalytic orientation to time that by nature cannot be understood chronologically, lest we fall into the trap of developmentalism and fail to recognize, and instead kill off, children's inner lives.

In chapter 3, Ionas Sapountzis, too, is thinking with Winnicott, as counter to a still growing emphasis in the field of School Psychology on standardized and other norm-referenced tests over all else they may learn through children's subjective experiences. "It is a stance," Ionas writes, "that denies not only the experiences these children convey in their drawings but the desire, however unconscious, to communicate something about themselves, to present themselves to an Other and to seek his or her understanding." Ionas provides an urgent discussion of the ways in which gender, race, and socioeconomic status contribute to the identification (or not) of disabilities. Though some policymakers and educators have positioned standardized tests as a tool to address inequity, here we see how that isn't inherently the case and might actually exacerbate inequitable educational outcomes. Children as young as fourth and fifth grade struggling to learn are already, Ionas finds, scared about being held back and not being able to go to college. Their fears are heartbreaking and are not unreasonable. Though we know this is also the result of structural inequity that we cannot easily resolve in our day-to-day work, Ionas points to things schools can do, such as creating initiatives to support parents. I find his chapter a sophisticated portrait of learning difficulty and disabilities because he shows us there is no simple or unidirectional explanation; instead, showing how multiple factors may exacerbate each other, for example, the emotional reactions of struggling to learn and the dynamic relationship between a child and parent throughout this struggle. Further, the language with which Ionas describes children (i.e., "an adorable tornado") will resonate with all who delight in or wish to make a deliberate practice of delighting in children during the moments they need us most. He positions children as wise, with the capacity to be deeply in tune with their own experiences, demonstrating exactly what it is he asks of the reader: to revere what Winnicott called children's "True Selves" as "sacred," with "a persistence and a faith in what can be found."

In chapter 4, Greta Carlson's case study of an incoming kindergarten client provides an additional portrait of how psychologists tasked with providing norm-referenced assessments may think psychoanalytically about the entirety of the testing encounter. Readers will enjoy, as I do, Greta's undeniable gift for weaving beautiful vignettes with accessible communication of theory-into-practice. Grappling, as do its preceding chapters, with conflicting theories about nature and environment, and of linearity and fluidity (e.g., Arnold Gessell and Anna Freud's respective orientations), Greta explores the notion, desirability, and limitations of "objective" developmental knowledge. The Gesell Developmental Observation–Revised (GDO-R) assessment, for example, she explains, is "chiefly characterized by describing, as opposed to explaining or analyzing," though the results of such evaluations are interpreted to make conclusions about a child's "developmental age" and to explain a child's performance in school. Alongside those quantitative assessment results, questionnaires provided to parents and teachers solicit inherently subjective reports of (what we are calling) the child's "self-control," "independence," and "cooperation with others," all constructs that may, as much as the quantitative assessments, construct and uphold ab/normalcy in schools. In reading Greta's work, I gained greater knowledge and optimism from the creative ways psychologists make use of data they are prescribed to collect (e.g., through dimensions of specific assessments) together with their equally systematic intuition (e.g., through relation). Historical theories of transference and countertransference (e.g., Melanie Klein and Otto Kernberg's respective departures from Freud) provide Greta further insight into the child's and psychologist's respective experiences of assessment. Demonstrating attention to a child's verbal and nonverbal expression during free play, and using psychoanalytic theory to consider the dynamic nature of test performance, Greta shows how these assessments provide her oft underrecognized opportunities for understanding dimensions of children's inner lives "instrumental to the motivation needed to learn and complete cognitive tasks" such as those that ultimately suggested her client's weakness in working memory and visual-spatial abilities. Especially compelling, I find, is Greta's multimodal attention to how her client ascribed different meaning to and through physical manipulatives. A child's observable in-the-moment emotional responses to testing materials, such as blocks, in relation to the varying ways in which they are expected to engage with those materials, Greta shows, provides insight into the same underlying desires and anxieties that may be evoked for children in the classroom. She positions assessment data as useful for the design of learning opportunities that not only remediate perceived cognitive deficits and capitalize on children's strengths for the purpose of achieving academic success, but also for facilitating a therapeutic environment for the child's general wellbeing: one in which they may "feel affectively contained and confident."

"Understanding what's really wrong"—this need for containment of which Greta writes—Michael Trout says, "often leads to intuitive and principled solutions—a promise not made when we settle merely for a diagnosis." In chapter 5, Michael provides portraits of multiple preschool-aged children, their teachers, and caregivers from his work as a mental health expert and consultant to schools. Michael characterizes teachers' work as fundamentally psychoanalytic, while acknowledging, as each of our authors does, the very separate projects of therapy and education. "Teachers are absolute masters," he writes, at empirical observation of children within context, at understanding children's behavior as communication, and using hypotheses about their communication to engage with children in ways that may meet their underlying needs. It is through infantile experiences of attachment and individuation from our earliest caregivers that we continue to discover ourselves and our worlds with others. Inquiry into a child's emotional experiences of attachment such as those of early loss, he finds, may direct us to everyday classroom practices through which the child's troubling internal working models may be disrupted. While experimenting with critical, inclusive changes to physical learning environments, he found "the most important interventions were the human ones." Teachers are capable, Michael argues, of "*holding*" an enormity of affect, of individual children and of groups, in order to facilitate, rather than shut down, such communication. This seeing and "holding," Michael explains, mirrors successful work in Analysis. "My belief has always been that Freud changed the world" Michael writes, "because he made some of his first patients feel *held*."

Teachers, so deeply failed by our social and political institutions, are also increasingly burnt out. It is within the context of growing class sizes and enormous pressure to demonstrate their competence through measurable student behavior and learning outcomes, Michael observes, that teachers set aside their relational strengths and strategies supported by psychoanalysis, with such serious consequences as the repeated expulsion of children from preschools. Michael is honest in ways that might validate teachers' lived experiences: he does not sugarcoat, for example, the exhausting difficulty of engaging with children whose moods overwhelm a classroom, or whose aggressive behavior suggests resistance to the very experiences of safety they may ask of us. His chapter is also tender, even whimsical, as he inhabits and welcomes us (back) into "waves of empathy" and "listening with our 'third ear,'" to "look carefully, to wonder without presuppositions, to imagine possibilities, to not be seduced by easy 'answers' or comforting diagnoses." It is a poignant reminder of all that is "in the room" with us, at all times: people and objects, seen through the ways in which we carry them. His practical examples provide a roadmap for returning to a space of curiosity about all that is "in the room" that can be difficult for anyone, even the most veteran, mindful, and emotionally aware educators, to maintain amid the day-to-day demands of working with children. I wish that every school had the funding for such consultants—and importantly, that professionals continue to be trained to think in the ways Michael has. Michael holds teachers with tremendous reverence and provides timely, much-needed language for those struggling to defend the advanced skills of those widely perceived as "just" "supervisors" of young children. I have assigned Michael's prior work (e.g., Koloroutis and Trout 2012; Trout 2020) to graduate and undergraduate students, and shared it with my colleagues, who have all found his ideas empowering, affirming of their gut feelings and professional identities.

Readers will see that Michael and Lesley Koplow, the authors of the following chapter and whose work I have also assigned to students (2002, 2008, 2021), each show, rather than tell, the sophistication of their thinking. In some of their respective prior books and articles, they have discussed psychoanalytic theory explicitly. In other writings of theirs, you would need to have foundational knowledge of psychoanalysis to recognize the way they make sense of a child or the practices they recommend to follow, for example, from Winnicott's ideas. It is not that other scholars in our fields are more pretentious or don't care about accessibility. Writing in this way is very challenging for those immersed in and thrilled by theory; moreover, most face crushing pressure to write things that challenge and appeal to peers, high-status journals, and publishers. It certainly remains a valuable exercise, supported by learning theories, for readers to interpret theory-heavy work for their own purposes and resist the urge to be told directly "so what?" We need both kinds of writing. You can rip my library of denser psychoanalytic texts from my cold, dead hands (and then enjoy them yourself!). I have, however, seen the ways theory can turn off both academic colleagues and my students who might otherwise be open to thinking psychoanalytically. I have been vulnerably challenged to shift my approach to teacher preparation after observing how reading can be discouraging, even damaging, to educators who are already made to feel from nearly every direction that they are not smart enough. I came to realize, as Michael discusses, the ways our education system already interferes with teachers' "felt sense of efficacy," their ability to confidently identify with their profession, justify their theory- and research-supported practices, and to find the connection and joy necessary to sustain themselves. I have seen and felt myself the ways that Michael's and Lesley's writing can support transformation, processes that professors are increasingly coming to see (or finally stop ignoring) as critical to teacher preparation.

Lesley Koplow is the founding director of the Center for Emotionally Responsive Practice at Bank Street College, a unique higher education institution dedicated specifically to preparing teachers and school leaders. New York is home to not only Bank Street and highly regarded degree programs with emphases in psychoanalysis such as New York University's and Adelphi University's (where Ionas Sapountzis and one of our series editors, Michael O'Loughlin, hold faculty positions) but has a long history of lesser-known therapeutic nurseries and psychoanalytic preschools. In chapter 6, Lesley describes her twenty-five-year-long *Teddy Bears in Classroom*

Practice project, a psychoanalytic approach implemented in hundreds of not just preschool but also elementary school classrooms, spaces in which knowledge of the infant-parent relationship remains far less discussed and applied. The "Teddy Bears" project stems from Lesley's early work as the director of a therapeutic preschool, where she observed the sophisticated, seemingly healthy ways in which children made use of beloved objects from home in their transition to a group setting: a setting characterized by reliable routines and in which psychotherapists engage in both individual and dyadic work with children and caregivers. Lesley was driven to bring elements of therapeutic nursery schools into general education settings, recognizing the benefits of expanded access for children who, due to systemic factors, are most in need of and yet least likely to access mental health care. Teddy Bears (i.e., "transitional objects") for everyone! (Winnicott 1971). Lesley's approach to understanding and facilitating individual development within classroom and home relationships shares aspects of those preceding chapters that privilege above all Winnicott's "holding environment": for Lesley, this is one in which sensitive, "good-enough" teachers afford children opportunities for safety and emotional integration through creative play. Chapter 6 features stories of using teddy bears with children facing some of the same perils as those in Lesley's prior studies, such as abrupt transitions in and out of foster care, food insecurity, and worries about physical safety in their homes, yet now radically transformed by the COVID-19 pandemic: a period of unprecedented fear and loss, difficult for even children without previously identified trauma to tolerate feeling and to verbalize. This emphasis on an emotionally facilitative environment may be challenging, as Lesley discusses, for schools to accept while under such great pressure to recoup pandemic "learning loss." And yet, observing children interacting with their teddy bears following the return to in-person schooling, Lesley saw children find themselves and others through a radical shift between isolation and community: indeed, saw children begin to repair their worlds. Teddy Bears proved, just as before, to be symbolic objects with which children can identify and assign attributes, find comfort and empathy (for themselves and others), and express themselves: facilitating developmental processes inseparable from "learning issues."

I first had the pleasure of visiting another New York psychoanalytic school, Little Missionary Day Nursery, in 2017, as I sought to understand what it is that distinguishes a "psychoanalytic preschool," and the ways in which those schools create inclusive environments for children with identified differences. There, I met Eileen Johnson, the school director and author of books advocating for the rights of children (2011) and describing an approach to engaging with children's emotions (2017). I observed she and the teachers at "Little Mish" employ an approach, she explains in chapter 7 of this volume, in which she continues to make mistakes and learn lessons:

failure, she argues, is inevitable and propels our understanding of children. Those who argue psychoanalysis doesn't "work" often diverge in their ideas about what it is they want to "work," what we may observe that indicates something has "worked," and what practitioners and clients must respectively document to claim such desired success. Eileen provides an incisive historical overview of parallel concerns in the institutionalization and nationalization of schooling, and the ways in which curriculum, "both the goal of school, and also the map by which the goal is reached" can so easily overshadow the role of attachment and relationships in learning. She understands the political expansion of mandated curricular materials "akin to how a narcissistic parent convinces a child of the parent's grandiose identity and secures the child's allegiance to that greatness—the child being used as a self-object, a vehicle for broadcasting the parent's good image to the world." "School can put the good of the institution," she worries, "or of society at large, at the forefront of its goals, and neglect the individuality of the child" so well documented in research, and yet for and with whom curriculum may not have been designed. In response to public concerns over school performance standards for children's development and learning outcomes, Lillian Katz (2007) suggested that we shift our attention from an outdated industrial model of schooling that positions education as a deliverable product, to consider the nature of *experiences* we ought to afford children.

In chapter 9, Joanna Fortune continues to grapple with just this. Her historical overview of psychoanalysis and early childhood education attends specifically to the ways in which the emergence of new psychoanalytic theories about play, and psychoanalysis-as-play, have and might shape schools. *Why* is it that psychoanalytic thinkers might argue for play-based approaches to preschool education? Are the things popularly referred to as "play" in formal education environments providing the "standards of experience" we're seeking? In the last few decades, Joanna explains, play-based early years education in Ireland has made a radical departure from previously favored Montessori and adult-structured learning. While necessarily expanding awareness and formalizing the value of play, Joanna finds its practice has not been simple in schools. One might arrange a school day in which there are periods of free play, construct school spaces, or provide materials that facilitate play, for example, but "what a program cannot prescribe is a playful state of mind . . . play is, moreover, a state of mind and a way of being." What I find stunning in Joanna's chapter is where she sees play, for example, in "the words we use, our prosodic vocalisations, our use of pitch, pace, pause and general musicality of our voices and in our facial expressions and use of humour." Play, Joanna contends, is both relational and neural. She reminds us, using both psychoanalytic theory and research in neuroscience, that it is through such shared affect that children explore and internalize relationships and understand and regulate their own emotions. It is such (practical!) play-fulness that facilitates children's experiences of safety: not only psychic but inseparably physiological.

In chapter 8,[1] I provide a portrait of my struggle to define and become a psychoanalytic educator during my first year as a lead teacher of three- and four-year-olds. It is a vulnerable story of days spent crying in my car, wanting so badly to ease children's anger and sadness in the classroom, and feeling like a failure for my inability to do so. As many teachers and school leaders do (Stearns 2020), I mistakenly thought my competence as an inclusive educator would be evident in the eventual absence of children's "negative" emotions and behavior, in the observable resolution of their inner conflicts. Eileen's discussion in chapter 7 of teachers' narcissism—their attachment to a particular role—provides a very apt window into my own. "While my behavior was fundamentally benevolent," Eileen writes, "it was also narcissistic in that I wanted to actuate my own vision: a comfortable child, a happy classroom, and me playing the role of benevolent teacher." My prior introduction to psychoanalysis led me to believe, in theory, children's behavior as indicative of their extraordinary ability to process unconscious desire and fear in new environments, and the necessity of facilitating spaces in which they can. I still struggled to engage with children therapeutically in ways that held true to those theories about learning, my ideas about the purpose of early childhood education, and my commitments to children. Professor and psychotherapist Gail Boldt (2019) shared similar anxieties she experienced during student teaching: "I have all of the theories in my head, but I don't know how to make them happen. There is a huge gap between what I know and what I can do" (26). In chapter 8 I provide brief excerpts of the advice that she and Michael O'Loughlin provided me, resembling Gail's host teacher's response: "You haven't learned yet how to let children fill that gap. You are still talking to yourself, to your own head. You aren't yet in relationship with the children" (Boldt 2019, 26). My anxiety, of course, did not immediately dissipate and continues to emerge in peculiar ways, but I did, through my engagement with professors and psychotherapists that year, develop simultaneous pride in my progress toward the stance of not-knowing characteristic of clinical psychoanalysts.

The third part of this volume provides portraits of psychoanalytic pedagogy in higher education, examining the learning and becoming of preservice teachers through the voices of both professors and their students. Though Katz's (2007) "standards of experience" was a discussion of those we coordinate for children, the same concept may be extended to professional training: what opportunities do pre- and in-service teachers typically have? What "standards of experience" might we hold and provide for emerging teachers? Every chapter in this text suggests that not-knowing is among the most important "standards of experience" for teachers. Michael Trout called this the task of becoming "brilliantly stupid" in a conversation we recorded as part of an instructional video library developed for students' asynchronous remote learning during the pandemic. My students, as I did, found relief, confidence, and inspiration in the permission to be "brilliantly stupid." The "brilliantly stupid" educator at any level, Michael explains, maintains one's professional knowledge and personal values while recognizing the inherent limits of one's own understanding, to dwell in a space of wonder about the o/Other's lived experience. It is exactly what Eileen Johnson continues to learn through the children at her school: "I am once again reminded that this is a lesson I have to constantly relearn. It is something therapists endeavor to keep in mind, as should teachers: Listening is the most important thing you can do. It must precede instruction, feedback or guidance." "Teachers should be liberated," she argues, "from the role of all-knowing expert and the need to engage constantly in presenting a positive self-image. They should be able to tolerate self-doubt and model vulnerability and self-reflection to pupils."

Clio Stearns shares some similar concerns with other authors in this volume about the ongoing professionalization of teaching and the problematic ways in which competency and proficiency are assigned to teachers and their students. In chapter 10, yet another beautiful weaving of vignettes and theory, Clio navigates her role as a professor of teacher education and illustrates the ways in which her psychoanalytic thinking has evolved through the supervision of student teachers. The chapter is new and especially compelling in its critical discussion of the ways in which we define trauma and those traumatized, and of apparent misuses and overuses of "trauma" in schools as an explanation and label for children's experiences and behavior. Clio points out that a child's subversion of classroom expectations, for example, may be as likely the product of his boredom as it may be communication of some internal developmental or relational conflict. Clio suggests we ought to consider both: a child's "behavior as a creative act, one that may have roots in something bad he has witnessed or experienced, but also one that is moving and changing his current environment into something else." In Clio's thinking with Christopher Bollas' concept of "psychic genera," it is not the healing of trauma for which teachers and classroom environments are demanded and responsible, but instead opportunities for creativity and newness—opportunities that may be afforded, agentively, by the very behaviors often interpreted as symptoms of trauma. Genera, "moments where real knowledge gets produced, where ways of relating, thinking, feeling and living alter" *are* education, Clio argues, while wondering, is facilitating newness the job of a professional teacher? Is our education system conducive to it? A problem even for those long thinking psychoanalytically, Clio articulates well, is its in/compatibilities with teacher licensing processes: for example, the process through which teacher candidates are expected to conduct observations of children, plan and implement discrete direct instruction, and demonstrate "high standards" for their students. While Clio finds tremendous value (and enjoyment!) in observing her student teachers' engagement with children during play and other unplanned encounters, this is not what she is expected by accrediting bodies—nor, in turn, what her student teachers expect her—to document of their professional capacities. "When an observer is only looking for certain things," Clio finds, "it removes a sense of import from the aspects of classroom life that do not fit on a checklist," which reinforces, I see, some of the same problems Eileen Johnson sees in "the narcissism of curriculum." Clio writes: "we are showing (children) that their present needs have to pay deference to a future adults are imagining for them." In spite of this system, Clio finds brilliance in her student teachers' everyday acts much the way that Michael Trout does: this "curiosity, born from genuine surprise," Clio observed, "leads to wonder and joy."

Chapter 11, written by Jim Garrett, and chapter 12, which I co-wrote with my students Carley Rader, Lydia Bingham, and Kailey Price, each discuss adaptations of psychoanalytic Work Discussion Groups for teacher education. Jim's chapter, originally published in the *Journal of Curriculum Theorizing* (2020), provides examples from his innovative observation seminar for pre-service teachers at the University of Georgia. His primary course assignment required each student to submit written reflections throughout the semester of self-identified, profoundly felt moments during their concurrent student teaching. Much like Esther Bick's original Work Discussion (Bradley and Rustin 2018) and previous adaptations that inspired our respective work (e.g., Lisman-Pieczanski and Blessing 2011; Alperovitz 2018), Jim's assignment dared students to re-present initial observations for Others while attempting to withhold judgment or interpretation, before exploring their inherently subjective dimensions: a productively disruptive challenge for practitioners in training. This too is a challenge for reflexive ethnographers in early childhood education, a parallel made explicit in chapter 12, but one that I also see implicit in Jim's chapter. Jim modeled this distinction for students, asking with careful and genuine curiosity, "What are the things that you are observing that make you interpret it as. . . ?" As each student's observations were read in class, Jim directed the group to free associate with specific words and phrases in their classmates' writing, which became "a grounding element for work that mirrors how dream elements function in psychoanalysis." Discussion of those associations aroused multiplicious, non-linear, expected and unexpected, verbal and not-yet verbal experiences of dreaming and change often unexplored in teacher licensure coursework.

Chapters 11 and 12 each demonstrate the brilliance of teachers ready to participate, emotionally and psychically, in what might be seen as "unconventional" or "impractical" instruction and assignments. Observation seminars, Jim and I each learned, are the product of each person in the room together. My co-authors Carley, Lydia, and Kailey showed up to class every week ready to think and ready to feel. They were deeply in tune with their emotional and physical experiences in both the preschool and university classrooms. They were earnestly, critically, and lovingly observant of not just themselves but their peers and their professor. They were willing to be vulnerable as we confronted the limits of our seeing. They set aside any understandable desire to know what their professor might want to hear, and any understandable desire to be told more expediently a standardized approach for what to do in their instruction and curriculum planning following each child observation. This was exceedingly rare in my nine years of university teaching, which tells me *not* that early childhood educators are not competent or capable of participating in Work Discussion, but that Work Discussion demands particular individual and collective labor (i.e. Katz's "standards of experience"), indeed, I would argue, healing work (O'Loughlin 2019). My co-authors seemed to benefit from opportunities that the seminar provided to discuss all of this, less afforded by other methods of teacher education, supervision, and staff group discussion, even their own psychotherapy.

This is a volume of polished, innovative work that reflects each of my co-contributors' tremendous intellectual, emotional, and creative capacities, and I am thrilled that a broader audience will have the pleasure that I have had of watching their thinking unfold. As a junior scholar, I remain starstruck that some of the people whose work and conference presentations most inspired me in graduate school have joined me in this volume (grad students, if you're reading this as I hope you are, the imposter syndrome does not go away. I wish you unencumbered joy, though I would be *far* more concerned if you never experienced imposter syndrome. I'll save a psychoanalytic interpretation of such anxieties for elsewhere and for now say that you'll accomplish it all anyway, and *you need not do it alone*). As an editor, I have been privy to more than their writing, and I would be remiss, in my dedication to advancing inclusion in the fields of psychoanalysis and education, to not also recognize the people behind the text. Scholars of psychoanalysis are uniquely qualified to craft therapeutic academic spaces and working relationships that reflect the theories to which we subscribe. And yet, many of those who preach reflexivity and therapeutic relationships in theory are unable or unwilling to turn the lens on themselves. After a decade in academia, I know that the grounded, curious, warm, and compassionate authors and series editors of this volume are among the exception, not the norm. Working with them was refreshing and renewed my optimism about academia that had years ago been beaten out of me. These authors and series editors are the people you want to have as speakers on your campus, as guest lecturers in your courses, and as collaborators on asynchronous course material, as several have for me and my students. These are the people to search for in conference agendas. You will be lucky to snag a seat in their audience, ask them questions, and play in the galaxies of their thinking. Offer to take them to coffee or lunch when you're in their city. Jump at any opportunity to observe their work in schools. I know first-hand that they will challenge you in wonderful ways, but also graciously open themselves to be challenged by you; they will treat you like you have something brilliant worth saying because you do. We must remain earnest students of each other, across disciplines, across career levels. I have been so deeply moved by my already wildly accomplished contributors' demonstrated commitment to just that. You can sit with us, literally and figuratively. I hope that you will. I will add to Lisa Farley's beautifully gutting conclusion of chapter one, "we can do more with our chances and childhoods," that we have futures, of psychoanalysis and of early childhood education, so very worth crafting together.

NOTE

1. I am indebted to the faculty and students in the Washington-Baltimore Center for Psychoanalysis' New Directions in Writing program for their support in revising earlier drafts of chapter 8. If you are looking for a supportive community that will refine, expand, challenge, and free your academic and creative writing, I can't recommend the program enough.

REFERENCES

Alperovitz, Sharon. 2018. "Fostering Psychic Transformation Through the Discipline of Infant Observation: The Eyes—and Mind's Eyes—Have It." *Psychiatry* 81, no. 1: 96–99.

Bloch, Marianne. 2013. "Reconceptualizing Theory/Policy/Curriculum/Pedagogy in Early Child (Care and) Education: Reconceptualizing Early Childhood Education (RECE) 1991–2012." *International Journal of Equity and Innovation in Early Childhood* 11, no. 1: 65–85.

Boldt, Gail. 2019. "Affective Flows in the Clinic and the Classroom." In *Affect in Literacy Learning and Teaching*, edited by Kevin M. Leander and Christian Ehret, 25–42. Routledge.

Burman, Erica. 2024. *Child as Method: Othering, Interiority and Materialism.* Taylor & Francis.

Danto, Elizabeth Ann. 2005. *Freud's Free Clinics: Psychoanalysis & Social Justice, 1918–1938.* Columbia University Press.

Danto, Elizabeth Ann, and Alexandra Steiner-Strauss, eds. 2018. *Freud/Tiffany: Anna Freud, Dorothy Tiffany Burlingham and the 'Best Possible School'.* Routledge.

Freud, Anna, and Dorothy Burlingham. 1942. *Young Children in War Time: A Year's Work in a Residential War Nursery*. George Allen & Unwin.

Freud, Sigmund. 1955. "Dr. Anton von Freund." In *The Standard Edition of the Complete Psychological Works of Sigmund Freud*, edited by James Strachey, 267–268. Hogarth Press.

Gaztambide, Daniel J. 2012. "'A Psychotherapy for the People' Freud, Ferenczi, and Psychoanalytic Work with the Underprivileged." *Contemporary Psychoanalysis* 48, no. 2: 141–165.

Johnson, Eileen. 2011. *The Children's Bill of Emotional Rights: A Guide to the Needs of Children*. Jason Aronson.

Johnson, Eileen. 2017. *Emotional Education: The A. R. T. of Teaching Children*. CreateSpace Independent Publishing Platform.

Kanter, Joel. 2018. *Face to Face with Children: The Life and Work of Clare Winnicott*. Routledge.

Katz, Lilian G. 2007. "Standards of Experience." *YC Young Children* 62, no. 3: 94.

Koloroutis, Mary, and Michael Trout. 2012. *See Me as a Person: Creating Therapeutic Relationships with Patients and their Families*. Creative Health Care Management.

Koplow, Lesley. 2002. *Creating Schools That Heal: Real-life Solutions*. Teachers College Press.

Koplow, Lesley. 2008. *Bears, Bears Everywhere!: Supporting Children's Emotional Health in the Classroom*. Teachers College Press.

Koplow, Lesley. 2021. *Emotionally Responsive Practice: A Path for Schools That Heal, Infancy–Grade 6*. Teachers College Press.

Lisman-Pieczanski, Nydia, and Deborah Blessing. 2011. "News from Washington DC: Infant and Young Child Observation Program." *Infant Observation* 14, no. 2: 224–226.

O'Loughlin, Michael, ed. 2013. *The Uses of Psychoanalysis in Working with Children's Emotional Lives*. Rowman & Littlefield.

"Our History." Anna Freud. Accessed April 25, 2024. https://www.annafreud.org/about/our-history/.

Phillips, Adam. 2007. *Winnicott*. Penguin.

Pyscher, Tracey, and Anne Crampton. 2020. "Possibilities and Problems in Trauma-Based and Social Emotional Learning Programs. Occasional Paper Series 43." *Bank Street College of Education*.

Stearns, Clio. 2019. *Critiquing Social and Emotional Learning: Psychodynamic and Cultural Perspectives*. Rowman & Littlefield.

Stearns, Clio. 2020. "Let Them Get Mad: Using the Psychoanalytic Frame to Rethink SEL and Trauma-Informed Practice." *Occasional Paper Series* 2020, no. 43: 22–32.

Trout, Michael. 2020. "The Centrality of 'Holding' in Infant Mental Health." Unpublished manuscript.

Winnicott, Donald. 1971. *Playing and Reality*. Tavistock Publications Ltd. Republished in 2005, Routledge Classics.

Young-Bruehl, Elisabeth. 2008. *Anna Freud: A Biography*. Yale University Press.

Part I

PSYCHOANALYTIC APPROACHES TO UNDERSTANDING CHILDREN AND CHILDHOOD

Chapter 1

Psychoanalytic Temporality

From Chronology to Duration in the Making of Childhood History

Lisa Farley

The idea of development as a linear ascent and acquisition of rationality has come into much-needed critique (Burman 2017, 2024; Dyer 2019; Gill-Peterson 2018; Land 2020; Levander 2017; Nxumalo 2019; Pacini-Ketchabaw et al. 2015; Pacini-Ketchabaw et al. 2016; Tesar 2016). Collectively, scholars within fields of Critical Psychology, Critical Childhood Studies, and Reconceptualist Early Childhood Education have challenged "modernist assumptions of truth, universality, and certainty" underlying conventional developmental frameworks (Blaise 2005, 3) and clarified how such frameworks reproduce Western epistemologies of time and being that marginalize children who disrupt, refuse, and/or exceed its linear scripts. Utilizing queer, feminist, posthuman, and anticolonial theories, scholars within these fields show how developmental frameworks enact, in the words of Hannah Dyer (2019), "the violence of normativity" (11). In turn, these scholars generate new metaphors—sideways growth, failure, queer kinship, postdevelopment, and antidevelopment—that spotlight the intersectional agencies and positions children embody as opening alternative ways of thinking about being, learning, and transformation (Burman 2017, 2024; Edelman 2004; Halberstam 2011; Kohan and Weber 2020; Land et al. 2020; Nxumalo 2019; Sakr and Osgood 2019; Stockton 2009).

A parallel critique of linear time can be found within contemporary schools of psychoanalysis, including scholars who engage with the above-named theoretical assemblages (Britzman 2003, 2011; Burman 2017, 2024). Of these thinkers, Erica Burman (2024) draws from psychoanalysis to propose a distinction between development and developmentalism. Whereas developmentalism is harnessed by political agendas aiming to impose hierarchy, adaptation to social norms, and apparatuses of exclusion, development can be understood as an uncertain process of making meaning from life's necessary contingencies and conflicts (Burman 2024, 10). Acknowledging that psychoanalysis has been "implicated in regimes of developmentalism," Burman (2024) also suggests it may "be used to counter" this very entanglement (198). In this latter sense, Burman (2024) reads psychoanalysis as a "critical resource" that "reverses traditional conceptions of causality" by offering a theory of "history as lived" (134). As lived, history is "a looping and iterative temporality" that opens an investigation into how "current contexts prompt recollection of earlier issues" and why knowing about this overlap can prompt a reimagination of both the past and future (Burman 2024, 156).

Building on contemporary discussions, this chapter offers a psychoanalytic theory of time that constructs development not in terms of chronology and hierarchy (i.e., "the idea that later forms build on and are built from earlier ones *to form better ones*"), but in terms of possibility and uncertainty (i.e., the idea that earlier forms run parallel to later ones and enable something else to occur) (Burman 2024, 10, original emphasis). As I will propose, psychoanalysis offers a theory of overlapping temporality that signifies as duration, or "a notion of time passing" (Birksted-Breen 2009, 39), that means dwelling with the "challenges of living as an embodied, often (and especially in very early life) vulnerable and helpless being" (Burman 2024, 134). To name vulnerability as a quality of being is not synonymous with the exclusionary construct of childhood innocence (Garlen 2019) but rather an admission that loss is the ground of existence. In psychoanalytic time, a different theory of development emerges: one that is recursive, disruptive, and, as Deborah Britzman (2009) argues, "uneven" (27). The implications of this argument are not only psychological but social and political. In highlighting dynamics of vulnerability and loss, psychoanalysis offers a critique of frameworks that construct these same dynamics as deficiencies belonging to "others" who continue to be marginalized by colonially produced ladders of developmentalism (Rollo 2018).

To elucidate these ideas, I turn to D.W. Winnicott's (1971) clinical invention of the Squiggle Game and his parallel theory of playing that *"takes time"* before having to *make sense* (Winnicott 1968a, 302, original emphasis). Playing is a creative and sometimes uncomfortable process that involves working through overlaps of time and making new meaning from what has already occurred but eludes consciousness. Through a reading of Winnicott's (1971) consultation with a nine-year-old child named Iiro, I illustrate how squiggles materialize psychoanalytic temporality, with a focus on how analytic time creates the ground to experience—again and anew—the affective force of past conflicts in the making of history as lived. Throughout, my analysis works in the space between social and clinical psychoanalysis to consider how a theory of psychoanalytic temporality can reframe the meaning of development by attending to the "ephemeral worlds" of psychic reality that instigate growth without repeating the hierarchical insistence that we grow *up* (Britzman 2011, 2).

PSYCHOANALYTIC TEMPORALITY

Within psychoanalysis, time is a tricky concept rather than a measure of chronology. Like no other discipline or discovery, Freud's theory of the unconscious bequeaths to us a complex internal structure that, in Britzman's (1998) words, "knows no time, no contradiction, indeed no negation" and in this sense, "tolerates all" (8). But while the unconscious "knows no time," psychoanalysis is not itself an escape hatch from temporality. It might instead be read as giving us a theory of why the "notion of time passing" is difficult (Birksted-Breen 2009, 39). As Jacob A. Arlow (1986) elaborates, "there is a deep-seated rebellion against the tyranny of time" because it instigates our earliest frustration of needs in having to wait and ends with the inevitable fact that we are "destined to lose the struggle against death" (507). Dana Birksted-Breen (2009) further explains that the opposing dynamic of timelessness poses its own difficulty that is felt as "timeless dread" made from the prospect of an experience with no end (42). Both time and timelessness are therefore difficult because, in the first instance, we are faced with mortality and, in the second, the overwhelm of boundless experience. Both Britzman (2006) and Burman (2024) highlight yet another difficulty in the belated quality of history that "is felt before its significance can be known" (Britzman 2006, 115). In this sense, history registers as an affective force that haunts the present and sets into motion what Dominick LaCapra (1987) calls "nonlinear, repetitive temporality" made from the unbidden return of conflicts that latch onto new objects and ideas in scenes of the present and future (226).

Psychoanalytic temporality therefore challenges chronological renderings of both development and history. As Britzman (1998) explains, the unconscious "unsettles the idea that the past—whether it goes under the name of development or history—can be laid to rest through the grasping of the proper order of events" (115). In educational contexts, too, analytic time departs from "the ordinary chronology of classrooms, grades, semesters, and years" because it refers to the affective return of early and forgotten scenes that interrupt progress narratives orienting efforts to teach and learn (Britzman 2003, 2). In psychoanalytic time, development is "uneven" (Britzman 2009, 27) and "can feel catastrophic" because it faces us with all we do not know and with what is difficult to know, and thus "signifies loss and empty space" (31). Psychoanalytic time therefore charges us to think about development as a reminder of incompleteness as our human condition: that none of us arrives at a state of total self-sufficiency, that we are driven by aspects of existence about which we know little, and that "there are always others" on whom we rely but who reside beyond our control (Britzman 2009, 29). Development is uneven because, as Britzman (2010) suggests, "Something about us does not grow up, and knowing this may return us to our oldest defences" (639).

Several psychoanalytic thinkers explain how such defenses work to stop and skip time (Arlow 1986; Birksted-Breen 2009, 2012; Green 2009; Kristeva 2010). For instance, André Green (2009) notes "the murder of time" (7) manifesting in repetitions that defend against creative processes—for Freud, mourning, and for Winnicott, playing—that are "capable of casting a fresh view on the past" (13). Julia Kristeva (2010) adds the idea of "abstract time:" a term she uses to describe a defensive condition that splits temporality into a "succession of immobile sections" in a bid to exact control over the fluctuations and losses that temporality implies (135). For Kristeva, abstract time disconnects the subject from the tempo of daily life and the rhythm of embodied relations that comprise being with others in the world (135). The key to loosening immobilized time resides in the labor of casting repetitions into what Kristeva (2010) describes as a "new temporality" or the "*mobility of duration*" (135, original emphasis). For Kristeva (2010), such mobility gives meaning to "unrepresentable dissociated passions" so that they may be experienced anew (135). In this sense, analytic time is a provision of containment needed to re-signify the impassioned return of unconscious material in ways that can serve creative living. Thus, while the "notion of time passing" may be difficult to bear, it is only through time passing that we may arrive somewhere different (Birksted-Breen 2009, 39).

Against this backdrop, the notion that development can be measured by linear stages can be read as its own murder that defends against the vulnerabilities and losses that accompany being-in-time. Burman (2017) takes up this line of inquiry in her earlier work, where she writes that "[a] psychoanalytic reading of developmental psychology offers glimpses into repressed themes of fear that underlie the scientific demand for control and prediction" (4). As Burman (2017) continues, psychoanalysis "enables a questioning of what lies behind the privileging of objectivity and control over the ambiguity, flux and ambivalence" of existence and the meaning of addressing these shifting processes in working with children (4). Thinking with Burman, the drive to objectivity—and developmental chronology—may defend against anxieties emerging from precisely the opposite condition: namely, that incompleteness is the ground of psychology. Such difficult knowledge is also why Burman (2017) describes psychoanalysis as the "repressed other of psychology" (104). To this, we can add that psychoanalytic time is the repressed other of chronology that involves "the reconnection of 'here and now' and 'then and there'" (Birksted-Breen 2009, 35) to create a "third dimension of time" where new meaning can thrive (Birksted-Breen 2009, 49). Development is, in this sense, "something that happens" to generate possibilities, rather than "a matter of social engineering" to be imposed in the name of progress and education (Burman 2024, 198).

THE DOING OF PLAYING: WAITING, SCRIBBLING, SQUIGGLING

While playing has been linked to Winnicott's theory of transitional space (Ogden 1995, 2021), Winnicott (1968a) also refers to a temporal quality of playing when he explains that "playing is doing" and that *doing things takes time*" (302, original emphasis). By emphasizing the doing of playing, Winnicott underscored the value of taking time with an experience before having to make sense of it. For Winnicott, playing is hard work and a method of "discovering the self through creative experience" (Lenormande 2018, 82). On this last point, Winnicott (1968a) made "a distinction between the meanings of the noun 'play' and the verbal noun 'playing'" (301). Much more than a rule-bound game or fun-filled event, Winnicott understood playing to be an existential process of ongoing self-discovery and psychic renewal, what Tamara Bibby (2018) describes as "the intensely serious business of living life creatively" (62). Playing is not, therefore, the opposite of reality, but a means to transform and connect more deeply to reality by infusing the world one inherits and finds with subjective "dream meaning and feeling" (Winnicott 1968a, 311). Through playing, it becomes possible to bend "phenomena from external reality" to serve "inner or personal reality" and thus to re-signify meaning in the service of creative living (Winnicott 1968a, 311).

Yet, critical scholars of childhood remind us that play more often repeats the exclusionary logics presuming to measure development, particularly in school contexts (Goodley and Runswick-Cole 2010). Because play is so often naturalized as a marker of development, children who do not play by normative rules are often constructed as lacking and as "non-playing" objects in need of "professional therapeutic intervention" (Goodley and Runswick-Cole 2010, 500). These critiques de-naturalize play by showing how its meaning is produced through dominant ideologies that uphold normative ideas about what it means to play and what it means to be a child at all (Jones, MacLure, Holmes, and MacRae 2012). In this context, Shin Ae Han and Joseph Tobin (2023) work against deficit narratives of "non-playing" to show how children may use play to experience the pleasures of "holding back and waiting" and "anticipation over participation" as empowering alternatives to linear temporal structures that define "appropriate" forms of playing in terms of individualism, mastery, and industry (8). Still, as much as play can be used to reify normative childhoods, the *denial* of children's play—whether in neoliberal, numbers-focused contexts of education (Genishi and Dyson 2009, 2012; Nxumalo 2019) or in colonially-produced conditions of war (Dyer and Georgis 2017)—interrupts children's access to "a site of radical creation in which the child tests out methods for rebuilding a world that has failed" (Dyer and Georgis 2017, 440).

When Winnicott distinguished the verb of playing from the noun of play, he too sought to loosen stereotyped meanings and developmental measures and instead to describe a more inclusive range of creative processes that serve spontaneity, meaning-making, and "the experience of aliveness" to which we all have a right (Winnicott 1960, 167). For Thomas Ogden (2021), who is thinking with Winnicott, aliveness can be defined as a state of being "in which an individual's ideas, feelings, and bodily sensations come to feel alive and real to him or her" (837). This feeling of aliveness can be contrasted with feeling false, unreal, or that one must hide to feel regarded and valued. Aliveness thrives in relationships, involving a feeling of, in Gail Boldt's words (2020), "being a vital *part of something*" that includes but is larger than the self (209, emphasis added). Winnicott's notion of playing as "doing" that "takes time" engages the real and relational qualities of aliveness because it invites a dwelling in depths of the unconscious with another person who can return its myriad meanings in a form that is both familiar *and* changed by the relation: that is, given back in a way that can be represented and rethought anew.

Presumptions and performances of analytic expertise indicate a failure to play on the part of the analyst—and that fuel repetitive responses and feelings of unreality. "There can be no witnessing," Britzman (2006) argues, when adults meet the surprises of children's play and questions with "premature explanations" or "wishes to enlighten" (128) that too often presume a child's deficiency (Farley 2018). By contrast, witnessing implies a duration that is both attentive and aimless, involving waiting without knowing: a position that Michael O'Loughlin and Almas Merchant (2012) describe as "limp" or "languid" (155). "The limp analyst," they explain, "waits for the child's unconscious to reanimate the analyst's interest. This reanimation leads to new aliveness in the analyst, which validates the existence and efficacy of the child's unconscious and allows for a new dynamic to emerge" (155). Analytic time is time in slow motion. The analyst must be willing to wait for meaning to emerge on a child's own time and to tolerate uncertainty without resorting to or skipping ahead to pre-set conclusions.

Returning to Birksted-Breen (2012), the analyst's position indeed "implies a withholding of immediate response and thus a duration" (819–820). As she explains it, the analyst's position is an embodiment of "the non-chronological time of reverie" that "suspends chronological time" (827). Birksted-Breen (2012) further links reverie to the analyst's "evenly suspended attention"—named above "languid"—that operates as a lightning rod for the patient's projected material and that the analyst takes in and, in time, returns in tolerable form, whether as an interpretation or in the case of Winnicott, a squiggle (819). In Birksted-Breen's (2012) words, reverie refers to the analyst's "mental processing and digestion of the patient's material" (821). Also called "reverberation time," reverie operates much like the to-and-fro of the Squiggle Game that symbolizes unassimilated material "in a rhythm which favours a temporality facilitating modification of the internal world and integration" (Birksted-Breen 2009, 44). "The time of reverberation," as Birksted-Breen (2009) elaborates, "is part of the experience of having feelings contained and made manageable" and does not operate by the external measure of clock time (40). In short, the tempo of the analytic relationship mirrors our earliest experiences of containment because it animates the non-chronological time of reverie, needed to transform unknown and seemingly immovable conflicts into history.

Outside the clinic, the non-chronological time of reverberation is mirrored in scholarship that reframes temporality within early childhood studies (Kohan and Weber 2020; Simms 2008). Significant to Winnicott's Squiggle Game, such reframing is often linked to arts-based methodologies with children (Sakr and Osgood 2019). Heather Malin (2019), for one, shows how the "act of art-making" with children is tied to meandering processes that are otherwise lost in developmental assessments that measure "completed art objects" against standardized images (13). Rachel Haydon and Lisa-Marie Gagliardi (2019), too, challenge the use of children's art objects to track individual development by underscoring the value of collaborative—and specifically, intergenerational—productions that facilitate connection and communication beyond any time-bound or finished product. Victoria Rijke (2019) further posits children's "scribble" as a postdevelopmental form inasmuch as it "is marked out by nonsensical, non-durable or illegible forms of transfer" (153). Not unlike Winnicott's use of the verb *playing*, Rijke (2019) draws on Roland Barthes to foreground the "'*ing*' suffix" in children's scribbles that illustrates "a continuing dynamic activity instead of something represented and complete" (173). As a form, scribble manifests a temporality of possibility that invites, as Rijke (2019) argues, "growth rather than development" insofar as it "remains unfinished, always" (173).

Whether or not squiggles can be read as art remains an open question; however, they may well be read as a postdevelopmental practice in their activation of non-linear time, mutuality, and incompleteness. They re-route the meaning of development from a linear and individual narrative to a collaborative and participatory work of history making. In what follows, I turn to Winnicott's (1971) therapeutic consultation with a nine-year-old child named Iiro to elaborate on the meaning of psychoanalytic temporality and the "doing" of playing as duration. Through the Squiggle Game, we catch a glimpse of "how the capacity to tolerate uncertainty enables a playing field to be established" (Armellini 2017, 16) and how, on this playing field, Winnicott and Iiro re-work older material through the lens of imagination in the creation of a new experience. That is, they show us how playing changes the past and future. At the same time, Winnicott claimed no expertise and instead took a languid position of both waiting for and welcoming unexpected meanings. The transformations made possible through this consultation, while not "clear-cut" (Winnicott 1971, 33), emerge from the doing of playing that also means centering duration and collaboration over chronology and expertise. Through the case of Iiro, we catch a glimpse of "the psychic time of learning" that involves attending to "obscure mental operations" and putting the affective conflicts they convey into time as the ground of embodying history as lived (Britzman 1998, 118).

ANALYTIC TIME IN THE CASE OF IIRO

The case of Iiro is one of many consultations that Winnicott undertook in a variety of settings, including Paddington Green Hospital and in his private practice. It appears alongside twenty other consultations in one of Winnicott's last publications and thus represents his late work. Winnicott had come to engage in therapeutic consultations with children instead of long or full-blown analyses to offer support for children needing a little extra boost or a helping hand in the ongoing work of living. The consultations center on a key psychoanalytic principle in that it is the patient who drives the topic of the session. As Winnicott (1971) writes, "these interviews are dominated by the child and not by me" (34). During consultations, Winnicott employed the Squiggle Game, a collaborative method of drawing that he began to use with children and youth as early as the Second World War (Farley 2011). The Squiggle Game began with Winnicott making a spontaneous stroke or mark in pencil on a square sheet of paper, which he then handed over to children to elaborate, revise, and/or modify. While visuality is the primary aesthetic of the Squiggle Game, the drawings produced by this method also engage and represent temporality, in large part, because they sketch out a space in which to put old and unthought feelings into time and to transform conflict into a meaningful history.

The drawings produced by the squiggle method are partial, affected, and not at all neutral. Winnicott (1971) readily acknowledged that "in no case would the same result have been attained if any other psychiatrist had been in my place" (31) and that "no two cases could be alike" because of his own humanity (34). There was also the humanity of the child that Winnicott (1968b) endeavored to call forth through the principle of "absolute freedom so that any modification may be accepted if appropriate" (320). With this last remark, Winnicott distinguished the Squiggle Game from other drawing methods used for therapeutic purposes in the early to mid-twentieth century, such as the Rorschach test, the Thematic Apperception Test (T.A.T.), and the Draw-A-Person Test, since the Squiggle Game did not carry a pre-set standard of what a child *should* create as a measure of normative growth (Farley 2011). Winnicott (1968b) went as far as to describe "defeat" if "something stereotyped were to emerge" and instead underlined the importance of "free participation," a distinguishing feature of the Squiggle Game, and which included that of the analyst (320). In relation to this last point, Winnicott (1971) also cautioned analysts against stereotyped interpretations, such as when "a therapist has interpreted a snake as a penis symbol" (35). This last idea highlights the anti-developmental character of squiggles in that they do not presume to measure a child against normative standards and instead welcome aesthetic moments of surprise—what Burman (2017) names above "ambiguity, flux and ambivalence"—that disrupt fantasies of "objectivity and control" implied within developmentalism (4).

The case of Iiro is also unique in at least two ways that nuance the meaning of analytic temporality. First, the case involves two different languages at work within a therapeutic context. Throughout, Winnicott spoke English and Iiro spoke Finnish. While Winnicott (1971) mentions their "excellent interpreter" Helka Asikainen, who was also a social worker and psychologist, he recalls that "she became quickly forgotten by both Iiro and myself" (37) because the communication between them unfolded without "much talking" (Winnicott 1971, 37) and through the "doing" of playing (Winnicott 1968a, 302). The case of Iiro therefore highlights playing as a creative process of transformation, which Winnicott (1968a) felt was downplayed in the analytic focus on the content of children's play. The case also illustrates how the gestural presence of being in a relationship can create a feeling of being understood even when language is not shared.

Second, the case of Iiro represents a child's relationship with his body and disability, and in this way stands as a reminder that child analysts have long been at work with diverse groups of children identifying across a wide spectrum. Still, scholarship exploring the relationship between psychoanalysis and disability studies remains relatively scant (for exceptions, see Farley 2018; Goodley 2009, 2011; Goodley, Liddiard, and Runswick-Cole 2018). Among studies that do examine such links, *social* psychoanalysis is most often identified as a productive framework through which to understand the process of splitting underpinning the systemic exclusion of disabled people within ableist and disablist structures (Goodley 2011; Kristeva 2010). Much less common, if at all, are studies that explore clinical psychoanalysis to surface generative practices with children, in large part, because of the implication of psychoanalysis in pathologizing difference and seeking normative treatment outcomes (Farley 2018). In this context, the case of Iiro may be read as an heir to this legacy inasmuch as Winnicott focuses on Iiro's internal world over the social structures disabling his experience. But it may also be read as a counterpoint to this legacy in that the consultation features Winnicott's efforts to support Iiro in representing the existential aspects of his disability not as a deficit, but as full of complex dynamics of desire, anxiety, surprise, and agency.

Winnicott met Iiro somewhat spontaneously during a trip to Lastenlinna, the Children's Hospital in Helsinki, Finland, where the analyst was invited to present casework to a group of psychiatrists, psychologists, psychiatric social workers, and nurses under the auspices of the World Health Organization (WHO). During that visit, Iiro was on the orthopedic ward. Winnicott (1971) engaged him in an interview so that the presenting case would be one with which the hospital staff was already familiar. This ostensibly meant that Iiro's interview was not a referral and did not show, in Winnicott's words, "any urgent presenting problem that would ordinarily involve a child psychiatrist" (37). Indeed, this was true of many of Winnicott's (1971) therapeutic consultations involving the squiggle method, for he viewed these meetings as "one way of getting into contact with a child" on the basis that we may all benefit from working through emotional concerns in the presence of an attentive and open listener (29). Winnicott (1971) even warned readers "against being excited" about finding therapeutic successes, because in most cases, "there will be no clear-cut result" (33). In this context, Winnicott's consultation with Iiro offers a poignant example of the therapeutic potential of communication without therapy, without the presumption of deficiency, and without the idea of a certain outcome.

The consultation begins with Iiro's interpretation of Winnicott's first squiggle. "It's a duck's foot" (38). For Winnicott, Iiro's comment "came as a complete surprise" and suggested his possible desire "to communicate on the subject of his disability" (38), about which Winnicott deliberately said nothing. Instead, he waded into the situation by reciprocating with a squiggle of a duck's foot, to which Iiro responded by drawing his own version of a duck's foot.

With the "subject of webbed feet" in clear view, Winnicott continued to "lean back and wait" for further communication on the subject (40). The next few squiggle drawings veered away from ducks and feet until Winnicott made one of Iiro's squiggles "into a rather awkward-looking swan" (44), which prompted a discussion of Iiro's great pleasure in swimming, a theme

Figure 1.1 Drawing of a Duck's Foot. Copyright © 1996 from *Therapeutic Consultations in Child Psychiatry* by D.W. Winnicott. Reproduced by permission of Taylor and Francis Group, LLC, a division of Informa plc.

that returned again and again in the consultation. About the swan, Winnicott supposedly belatedly said that he "was vaguely continuing the duck theme" even though he did "not remember thinking this out" on account of being "engaged in the game that [they] were both enjoying" (44). Iiro made Winnicott's next squiggle into a shoe while asserting its completeness—"it did not need anything doing to it" (45)—the meaning of which would emerge later on.

Moments later, Winnicott's implication in the theme of hands and feet became more intentional when he drew an image that "was rather deliberately shaped so that [Iiro] could have made it into a hand" (46). "Whether this was right or wrong," Winnicott did not say, except to admit his spontaneity in the doing of playing: "I felt like doing it" (46). At this same moment, Winnicott noticed Iiro's own spontaneous gesture in his "unwillingness to look at his own hands," an observation about which Winnicott decided to not "make any remark" (46). That is, Winnicott did not make an interpretation, but rather allowed for the duration of time and doing of playing to continue in their unfolding. Next, Iiro made a squiggle of a hand that, when prompted to share "what he was thinking," he exclaimed, "It just happened"—leading Winnicott to suggest "*he had surprised himself*" (47, original emphasis), suggesting the emergence of meanings about which he himself did not have conscious awareness. In this unexpected moment, Winnicott also noticed that Iiro "was now near to looking at his own hand" (47). Notably, Winnicott did not intervene with an interpretation but "allowed things to rest a little" and so created a space to dwell in time as the doing of playing continued (47).

The next squiggle stayed with the theme of hands, when Iiro made a squiggle featuring an angle that "was almost exactly the same as the angle between two prominent fingers of his left hand" that were "three or four inches away from the drawing, holding down the paper" (48).

At this point, now the twelfth squiggle, Winnicott speculates about the meaning implied in their drawings so far: "It is like your left hand, isn't it!" (48). Iiro responded with some agreement, saying, "Oh yes, a bit" (48), and then began to tell Winnicott about his past and future operations, as well as to share that "his feet were the same"—recalling to Winnicott's mind Iiro's earlier drawing of the shoe (48). He also shared his desire "to be able to play the flute," prompting Winnicott to ask, "What would you like to be when you grow up?" (49). In response, Iiro offered that he "will be like daddy, a building contractor" or "like the man who teaches handicrafts at school" (49). At this point, Winnicott made a mental note of two ideas: the first, that Iiro seemed "almost too compliant," and second, that Iiro seemed to be grappling

Figure 1.2 **Drawing of a Hand.** Copyright © 1996 from *Therapeutic Consultations in Child Psychiatry* by D.W. Winnicott. Reproduced by permission of Taylor and Francis Group, LLC, a division of Informa plc.

with the "difficult idea that he would like to be able to do the very things that his condition would make difficult or impossible" (49). In attributing difficulty to Iiro's "condition," Winnicott did not name or challenge the ableist and disablist world in which they both lived. In this way, the consultation lays bare how a psychoanalytic focus on the internal world can overlook an examination of disabling environments and ideologies (Michalko 2002) that seek to designate which children are and are not imagined as having viable futures in a range of endeavors, including "building," "handicrafts," and "teaching."

In this same context, it is also important to note that Winnicott (1971) invited Iiro to notice the emotional impact of such exclusions by asking him to contemplate why he might feel "cross" (49). That is, Winnicott invited Iiro to contemplate how his future aspirations may be linked to normative expectations and an archive of anger. In response, Iiro underscored his agency by way of a negation: "I'm never cross. It is my own choice. I choose to be operated on" (49). Iiro's articulation touches on a body of literature that frames agency as a relational effort: i.e., what children make happen in the context of relationships and normative discourses aiming to corral differences into normative (and neoliberal) outcomes (Garlen et al. 2022; Karmiris 2023; Komulainen 2007; Puar 2017). While Winnicott was not privy to these discussions, his psychoanalytic orientation meant he was prepared to think about conflict at the core of agency, and specifically how Iiro's desires for himself may be affected by his dependency on love and loss. In probing whether Iiro might feel cross, Winnicott opened a space in which he might speculate about how his future aspirations inherit social expectations, how the desire to fit in can be linked to the anger of being excluded, and why the choices we make for ourselves can provoke more questions than they do answers.

Returning to the case, Winnicott and Iiro delved more deeply into conflict in the context of Iiro's creation of yet another water creature that he called an eel. While it "was eel season in Finland" at the time, thus indicating the influence of the material world, Winnicott also probes interiority, or what Iiro might want for and from the eel, asking, "Shall we put it back in the lake or cook it and eat it?" (50). Iiro quickly states his intention: "We will let it go back and swim in the lake because it is so small" (50). Taking into consideration the eel's smallness and Iiro's own pleasure in swimming, Winnicott now speculates that Iiro may identify with the eel, using the underwater creature to communicate something about his own unknown history of desire, and that prompted Winnicott finally to offer an interpretation:

> If we think of you as small, you would like to swim in the lake or swim on the lake like the duck. You are telling me that you are fond of yourself with your webbed hands and feet and that you need people to love you that way as you were when you were born. Growing up, you begin to want to play the piano, and

the flute and to do handicrafts and so you agree to be operated on, but the first thing is to be loved as you are and as you were born. (50)

The interpretation is deep, surfacing a desire for love—and accompanying possibility of its loss—as the condition of existence. Once again, Winnicott's interpretation does not offer a position on whether Iiro should or should not undergo treatments, for this is not the work of psychoanalysis. Rather, Winnicott's interpretation sets conflict into analytic time, where Iiro may contemplate his desire before having to worry about the future others may desire for him.

Winnicott's interpretation prompted Iiro to add another detail that Winnicott did not know previously: "Mother has the same thing that I have got" (50). Soon thereafter, Iiro drew a replica of his left hand, punctuated by an explicit comment about the repetition of this motif: "It's the same again!" (51). As before, Winnicott does not offer an interpretation and instead allows for the unfolding of experience in the presence of "evenly suspended attention" (Birksted-Breen 2012, 819). The very last squiggle is started by Winnicott, who then hands over to Iiro, who, as Winnicott recalls, "quickly saw what he wanted, putting an eye and the webbed feet and again he said: 'It's a duck'" (53).

 In contrast to the straight angles and stark lines of their previous squiggles, this final drawing is thick with curves. As Winnicott speculates, this fulsome bird brings them back to the beginning of the consultation, this time with the difference of Iiro's "reinstatement of his love of himself" (53). As if to punctuate this moment of feeling loved in and as himself, Winnicott asked Iiro to inscribe his name and age on this last drawing, which he did. For at least five years after their meeting, Iiro wrote letters to Winnicott that were often accompanied by photographs of his dog and friend while fishing on a lake: activities that may be read as evidence of the ongoing doing of playing in Iiro's life.

Following the consultation, Winnicott had occasion to meet with Iiro's mother at her request, and that was again translated by social worker and psychologist Helka Asikainene. During this meeting, the mother explained to Winnicott she had been anxious about the congenital nature of her condition, which came to the fore upon Iiro's birth. At first, the mother recalls her feelings of devastation, which were soon allayed by the possibility of having "his fingers and toes mended by persistently using the orthopaedic surgeon" (54). The mother also spoke of her guilt and superlative love for Iiro when she thought about the promise of surgical intervention, saying: "I have loved him more than the others" (54). However, the mother's alignment of love with "mending" repeats a common trope of overcoming that, as Amanda Apgar (2023) argues, justifies "normalizing" interventions that assume disability "can

Figure 1.3 Drawing of a Duck. Copyright © 1996 from *Therapeutic Consultations in Child Psychiatry* by D.W. Winnicott. Reproduced by permission of Taylor and Francis Group, LLC, a division of Informa plc.

and should be corrected" (17; see also Michalko 2002; Titchkosky 2007). The "logic of cure" implied inside this trope "responds not by changing the world, but by attempting to change the body" (Apgar 2023, 17) and thereby constructs "happily ever after" in terms of a child "fitting in" (Apgar 2023, 19).

The case of Iiro reflects some of this history and thus frames development as a complex negotiation among a child's embodiment of self, desires for love and belonging, future aspirations, fears of loss, and family ties as these dynamics are also submerged in dominant ideologies of developmentalism that more often "limit rather than enable" (Burman 2024, 198). The case therefore invites us to name psychical processes—including desire, choice, guilt, and relief—as effects of inherited structures and legacies to be represented and reimagined, rather than as innate and unchanging traits (Ahmed 2010; Eng and Han 2019). The case of Iiro also invites a psychoanalysis *of* the social world—and its relentless "culture of the perfect child"—as its own pathology: what Kristeva (2010) calls a "malaise" that denies all that is "imperfect about the human condition" by projecting lack onto those it constructs as 'other' (255; see also Young-Bruehl 2012).

As much as the case of Iiro exposes how the malaise of ableism presses down on a child's humanity, it illustrates how the act of playing gives time over to work through the residual effects of this inheritance. Indeed, the to-and-fro of Iiro and Winnicott's squiggles symbolize an affective force of history that quietly shadowed Iiro's future aspirations, just as these little drawings offered an occasion to situate Iiro's own desires in relation to—but not necessarily determined by—the future desired for him. The case of Iiro therefore sketches a theory of development as a creative labor of working through conflict, rather than an assimilation to pre-set outcomes. In this context, Iiro's stated desire to change and his unspoken desire to be loved as he was born need not stand in opposition, but rather underscore the value of symbolizing conflict in the making of childhood history as lived.

DURATION: ON DEVELOPMENT BEYOND DEVELOPMENTALISM

Metaphorically and materially, developmentalism segments time into a chronology that imposes hierarchy and entrenches normative conceptions of learning and growth. In this sense, there remains good reason to critique the notion of linear time at the core of conventional developmental discourse. However, the seemingly opposite idea of timelessness is not an escape hatch from the limits of chronology. The timelessness of the unconscious can be its own terror, invoking fantasies and fears that are not necessarily experienced as freedom. Timelessness can also open onto a social and political abyss of exclusion. As Jonathan Silin (1995) reminds us, the idea that children can or should be taken "out of time" aligns with the troubling (and seemingly timeless) ideal of childhood innocence that protects the most privileged and severs children's lived experiences from "the worlds in which they occur and the interactions that give them shape and substance" (50–51). It can be a relief for a child to experience duration and use that time as a critical resource to give shape and substance to seemingly endless conflicts by setting them into the rhythms of the social world and tempo of life itself.

Psychoanalytically, the antidote to chronology is not timelessness, but duration. Duration gives shape and substance to the force of past conflicts by bringing them into the narrative relief of history, where history refers not to a "proper order of events" (Britzman 1998, 115), but to a circuitous labor of re-signifying old plots as the ground for their continual renewal without a set destination. The mobility of duration therefore offers a vantage point from which to be critical of developmentalism without at the same time doing away with the fact of development as "something that happens" beyond the limits of chronology (Burman 2024, 198). Duration is a reminder that development is uneven, that history returns, that conflict is never fully resolved, and that incompleteness is a condition of being and feeling alive. Duration is a reminder that while we cannot escape time, history is not already written and that through history, we can do more with our chances and our childhoods.

REFERENCES

Ahmed, Sara. 2010. *The Promise of Happiness*. Durham: Duke University Press.

Apgar, Amanda. 2023. *The Disabled Child: Memoirs of a Normal Future*. Ann Arbor: University of Michigan Press.

Arlow, Jacob A. 1986. "Psychoanalysis and Time." *Journal of the American Psychoanalytic Association* 34, no. 3: 507–528.

Armellini, Marco. 2017. "Introduction to Volume 10." In *The Collected Works of D.W. Winnicott: Volume 10*, edited by Lesley Caldwell and Helen Taylor Robinson, 3–21. Oxford: Oxford University Press.

Bibby, Tamara. 2018. *The Creative Self: Psychoanalysis, Teaching and Learning in the Classroom*. London: Routledge.

Birksted-Breen, Dana. 2009. "'Reverberation Time,' Dreaming and the Capacity to Dream." *International Journal of Psychoanalysis* 90, no. 1: 35–51. DOI: 10.1111/j.1745-8315.2008.00118.x.

Birksted-Breen, Dana. 2012. "Taking Time: The Tempo of Psychoanalysis." *International Journal of Psychoanalysis* 93, no. 4: 819–835. DOI: 10.1111/j.1745831 5.2012.00597.x.

Blaise, Mindy. 2005. *Playing it Straight: Uncovering Gender Discourses in the Early Childhood Classroom*. New York: Routledge.

Boldt, Gail. 2020. "Theorizing Vitality in the Literacy Classroom." *Reading Research Quarterly* 56, no. 2: 207–221. DOI: 10.1002/rrq.307.

Breslow, Jacob. 2021. *Ambivalent Childhoods: Speculative Futures and the Psychic Life of the Child*. Minneapolis: University of Minnesota Press.

Britzman, Deborah P. 1998. *Lost Subjects, Contested Objects: Toward a Psychoanalytic Inquiry of Learning*. Albany: State University of New York Press.

Brtizman, Deborah P. 2003. *After-Education: Anna Freud, Melanie Klein and Psychoanalytic Histories of Learning*. Albany: State University of New York Press.

Britzman, Deborah P. 2006. "Little Hans, Fritz, and Ludo: On the Curious History of Gender in the Psychoanalytic Archive." *Studies in Gender and Sexuality* 7, no. 2: 113–140. DOI: 10.2513/s15240657sgs0702_1.

Britzman, Deborah P. 2009. *The Very Thought of Education: Psychoanalysis and the Impossible Professions*. Albany: State University of New York Press.

Britzman, Deborah P. 2010. "On the Madness of Lecturing on Gender: A Psychoanalytic Discussion." *Gender and Education* 22, no. 6: 633–646. DOI: 10.1080/09540253.2010.519579.

Britzman, Deborah P. 2011. *Freud and Education: An Introduction*. New York: Routledge.

Burman, Erica. 2017. *Deconstructing Developmental Psychology*. London and New York: Routledge.

Burman, Erica. 2024. *Child as Method: Othering, Interiority and Materialism*. London and New York: Routledge.

de Rijke, Victoria. 2019. "'It Might Get Messy, or Not be Right:' Scribble as Postdevelopmental Art." In *Postdevelopmental Approaches to Childhood Art*, edited by Mona Sakr and Jayne Osgood, 153–176. London: Bloomsbury.

Dyer, Hannah. 2019. *The Queer Aesthetics of Childhood: Asymmetries of Innocence and the Cultural Politics of Childhood*. New Brunswick: Rutgers.

Dyer, Hannah and Dina Georgis. 2017. "Play Interrupted: Love and Learning amidst Difficult Futures for the Children of Gaza." *Review of Education, Pedagogy, and Cultural Studies* 39 no. 5: 431–445. DOI: 10.1080/10714413.2017.1372973.

Edelman, Lee. 2004. *No Future: Queer Theory and the Death Drive*. Durham: Duke University Press.

Eng, David and Shinhee Han. 2019. *Racial Melancholia, Racial Disassociation: On the Social and Psychic Lives of Asian Americans*. Durham: Duke University Press.

Farley, Lisa. 2011. "Squiggle Evidence: The Child, the Canvas, and the Negative Labor of History." *History and Memory* 23, no. 2: 5–39. DOI: 10.1057/pcs.2015.59.

Farley, Lisa. 2018. *Childhood Beyond Pathology: A Psychoanalytic Study of Development and Diagnosis*. Albany: State University of New York Press.

Garlen, Julie C. 2019. "Interrogating Innocence: 'Childhood' as Exclusionary Social Practice." *Childhood* 26, no. 1: 54–67. DOI: 10.1177/0907568218811484.

Garlen, Julie C., Debbie Sonu, Lisa Farley, and Sandra Chang-Kredl. 2022. "Agency as Assemblage: Using Childhood Artefacts to Examine Children's Relations with Schooling." *Journal of Childhood, Education & Society* 3, no. 2: 122–138. DOI: 10.37291/2717638X.202232170.

Genishi, Celia and Anne Haas Dyson. 2009. *Children, Language, and Literacy: Diverse Learners in Diverse Times*. New York: Teachers College Press and Washington, DC: National Association for the Education of Young Children.

Genishi, Celia and Anne Haas Dyson. 2012. "Racing to the Top: Who's Accounting for the Children?" *Bank Street Occasional Paper Series* 27: 18–20. DOI: 10.58295/2375-3668.1067.

Gill-Peterson, Julian. 2018. *Histories of the Transgender Child*. Minneapolis: University of Minnesota Press.

Goodley, Dan. 2009. "Bringing the Psyche Back into Disability Studies: The Case of the Body with/out Organs." *Journal of Literary & Cultural Disability Studies* 1, no. 3: 257–272. DOI: https://www.muse.jhu.edu/article/365203.

Goodley, Dan. 2011. "Social Psychoanalytic Disability Studies." *Disability & Society* 26, no. 6: 715–728. DOI: 10.1080/09687599.2011.602863.

Goodley, Dan, Kristy Liddiard, and Katherine Runswick-Cole. 2018. "Feeling Disability: Theories of Affect and Critical Disability Studies." *Disability & Society* 33, no. 2: 197–217. DOI: 10.1080/09687599.2017.1402752.

Goodley, Dan and Katherine Runswick-Cole. 2010. "Emancipating Play: Dis/abled Children, Development and Deconstruction." *Disability and Society* 25, no. 4: 499–512. DOI: 10.1080/09687591003755914.

Goodley, Dan, Katherine Runswick-Cole, and Kristy Liddiard. 2016. "The Dishuman Child." *Discourse: Studies in the Cultural Politics of Education* 37, no. 5: 770–784. DOI: 10.1080/01596306.2015.1075731.

Green, André. 2009. "From the Ignorance of Time to the Murder of Time: From the Murder of Time to the Misrecognition of Temporality in Psychoanalysis." In *The Experience of Time Psychoanalytic Perspectives*, edited by Jorge Canestri and Leticia Glocer Fiorini, 1–19. New York: Routledge.

Halberstam, Jack. 2011. *The Queer Art of Failure*. Durham: Duke University Press.

Heydon, Rachel and Lisa-Marie Gagliardi. 2019. "Reconceptualizing Early Childhood Art: The Lessons of Intergenerational Art Curricula and Postdevelopmental Theorizing." In *Postdevelopmental Approaches to Childhood Art*, edited by Mona Sakr and Jayne Osgood, 87–110. London: Bloomsbury.

Jones, Liz, Maggie MacLure, Rachel Holmes, and Christina MacRae. 2012. "Children and Objects: Infection and Affection." *Early Years: An International Research Journal* 32, no. 1, 49–60. DOI: 10.1080/09575146.2011.593029.

Karmiris, Maria. 2023. "Reading Silences/Silent Readings: Disrupting the Hegemony of Voice In Research with Disabled Children." *Childhood* 30, no. 2: 116–128. DOI: 10.1177/0907568223116437.

Kohan, Walter Omar and Barbara Weber, eds. 2020. *Thinking, Childhood, and Time: Contemporary Perspectives on the Politics of Education*. Lanham: Lexington Books.

Komulainen, Sirkka. 2007. "The Ambiguity of the Child's 'Voice' in Social Research." *Childhood* 14, no. 1: 11–28. DOI: 10.1177/09075682070685.

Kristeva, Julia. 2010. *Hatred and Forgiveness*. New York: Columbia University Press.

LaCapra, Dominick. 1987. "History and Psychoanalysis." *Critical Inquiry* 13, no. 2: 222–251.

Land, Nicole. 2020. "Tending, Counting, and Fitting with Post-Developmental Fat(s) in Early Childhood Education." *Contemporary Issues in Early Childhood Education* 23, no. 1 (February): 1–16. DOI: 10.1177/1463949120907383.

Land, Nicole, Cristina Delgado Vintimilla, Veronica Pacini-Ketchabaw, and Lucille Angus. 2020. "Propositions Towards Educating Pedagogists: Decentering the Child." *Contemporary Issues in Early Childhood Education* 23, no. 2 (September): 1–13. DOI: 10.1177/146394912095352.

Lenormand, Marie. 2018. "Winnicott's Theory of Playing: A Reconsideration." *The International Journal of Psychoanalysis* 99, no. 1: 82–102. DOI: 10.1080/00207578.2017.1399068.

Levander, Caroline F. 2017. *Cradle of Liberty: Race, the Child, and National Belonging from Thomas Jefferson to W. E. B. DuBois*. Durham: Duke University Press.

Malin, Heather. 2019. "Art-Making as Activity: How Children Make Meaning Through Art." In *Postdevelopmental Approaches to Childhood Art*, edited by Mona Sakr and Jayne Osgood, 13–28. London: Bloomsbury.

Michalko, Rod. 2002. *The Difference That Disability Makes*. Philadelphia: Temple University Press.

Nxumalo, Fikile. 2019. *Decolonizing Place in Early Childhood Education*. New York: Routledge.

Ogden, Thomas H. 1997. "Some Theoretical Comments on Personal Isolation." In *Encounters with Autistic States: A Memorial Tribute to Frances Tustin*, edited by Theodore Mitrani and Judith L. Mitrani, 179–194. Lanham: Jason Aronson.

Ogden, Thomas H. 2021. "What Alive Means: On Winnicott's 'Transitional Objects and Transitional Phenomena'." *International Journal of Psychoanalysis* 102, no. 5: 837–856. DOI: 10.1080/00207578.2021.1935265.

O'Loughlin, Michael and Almas Merchant. 2012. "Working Obliquely with Children." *Journal of Infant, Child, and Adolescent Psychotherapy* 11, no. 2: 149–159. DOI: 10.1080/15289168.2012.675820.

Pacini-Ketchabaw, Veronica, Sylvia Kind, and Laurie L. M. Kocher. 2016. *Encounters with Materials in Early Childhood Education*. New York: Routledge.

Pacini-Ketchabaw, Veronica, Fikile Nxumalo, Laurie Kocher, Enid Elliot, and Alejandra Sanchez. 2015. *Journeys: Complexifying Early Childhood Practices through Pedagogical Narration*. Toronto: University of Toronto Press.

Puar, Jasbir K. 2017. *The Right to Maim: Debility, Capacity, Disability*. Durham: Duke University Press.

Rollo, Toby. 2018. "Feral Children: Settler Colonialism, Progress, and the Figure of the Child." *Settler Colonial Studies* 8, no. 1: 60–79. DOI: 10.1080/2201473X.2016.1199826.

Sakr, Mona and Jayne Osgood, eds. 2019. *Postdevelopmental Approaches to Childhood Art*. London: Bloomsbury.

Shin, Ae Han and Joesph Tobin. 2023. "Using Walter Benjamin to Rethink Children's Non-Participation in Play Activities." *Contemporary Issues in Early Childhood*, online first, 1–15. DOI: 10.1177/14639491231206944.

Silin, Jonathan. 1995. *Sex, Death, and the Education of Children: Our Passion for Ignorance in the Age of AIDS*. New York: Teachers College Press.

Simms, Eva M. 2008. *The Child in the World: Embodiment, Time, and Language in Early Childhood*. Detroit: Wayne State University Press.

Stockton, Kathryn Bond. 2009. *The Queer Child: Or, Growing Sideways in the Twentieth Century*. Durham: Duke University Press.

Tesar, Marek. 2016. "Timing Childhoods: An Alternative Reading of Children's Development through Philosophy of Time, Temporality, Place and Space." *Contemporary Issues in Early Childhood* 17, no. 4: 399–408. DOI: 10.1177/1463949116677792.

Titchkosky, Tanya. 2007. *Reading and Writing Disability Differently: The Textured Life of Embodiment*. Toronto: University of Toronto Press.

Winnicott, D. W. 1960. "Ego Distortion in Terms of True and False Self." In *The Collected Works of D.W. Winnicott, Volume 6*, edited by Lesley Caldwell and Helen Taylor Robinson, 159–171. Oxford: Oxford University Press.

Winnicott, D. W. 1968a. "Playing: A Theoretical Statement." In *The Collected Works of D.W. Winnicott: Volume 8*, edited by Lesley Caldwell and Helen Taylor Robinson, 299–312. Oxford: Oxford University Press.

Winnicott, D. W. 1968b. "Letter to L. Joseph Stone, 18 June." In *The Collected Works of D.W. Winnicott: Volume 8*, edited by Lesley Caldwell and Helen Taylor Robinson, 319–320. Oxford: Oxford University Press.

Winnicott, D. W. 1971. "Therapeutic Consultations in Child Psychiatry." In *The Collected Works of D.W. Winnicott: Volume 10*, edited by Lesley Caldwell and Helen Taylor Robinson, 37–55. Oxford: Oxford University Press.

Young-Bruehl, Elizabeth. 2012. *Childism: Confronting Prejudice against Children.* New Haven: Yale University Press.

Chapter 2

Contemporary Gender(s)

Reconsidering Freudian, Postfoundational, and Psychoanalytic Perspectives for Educators and Practitioners

Janice Kroeger, Christopher Konieczko,
Dana Oleskiewicz, Alexandra C. Gunn,
and Andrea Sanchez

YESTERDAY: OLD IDEAS

In this chapter, we grapple with historical conceptualizations of gender, mostly interrogating Freudian- and Piagetian-derived concepts in relation to postfoundational theories. We describe current manifestations of gender and sexuality, navigating toward a contemporary understanding of gender within critical feminist–informed definitions of care and practice. We ask these questions:

- What is responsive when new forms of social understanding and technology-assisted gender constructions are available?
- What are supportive responses to gender-diverse young people?

Drawing from inclusive psychoanalytical frameworks and wielding new questions about how teachers and others who work with children have traditionally understood gender or gender permanence (informed by late nineteenth-century constructs), we reconsider gender construction within contemporary critical feminist and queer social theory. We focus on constructs of childhood, including new thinking about gender diversity and gender-diverse childhood(s) that are informed by parents and children and are written for the care workers who support them.

In this chapter, we reconsider many of the ways educators have been taught about children, childhood, sexuality, and gender, and the practices of care workers of all types, because we are largely influenced by Freudian theories and Piagetian constructs taken up and promoted via Western developmental psychology. We (the authors of this chapter) are challenged by an eclectic blend of older and newer ways of thinking about childhood, gender, and sexuality, and we are advancing new ways of thinking that are informed by deconstructions of developmental thought (Burman 2011), as well as reconsiderations of ethical responsibility to queer children informed by queer and trans theories (Chapman 2023; Steele and Nicholson 2020). Our backgrounds and experiences vary: Alex and Janice were trained in an earlier time of teacher education, having finished doctorates in the early 2000s; Chris is educated in clinical counseling, itself using many forms of psychoanalysis; Dana is educated in environmental and biological sciences and is earning a Ph.D. in cultural studies; and Andrea is currently earning a Ph.D. within early childhood teacher education.

Freudian constructs, produced as normative, have dominated the late twentieth and early twenty-first centuries in conjunction with developmentalism, and they still hold sway within the teacher training and practice milieu (Counterman and Kirkwood 2013; Flanagan 2011; Wurtele and Kenny 2011). Freudian ideas are often presented and dismissed as outdated. Nevertheless, more contemporary ideas about deconstructing gender (or understanding gender beyond a binary construct), which are more closely aligned with the healthy development of queer children, are only briefly mentioned in a child development textbook (Trawick-Smith 2022). Poststructural, feminist, or queer studies are not mentioned in contrast to Freud's (or Piaget's or Kohlberg's) work; however, those constructs have gained purchase in many disciplines associated with youth, such as childhood studies, psychiatry, social work, and counseling. We hope to influence continued progress in a direction of understanding gender and sexuality more fully in the field of childhood education because for some children, Freudian constructs and the unconscious ideals proliferating from them are counterproductive—and even harmful—especially considering the conservative U.S. legislative actions that are undermining gender-affirming care today.[1]

Freudian theory has implicitly dominated constructs of family life, gender, and sexuality. This dominance persists despite steady countermanding examples from cultural anthropologists, feminists, and other social scientists, who have demonstrated that the breadth of interpretation of gender expression and sexuality across the world and across time is substantial (Coward 1980; Quinn and Luttrell 2008; Mimica 2008). Many scholars argue that theories such as the Oedipus complex are artifacts of colonialism and the patriarchal father-headed household of a bygone Victorian era (Burman 2011; Coward

1980). Compulsory heterosexuality and the "ideal" nuclear family have been primary drivers of reproduction and social modeling for the past two centuries; nevertheless, family types and sexualities beyond the psychological construct of "normal" have proliferated, gaining a substantial hold for us to reconsider what is healthy for children (Cornell University 2015; Heilman 2008; Rich 1980; Tasker and Golombok 1997).

We (the authors) think, as many scholars do, that a child's ability to define themselves as a gendered or sexual being is one of the child's most basic human rights. Therefore, it is necessary to scrutinize institutional practices, legalities, and binary categorizations of self (which have been codified into law in many places) (DePalma and Atkinson 2010; DePalma 2013; Field and Mattson 2016; Paechter 2017; Rosky 2013). We also know that contemporary children will pick and choose from the human activities and cultural models available to them, as their parents did before them have, which will ultimately shape their own sexuality and gender identity within culture as they grow. Conceptualizations of gender identity that are narrowly defined with Freudian and Piagetian constructs have not kept pace with changes in human behavior or historical changes in families. Nevertheless, a child's gendered self largely comes to be understood by the individual within a time frame of childhood, and it is often supported by care professions and families (using psychoanalytic frameworks). Children whose gender transcends a binary definition are particularly impacted by unconscious or deliberately narrow expectations for their identity and behavior from the adults around them.

TODAY: NEW QUESTIONS

How to support children psychoanalytically in classrooms, communities, homes, and clinics always depends on these factors: when and how children bring topics up, how they choose to express themselves, how they ask questions and come to learn, and how adults support them. Gender and sexuality are complicated subjects for many care workers. However, owing to queer activism(s) and the lived experiences of trans and intersex individuals, the recent conceptual contributions of intersectionality and feminism(s), and supportive health care, transgender people have taught us that "gender development and sexuality identity development are two separate developmental tracks" which are "crossing at certain points" (Ehrensaft 2017, 59; Kroeger 2023; Stryker 2008). Moreover, what is spoken about or understood between children and adults regarding young children's gender development largely depends on adults who either help them gain clarity about gender and sexuality or ignore their questions.

For example, in early childhood classrooms around the world, young children have persistently and knowingly participated in cross-gender play. They have openly performed nonconforming behavior throughout childhood despite strong objections and even sanctions from peers, teachers, and parents alike. Examples include dressing in clothes or playing with toys considered "wrong" for their gender. This cross-gender experience of play includes cis- and transgender children (Alegria 2016; Ehrensaft 2014; Gunn 2008, 2023b; Kroeger, Recker, and Gunn 2019; Surtees 2005; Taylor and Richardson 2004). In Gunn's (2023b) description of boys playing cars and families in the sandpit, one boy confidently suggests his peer take the role of mum so they can play their story of "mums, dads, kids, and cars" despite there being no girl children immediately playing in their group. Ultimately, the invitation wasn't taken up by the boy who was nominated to be "mum" but gender fluid play and expressions are regularly observed in early childhood play.

Classroom studies across many decades have shown that young children are exceptionally astute and often imitate and attempt to understand romantic love and human sexuality, even if not directly taught how to think or what to think about social behavior by the adults around them (Blaise 2010; Cahill and Theilheimer 1999; Sotevik 2023; Surtees 2005). For example, we presume children's frequent and detailed performative play around sexuality (especially straightness) is to explore and examine both what they see and what they are "trying on" for themselves at present, which might inform the performances of their future selves (Blaise 2010). In Sotevik's 2023 work, Swedish children incorporate descriptions of love, kissing, and being married into their play and craftworks, often along heteronormative lines; however, when children's talk or classroom experience create openings to the possibility of same-sex love, teachers and children are extremely quiet. However, when queer love is brought by children into play in classrooms as observed by researchers, classroom teachers' acknowledgment of that love is notably absent (Cahill and Theilheimer 1999; Sotevik 2023). Questions among practitioners about adequate responsiveness within children's discussions of romance, whether it is between individuals of the same or different gender, are acknowledged but within dominant heterosexual matrices, which leave little room for maneuvering gender outside of binary constructs (Blaise 2010; Cahill and Theilheimer 1999; Sotevik 2023). In other words, though research accounts acknowledge the complexities of children's gender and sexuality knowledge or development, largely missing in schools is recognition of queer identities and lives.

For many decades, the field of early care has been coached to be non-sexist, offering play roles and materials to expand gender roles and reduce and interrupt gender bias (in the workplace and in homes), largely within the construct of gender equality (Liben and Bigler 2017). Today's questions about gender are more complicated. As we (authors) contemplate the complexity of LGBTQI issues in classrooms, we know an entirely different epoch is upon us—one in which children are still asking questions about gender—but the answers have gotten messier. In addition, gender-diverse children and their parents are reframing gender identity as they navigate children's agency in their own development (Kroeger et al. [in review]). In a larger sense, community and culture seem to be revisiting questions of what gender *is*, and the field of early childhood continues to re-examine gender, as gender identities proliferate.

In this chapter, we might better conceive of how we can honor gender-diverse young children's identities as they come to know themselves in our classrooms. Gender-diverse children are described in the literature as children, whose "internal experience of their gender does not align neatly with their physical characteristics" (Frye 2022, 34). Alex and I are learning from our research with parent and teacher advocates of gender-diverse children (Gunn and Kroeger, in press; Kroeger, Gunn, Oleskiewicz, Konieczko, and Sanchez [in review]) that young children are also telling their parents who they are as gendered beings and asking questions that illuminate the young child's tremendous sophistication. In gender-affirming families, those questions (and answers) are complex, thorough, and optimistic (Kroeger et al. [in review]). At the very least, it is imperative that adults learn to distinguish the concepts of sexual orientation and gender identity and that they be equipped to support gender-diverse children and their peers who are growing up in classrooms and schools in new and different ways (Chapman 2023; Kroeger and Regula 2017; Nutt 2015; Steele and Nicholson 2020).

We use the term *gender-diverse children* because it describes the full range of trans, cis, gender fluid, gender nonbinary, or nonconforming identities that children may come to inhabit as adults, as identities are likely to emerge in the earliest years and solidify as children grow. Gender identity performed by young children does not usually denote sexuality (or sexual identity), but children's expressions often show a complex understanding of sexuality or romantic relationships (Blaise 2010; Cahill and Theilheimer 1999; Sotevik 2023). We work from queer-informed frameworks in this paper, because of the complex history of, but lesser-known body of knowledge circulating within intersex and transgender experience, marshaled forth largely by the queer rights movements, which hold promise to inform psychoanalytic support mechanisms (Gill-Peterson 2018; Steele and Nicholson 2020; Stryker 2008).

For many children, cross-gender play is episodic. For others, it is persistent, and regardless of how children express gender, gender expression in childhood does not predict the child will come to be identified as trans or lesbian, gay, or bisexual as an adult. At least one longitudinal study does suggest that children who expressed significant interest in cross-gender-typed behavior in preschool years were more likely to identify as belonging to lesbian, gay, or bisexual categories as adults (Li, Kung, and Hines 2017). While the individual instances of gender-diverse expressions in early childhood that may eventually manifest as [gender dysphoria[2]] in middle childhood or adolescence might be relatively rare, the struggle of young people who appear to be one sex at birth but who identify with the other sex before puberty has become more apparent in public life, medical, social support services, pediatrics, and anthropological accounts (Ehrensaft 2017; Frye 2022; Mimica 2008). We bracket the term [gender dysphoria] because the term pathologizes something that also happens across cultures and is historically present and valued differently across human history and place (Gill-Peterson 2018; Halberstam 2018; Stryker 2008). Writers on trans and intersex culture from various disciplines argue that what is new about transgender development is the complexity of hiding or revealing this social identity in our time, especially in schools, because of the complex legal, mental health implications and navigation of heteronormative culture (Gill-Peterson 2018; Halberstam 2018; Nutt 2015).

Today, gender-nonconforming children are well known in medical literature and in the public sphere (Ehrensaft 2017; deMayo, Jordan, and Olson 2022; Nutt 2015; Turban and Ehrensaft 2018), and under significant political attack. Author Jules Gill-Peterson (2018) argues for a more knowledgeable public as she writes about a history of trans childhoods, denoting, "If trans children cannot mortgage the future to pay for civil rights that they lack today, the past century might serve to deepen the public reality of their lives, challenging anti-trans forces" (196). Additionally, trans youth identity emergence challenges parents and the larger public, who question the reality of the experience (Frye 2022, 34), but those professionals who have studied and written about gender and sexuality know that gender (and sexuality) has always been more complicated than unresolvable bifurcated debates or public opinion. One who pokes at the very concept of gender will find salient intersex conditions along with the historical presence of humans who are transgender. In addition, one will find interpretations and enactments of gender that complicate the very fabric of the binary notion of gender that is proliferating in nearly all but the most recent developmental psychology.

In this chapter, we pose some simple arguments for keeping some elements of Freudian theory and psychoanalytic processes alive. For example, Freud's work established and allowed for the uncovering and releasing of emotions from the unconscious; moreover, he was among the first to consider free association, fantasy, and the role of psychoanalysis as a process to move desire from the unconscious to conscious awareness (Crain 2014). We aim to contribute to gender-affirming psychoanalytic processes among care workers—who care for and about gender-diverse childhoods—and we reframe gender and sexuality in classrooms to reconsider childhood more broadly. To provide adequate backdrop information, we first consider some aspects of developmental and psychoanalytic theories, and then we integrate the changing terrain of gender and implications for practices today. Our efforts support care workers who will engage in processes of affirming gender-diverse childhoods.

CONSIDERING FREUDIAN CONSTRUCTS AND OTHER IMPORTANT HISTORIES

Freudian Theories (Foundational and Regulatory)

In early twentieth-century scientific studies of children, norms for children's development, and other branches of social science were often informed by Freudian concepts (including gender and sexuality). Freud's ideas influenced and shaped gender and sexuality in psychology, anthropology, and child study movements within Vienna, Paris, and America from the inception of his first publications to the present day (Alcabes 2022; Crain 2003; Noppe 2002; Sangren 2008). Freud wrote prolifically about sexuality and children in a series of essays, the first of which contributed to the development of a theory of sex (Freud 1925a; Gunn 2008). In a second essay, his thinking proliferated toward sexual aberrations (Freud 1925b; Gunn 2008), establishing a line of reasoning between what was to be considered normal heterosexual sexuality and so-called *abnormal* nonheterosexual sexuality. In his essay concerning infantile sexuality, Freud further accounted for variations in normal heterosexual sexuality development in children and adolescents.

In contrast, anthropologists objected to many of Freud's constructs as cultural essentialisms. For example, Bronislaw Malinowski attempted to counteract the familial configuration of the mother–father–infant triad toward a matrilineal complex, showing cultural variations in sexuality and power in Trobriand Islanders (Murray and Darnell 2000; Sangren 2008; Malinowski 1927). Margaret Mead also went on to document and countermand images of Western familial and adolescent stress by studying Samoan adolescence, showing an emergence of sexual relationships among adolescent girls as self-chosen, sometimes with more than one partner, and unconnected to marriage and procreation (Shankman 2021, 33). In her further works, the nuclear family was countered, as her fieldwork contributed to the analysis of multi-household memberships of children among extended familial arrangements, and she exposed the great amount of variation in men's and women's roles in parenting and wealth management among the Arapesh, Mundugumor, and Tchambuli (Shankman 2021). Mead's work often upstaged conservative American gender ideals throughout her life in anthropology (Shankman 2021).

In contrast to anthropology, feminist and queer scholars have used ideas from Foucault to reframe Freud's work as creating the "normal citizen" largely constituted as heterosexual (Richardson 2004). Others have argued that Freud's work framed the heterosexual child as the standard against which all children's normal heterosexual sexual development might be compared (Gunn 2008). Judith Butler argued further that Foucault's conceptual move from sex and sexuality to bodies and desire allowed greater maneuverability within human thought, experience, rights, and cultural constraint, answering the regulating function of society (Butler 1999).

Postfoundational theorists (critical, postcolonial, feminist, and post-structural) have deconstructed Freud's work, reminding practitioners that sexual activity in young children was thought unnatural and an imposition of "physical and moral, individual and collective dangers" during Freud's lifetime (Foucault 1978, 104). Current thinking among some childhood experts recognizes children's complexity and nuanced behavior toward their individual performances of gender, utilizing Judith Butler's analysis of Foucault's concepts of bodies and desire and heterosexual matrix (Blaise 2010; Butler 1999; Paechter 2017). Notions that children were "deemed to be naturally without a sexuality" framed within childhood innocence have been supplanted by children's right to exist as meaning makers and autonomous beings, constructing their own gender and sexuality (Kroeger et al. 2019; Paechter 2017; Richardson 2004). Care workers have often taken on roles of protectors, with the belief that . . . [children] . . . could potentially "be sexualized" by others who might exploit them (Tait 2001, 44). Additionally, it is worth noting that fears related to child protection are often framed in relation to homosexuality and trans people, misconstruing men, gay men, and "drag queens" as particularly dangerous and likely to sexualize children or make children gay or trans[3].

The reasons that psychoanalytic approaches matter in care roles are that care workers are often the first to observe children's play. Care workers support families in parenting roles and give care to children while teaching them and their peers how to adapt to each other and demonstrate healthy social-emotional skills. Care workers also teach young children how to exist civilly in a larger community of learners throughout childhood. Parents, conversely, are often held accountable for children's psychosexual development (Shulman 2021) with very little or no attention paid to educators' roles in children's psychosexual development in schools (although heteronormativity is instantiated via social transmission) (Paechter 2017). Psychoanalytically, care workers of children (teachers, school psychologists, counselors, etc.) have a role to play in helping parents and other students accept and include gender-diverse students' identity and presence in public spaces (Chapman 2023; NASP 2014; Kroeger and Regula 2017; Steele and Nicholson 2020).

We can recognize psychoanalytic traditions as having their origin in post-Victorian era gender relations, in which women, many men, and especially children, did not have sovereignty—and in which ambivalent, conflicting, and pathologizing statements are made concerning homosexuality (Hodges 2011) but also in reference to today's post-foundational attempts to deconstruct Freud's work historically. In some accounts of Freudian psychoanalysis (Crain 2014), we might see traces of why he focused so heavily upon sexuality and gender. Freud's "patients repeatedly told stories about how their parents had committed the most immoral sexual acts against them as children—stories that Freud finally concluded must mainly be fantasies" (p. 250). Freud's own history of conflicts with his father as well as his father's death contributed to his construction of the Oedipus complex, which he described and discussed with a following of younger scientists and writers, who participated in psychoanalysis and eventually developed their own complex theories about human consciousness, or contributed to ideas about how psychoanalysis should proceed. For example, Alfred Adler and Carl Jung as well as Melanie Klein were among his early followers (Baker and Carlson 2017; Crain 2014; Freud 1914a).

Those practicing psychoanalysis today know that beliefs about sexuality, fantasy, and protections of young people have informed professional development somewhat in accordance with Freudian theory, including psychoanalysis (Hodges 2011). Freudian ideology (and other developmental theories) has followed into parenting and teaching, many times implicitly reinforcing children's sexuality in accord with unacknowledged but stringent expectations and cultural standards of heteronormativity and the gender binary (Counterman and Kirkwood 2013; Crain 2014; Gross 2024; Noppe 2002). However stalwart the influences of Freudian theories are on modern constructs of heterosexual sexual development, it is important to note that Freud himself (and his daughter Anna Freud) did not think children were able to be part of psychoanalysis, because their necessary "defenses were not developed." But many predecessors of Freud's work successfully worked with children, furthering psychoanalysis (Baker and Carlson 2017, 57). For example, modern psychotherapy includes both Adlerian theory, which is often focused on attachment relationships, with goal-oriented lifestyle adjustments in work, love, and friendships with a goal of advancing individual well-being, and Kleinian theory, which encompasses play therapies, object relationships, and emotional transference (with the therapist), centered around the person's larger life goal of holistic adaptation to maladaptive behavior.

Both contemporary psychoanalytic perspectives of Adler and Klein (unlike early Freudian perspective) agree that for children, creating relationships where "one has a sense of belonging, whether to the primary caregiver or a larger entity is the key" to returning to (or maintaining) psychological health (Baker and Carlson 2017, 167).

In Michael Trout's chapter of this book, Trout argues that psychoanalysis is often disregarded in care work precisely because of its association with Freud. And yet, neo-psychoanalytic approaches have transformed radically in the past century and thus cannot be undervalued in approaches to care with young children and families. We endorse holistically those psychoanalytic perspectives which support the health and safety of gender-diverse children, appreciating the power of contributors like Alfred Adler and Melanie Klein.

Since the publication of Freud's earliest research, psychoanalytic approaches branching from his contributions have helped to establish foundations of practice that have been long-lasting and productive for many marginalized individuals and communities. Freud's work also valuably asserted the orthodoxy of the child as a recognized sexual being (Crain 2004; Tait 2001). However, some of the underlying norms of development concerning what children were to do and at what ages, and what problems they were (made to resolve) within gender (and sexuality) have remained explicitly heteronormative and refuted (Hodges 2011). Unfortunately, Freud's early conceptual thinking omitted sexual expressions and identities beyond heteronormativity, making them aberrant (which they remain) in mainstream public discourse. For example, consider laws that assert the legitimacy of only the male or female binary gender (or body) and the denial of access to legitimate health care, such as psychoanalytic support (within holistic psychological, medical, and legalistic support) for gender-diverse youth.

Freud's notions of psychosexual development or psychoanalysis are featured among materials in some health care, social worker, adolescent and infant developmentalists, educators, as well as physicians and medical personnel documents (Gross 2024; Shulman 2021; Steinberg 2017). Freud argued that three important erogenous zones become the center of children's sexual interests in their early years and that the early childhood child progresses through the oral[4], anal and Oedipal stages until the age of around six years, where the Oedipal complex became resolved (Skolnick 1986). Freud's Oedipus complex is posited as a normal emotional crisis brought on when children's natural sexual impulses toward their opposite-sex parents lead to the development of guilt (on the part of the child) and jealousy (about their same-sex parent). The complex is said to occur in two important life stages: early childhood and adolescence. If successfully resolved, the development of conscience and of adult heterosexual identity will occur. This is how many of us learned about childhood sexuality as students of early childhood teacher education. Freud's perspectives remain powerful in teachers' learning and in professional publications of the present day, even if only briefly mentioned (Crain 2014; Gross 2024; Hendrick 2001; Honig 2000; Tobin 1997).

However, within attempts to move beyond Western imperialism within development frameworks, a transgender recognition is emerging (Steele and Nicholson 2020; Trawick-Smith 2022).

Freud considered that forms of non-heterosexual sexuality were examples of arrested development and unresolved conflicts of childhood. In the Oedipal configuration, the binary of normal heterosexuality/abnormal (or pathological) non-heterosexual sexuality is produced. These notions of healthy and normal heterosexual sexuality expressed in Freud's work help shape our sense of what we should, can, and must do as care workers: construct children heterosexually. Along with this thinking of normal, we form ideas of abnormal. Combining notions of normal psychological development with heterosexual sexual development subsequently marks non-heterosexual sexuality as abnormal. Freud's theories facilitate a host of understandings about sexualities proper and perverse (Gunn 2008). The original Freudian stage theories are also considered one of many regulatory discourses about children's sexuality. In some instances of human development and psychiatry, the stages of lesbian, gay, and bisexual identity are theorized developmentally (Savins-Williams and Cohen 2015), noting that most lesbian, gay, and bisexual individuals forgo sexual confusion or mental illness. Additionally, mentions of the sexuality of lesbian, gay, or bisexual adolescents are described in relation to safe sexual activity, but not to the development of healthy development or identities per se (Steinberg 2017).

In *Histories of the Transgender Child* (2018), Jules Gill-Peterson details the medicalization of trans people over the past century. She documents that gender-diverse and nonconforming children are not a new phenomenon through the examination of medical records, especially those of intersex individuals. The idea of binary sex based on gonadal appearances and reproductive capacity was transformed conceptually in early twentieth-century life sciences. Gill-Peterson argues that even the term "gender" came to be known as a signifier, first medically to describe the complexity of the intersex body and then through implications from feminist theories to come to include social implications (2018). In the early 1900s, a diagnosis of *hermaphroditism* (today entitled intersex condition) was given to a young child in 1915 and is one of the earliest documented cases on record of a child's body being altered to conform more fully to a heterosexually idealized binary appearance (Gill-Peterson 2018).

We do not conflate intersex conditions and trans identities here but see the intersection of these two types of gender-diverse identity formations as a turning point for the complexification of binary gender constructs (Kroeger 2023; Kroeger and Regula 2017; Steele and Nicholson 2020). Variations of sex characteristics (appearances of the body) are documented, and at least forty variations of intersex conditions exist (Carpenter 2018). Medical procedures such as hormone alterations and cosmetic or reconstructive surgery for intersex and transgender people began in the early 1900s but had historically been performed upon intersex people regularly, to make the appearance of an intersex body match heterosexual ideals. Medical professionals often endorse "the option of genital surgery to assign the child a 'stable' gender to erase the perceived stigma of body differences, which is regarded as having the potential to cause the child significant suffering" (Murray 2009, 266). Without individual autonomy or consent, such surgeries were and are (still) carried out within infancy and early childhood; this "pathologizing" of the intersex body is to ensure a "masculinizing or feminizing" appearance dependent upon "heteronormative expectations for surgical outcomes" and is highly criticized within declarations of universal human rights (Carpenter 2018, 207–208). Intersex surgeries are purported to be invasive, repetitive, and make children endure painful procedures which damage tissue, create a loss of sensation, and wield a host of trauma and psychological problems; and moreover, are considered by many a tremendous human rights violation (Breen and Roen 2023; Carpenter 2018; Murray 2009).

Increased insights into endocrinology, psychology, and medical intervention for intersex patients have contributed to many advocates calling for a rejection of "gender" as a binary construct, marshaling in a host of questions, for example, about intersex persons' rights (Carpenter 2018; Gill-Paterson 2018; Murray 2009). The World Health Organization has taken a stance on sexual health, in which persons have a right to a state of physical, emotional, mental, and social well-being in relation to sexuality. Along with this is a right to freedom from discrimination, a right to privacy, freedom from violence and coercion, and the right to education, information, and access to health services (Carpenter 2018).

Even if newer and emerging work from pediatrics and transgender social work, psychiatry, and psychological care has come to include gender-affirming care—and the reader recognizes with us the limitations of a gender binary as established in some contemporary developmental, clinical, and social work literature (Turban and Ehrensaft 2018)—the everyday person (as well as those in teacher education and other professional spheres) still has little exposure or knowledge about intersex or transgender histories and consequently misunderstands contemporary gender unless scholars who educate in various professions choose to engage rather than avoid this controversial topic. Scholarship in transgender theory has also recently emerged, providing context in the academy that, given time scholars hope will likely result in a better understanding among the public (deMayo, Jordan, and Olson 2022; Nagoshi et al. 2023; Steele and Nicholson 2020). But this will only happen if the information given here enters mainstream knowledge bases.

In the next section, we elucidate and problematize constructs from Piaget's and Kohlberg's thoughts on cognitive development (and gender), which may help us to consider how to best support young children within gender diversity. We write this section to lay a foundation for the types of psychoanalytic approaches that might be useful for practitioners as they consider supportive settings for children and parents. We pick and choose the most useful ideas from these theorists to navigate gender complexity as we see it.

BORROWING FROM OR EXPUNGING PIAGET?

Piaget-Derived Theories (Use with Caution)

Care workers are often taught from Piagetian-derived ideas of cognitive development in relation to gender permanence (Crain 2015), and some contemporary texts address gender beyond the binary by explicitly including transgender and gender-diversity ideas related to preschool children (Chapman 2023; Steele and Nicholson 2020; Trawick-Smith 2024), but most do not.

Schema was Piaget's description of how children learned cognitive rules for games and life and were based on interactions and experiences with others, in combination with shifting more abstract concepts (Ginsburg and Opper 1969; Piaget 1965). Piaget conjectured, through his observation of children, that cognitive growth occurs as children begin to understand and apply social reasoning to their cognitive schema, informing and supporting their own "rules" as internal thoughts grew in sophistication across time and in relation to novel experiences. Piaget's original ideas were applied to such things as games (marbles), math concepts, and social interactions with more experienced peers or adults (Piaget 1965). Care workers have always known that as cognitive schema is applied to the interaction between gender-diverse children and society today, the issues are more complex than marbles and math problems.

Lawrence Kohlberg, Piaget's predecessor, created the term gender constancy to describe the stage-like manner between ages three and seven, in which gender labeling, gender stability, and gender congruence occurred (Crain 2005; Kohlberg 1966). In Kohlberg's work, the construct of gender constancy arose as an invariant human property that he claimed children become aware of and remained stable across time. Kohlberg (1966) argued that children would begin to understand that superficial changes in appearance (like a haircut) do not alter gender (Noppe 2002). As authors, we notice, within the process of social transitioning among younger trans-identified children and with the advent of gender-altering technologies (like hormone suppressors), that gender constancy, including the ages at which children might know their gender (and declare it), is not stable or predictable (and perhaps even in Kohlberg's time, never was).

Parents' conversations with children—giving them facts and current awareness of gender nonbinary constructs, with ideas to consider about trans identities, or about what is possible with the help of health care—along with children's own internal sense of gender in relation to the appearance of their body, create discursive and conceptual shifts in which the modern construct of the gender binary has changed (Kroeger et al. [in review]). We think that "mind over matter" matters, because a child's cognition (informed by conversations with adults about the acceptability/unacceptability of exploring gender in the early years) along with the child's sense of self will ultimately lead to the child's own internal sense of gender. Feminist theorist and social scientist, Sandra Bem argued for "aschematic" gender socialization, to broaden parenting around social roles and gender (Liben and Bigler 2017); and subsequently the changes in society that intersex and trans rights have harkened allow caring professions to argue that the stability of the gender binary has been replaced with variable "potentials" for gender (Jackson and Bussey 2023).

Cognitive constructs derived from Piaget and Kohlberg already assume that the cognitive capacities of the child will be altered and informed by the child's self-socialization (within their culture) (just as psychoanalytic and cultural anthropological disciplines had derived) as well as adult interactions. In today's reality, a child's early cognitive capacity may lead to a gender-diverse sense of self rather than a strictly gender binary one, regardless of what adults do or do not do. Also, we do not know if Piaget or Kohlberg came to these conclusions, but assume they, like Freud, considered all gender expressions beyond binary explanations to be aberrant.

To our knowledge, neither child development theories nor Freudian constructs have ever attempted to explain transgender experience (except as deviant or aberrant), nor did such ideas acknowledge the historical and biological presence of intersex persons' experiences; furthermore, developmental theories prove restrictive, especially in the many cases where the parent advocates who are adults are more "knowledgeable" in a cultural and social sense than their conservative "time-space" deems popular. For example, a parent who wishes to be supportive and honest with their gender-nonconforming child yet lives in an oppressive environment may shield that child, encouraging them to do gender differently in various settings based on safety, or attempt to alter the spaces in which the child is educated (Kroeger et al. [in review]). In the case of a parent who does not recognize gender diversity but has a child expressing gender expansively in an accepting and accommodating educational environment, they might experience the dissonance created between home and school and grow to reconcile the limitations of their thinking, accepting the child's play and gender expression more fully (Kroeger and Regula 2017). Additionally, children will be learning about gender all the time, with and without direct intentional adult support.

For young children, thinking about gender and doing gender will drive gender identity (Blaise 2010). Young children will always be learning and doing what they will and are internally driven, regardless of an adult's interventions, sanctions, or supports. In other words, avoiding gender will not prevent those who are inclined to express gender in an expansive manner from doing so. Recent psychiatric and medical care literature suggests that

> One's assigned sex at birth may differ from one's core identity, not because of poor parent handling or infantile confusions, but because of brain and mind gender messages overriding signals from genitalia, chromosome, or parental expectations . . . this phenomenon . . . has been referred to as 'neurological sex', defined as a uniform standard of legal sex based on gender identity, in which brain messages are privileged over anatomy and chromosomes in determining an individual's authentic gender. (Vanderhost 2015) (Turban and Ehrensaft 2018, 1230)

We have illuminated some ways in which traditional models of gender and sexuality development within foundational theories of Freud, Piaget, and Kohlberg's work fail to account for gender diversity, complementing Collopy's work (this edition) which recognizes that psychoanalysis's popular twentieth-century emergence co-occurred with mainstream developmental theories (yes—Piaget read Freud's work). Additionally, we provided some conceptual underpinnings of a history of sexuality, intersex conditions, and trans-youth development, noting absences in the literature in early childhood, to help us reassess current needs for social support systems for young people. The care fields of childhood will continue to shift within a larger framework of what constitutes responsive professional practice.

GENDER AND ITS PERMANENCE AMONG CARE(ING) WORKERS

One might interpret that our desire in writing this chapter is to prepare for the increasingly present gender-diverse and transgender youth (Ehrensaft 2017; Turban and Ehrensaft 2017). This is the case; at the heart of several of our shared research projects are questions about what the care worker's and teacher's responsibility is to gender-diverse children and their parents.

We wrote this chapter because we know that teachers and other care workers deserve tools which go beyond outdated constructs. Contemporary reasoning is at the ready to navigate the bifurcated political climate in a complex, holistic, and thoughtful manner. Mainstream textbooks on development do not yet describe the depth or complexity underlying some expressions of gender or gender-crossing experiences among children, and we have found that intersex and trans-informed identity formation is largely absent in mainstream childcare textbooks, though it is present in many health and counseling disciplines (Cuadra et al. 2024; Gross 2024; Schnabel and Keuroghlian 2023). Many contemporary anti-bias texts also replicate outdated cognitive models of gender permanence or do not name transgender bias within anti-bias approaches. We know that cross-gender identifications (gender-diverse individuals) are prevalent historically and are estimated to make up between 1.2% and 2.7% of adolescents (Zhang et al. 2020). The proportion of cross-gender identifications, which only include transgender youth, makes up as much or more than 0.53% of the population or as many as 1/189 people (Crissman, Berger, Graham, and Dalton 2017; Gates 2016). The upsurge in the need for services and support is long overdue, playing out in classrooms, schools, community centers, health care and counseling support services, and the political arena.

Although it is common for all children to explore a range of gender expressions in early childhood settings, we will not know the outcome of many young gender-diverse people's identities based upon their actions in the early years, middle childhood, or adulthood. Many gender-diverse individuals evolve in their identifications over their lives. We've learned from the literature that gender diversity itself is not problematic, but as gender-diverse young people experience trans-hatred, "Internalizing psychological problems" like anxiety, depression, and suicidality might become salient. Gender-affirming care providers surmise that poor mental health outcomes experienced by gender-diverse youth are "thought not fully to be caused by the condition of cross-gender identification" but are "secondary to minority stress and dysphoria associated with one's body developing in an incongruent fashion to one's gender identity" and from society's "reactions to their gender presentations" (Turban and Ehrensaft 2018, 1232). In other words, the social reactivity to such children is largely negative (perhaps becoming more negative as students age), and this causes their social and psychological problems.

In the family psychology field, there is evidence that healthy family functioning in general, and prior to the child's disclosure (as trans, non-binary, or genderqueer) is associated with better mental and physical health outcomes (Heatherington and Lavner 2008). Newer research suggests that affirmative treatment protocols (gender-affirming care, including psychological, social, and medical) have the potential to improve the higher rates of mental health difficulties, anxiety, depression, and suicidality (Tordoff et al. 2022).

HOW MIGHT PSYCHOANALYTIC(S) BE
APPLIED TODAY?

We have laid some foundational concepts to support gender-diverse children while also deconstructing aspects of Freudian, Piagetian, and Kohlberg's influences upon gender and sexuality in Western thought. Although we critiqued Freudian concepts, we do not equate psychoanalysis with (only) Freud's contributions. We do think cognitive schemas supported in psycho-analytic traditions are important because they assist children in overcoming their own helplessness, sense of powerlessness (or wishes for control), and might help individuals reconcile their fantasies, their emotions, and personal defenses or cope with the effect of their presence in settings (Martin and Ruble 2004). Active listening and unconditional positive regard, central to any therapeutic setting, make sense for gender-diverse children and their families. In relation to adult responsiveness to children, whether it be in classrooms, therapy settings, play groups, or other care settings, all children deserve to be listened to; their wishes and ability to make meaningful sense of themselves and the world matter. Gender-diverse children also deserve to have power. Care workers are to be open-minded and unprejudiced in their capacities of caring within psychoanalytic approaches (Breaux and Thyer 2021).

In our work with parents as advocates of gender-diverse children, we find that parents are creating healthy niches in the home in which children can find gender expressions that suit them as they explore and grow (Kroeger et al. [in review]). Families and parents are the first adults to give gender-diverse young people the language and environment to understand gender and sexu-ality; they give children permission to express themselves and affirm their changing identities (Kroeger et al. [in review]). In our work listening to par-ents of gender-diverse children, terminology is very salient, with many fami-lies working hard to understand newer medical, social, psychological, legal, and rights-based language(s). Parents (just like care workers) must unlearn many of the constructs of heteronormativity expressed in schools and larger settings (DePalma 2011; Kroeger et al. [in review]). What might be helpful in care settings, then, is an intentional regard for the meaningfulness of a child's gender expression as well as a recognition of their autonomy. Care workers' roles are to help the child understand themselves (and the world) and recog-nize what desires, activities, and self-expressions are relevant to them, giving them skills and confidence to navigate the world as they grow.

Everything that might be done within a psychoanalytic approach that is gender-affirming would be helpful to individuals as they safely navigate their internal and external experience. Perhaps one would integrate the conscious desires of the child into classroom experiences and help a child's peers respectfully navigate a gender-inclusive reality. For some care settings, this may mean helping the child to recognize their unconscious reality (desires and fears) within a material reality (of safety and support). In other words, helping the child to navigate the culture in which they exist and more fully understand their individual autonomy and self-expression through things such things as dress, clothing, hair, make-up, and names, as well as naming and understanding other subjective forms of self-expression, could be under a psychoanalytic approach. At older ages, care will mean helping a child understand sexuality in relation to gender development, or it might mean helping a child flesh out their "desires" (to be like or unlike others of one's gender) or navigate their romantic feelings toward others. As a child's cognitive schema is made "aware" of gender-diverse constructs, trans-, non-binary (etc.), a child's unconscious desire (with verbalization and recognition) might supersede fears (such as lack of support), helping the individual navigate their gender identity within a conscious reality.

As care workers, we are reminded that fluidity is tantamount to constructs of gender and sexuality; for us, gender and sexuality are more than biology and the appearance of the body; and they are more than the social constructions allowed by culture. Allowing children to have the first say in their own gender and sexuality development with the support of psychoanalytic perspectives is helpful. We draw upon gender-affirming care models which state that

> Many individuals continue renegotiating their gender throughout childhood or adulthood, with no observable detriment to their mental health. Youth may establish a cisgender identity and not embrace a heterosexual identity, with no aspersion to their emotional well-being. A significant number of individuals experience a gender identity that does not match their gender assigned at birth, and this can be a long-lasting identification. (Turban and Ehrensaft 2018, 1230)

Although the ideas presented here are underrepresented in most care theory related to teaching, work like ours can complexify most if not all long-standing theories of development and teaching in care settings (Chapman 2023; Steele and Nicholson 2020).

UTILIZING CRITICAL AND QUEER FEMINISMS WITHIN TEACHER EDUCATION

As part of our own intellectual undoing of our historical investments in a binary gender and heteronormative sexuality construction, we have needed to navigate for ourselves and our students; often "reteaching" ourselves, using an eclectic blend of legal, pediatric, theoretical, feminist, psychoanalytic, therapeutic, and philosophical works, as a means of talking back to oppressive systems of thought. We have also had to develop educational materials about gender and sexuality, recognizing the historical underpinnings of a field of study, while pivoting and welcoming how practices, terminologies, and constructs are changing quickly. Going against mainstream thinking has not been an easy task.

Conservative forces would like us to believe that gender is binary and that sexuality is only to be performed between masculine and feminine cis-gendered bodies. Furthermore, conservatism prescribes that all other expressions of humanity and gender or sexuality are immoral, indecent, and wrong, or absent of love or respect. Choosing to interrogate and deconstruct gender or sexualizing discourses of schooling is part of strong movements recognizing that discourses and categorial associations between biology, social practice, and self are queer and always have been (Blaise 2010; DePalma 2013; Gunn 2008). Because care workers are likely to be caught in the webs of their own histories of morality and reason, as well as fear and uncertainty, it is important to remain conscious. When a parent requests a change in gender-normativity in classrooms, the care worker must acquire skills to navigate controversial but necessary terrain. While some educators and care workers may believe it is wrong to "give children ideas," others (like us) know that it is wrong not to.

First, educators need new language and terminology with which to understand gender and sexuality. This knowledge and language exceed historical Western developmental norms, ages, and stage configurations, and it is one that recognizes gender and sexuality beyond our fixed binary gender and normative heterosexual constructs. As Alex and I go about working with students, we go beyond the general development described in mainstream textbooks by presenting the complex hormonal influences upon the body and the brain (after the gonadal sex is established) and illuminate the instances in which biology becomes less predictable, producing intersex bodies, or when the body's sex (determined on appearance at birth) conflicts with the individual's sense of self. By far, educators' requests for professional learning in relation to gender and sexuality emphasize language and terminology as one of the most urgent priorities as we increasingly note the failings of our historical teachings. Second, we strive to help adults recognize the diverse and expansive understandings and practices of gender and sexuality today. We include in table 2.1 a small list of gender and sexuality-related terms we have used in our research to help readers navigate and comprehend the changing concepts and language. This is by no means an exhaustive list, but we have found it useful in our own work with advocate parents and teachers.

Table 2.1 Glossary of Terms for Gender-Diverse Childhoods

Term	Definition
Anti-Bias	Anti-bias curriculum (Derman-Sparks, Edwards, and Goins 2020) is an early childhood approach taken up by professionals in which bias stemming from racism, classism, sexism, and gender is recognized. Bias is to be disrupted and replaced with factual information and appropriate terminology to express and respect human diversity.
Cisgender	(pronounced sis-gender) A term to describe a person whose gender identity matches the biological (gonadal) sex they were assigned at birth.
Gender Conforming	A person whose gender expression is consistent with cultural norms expected for that gender. According to dominant Western gender norms, boys and men are or should be masculine, and girls and women are or should be feminine. Not all cisgender people are gender conforming, and not all transgender people are gender conforming.
Gender Binary	The idea that gender is strictly an either/or option of male/man/masculine or female/woman/feminine based on one's assigned sex at birth. The gender binary is considered to be limiting and problematic for everybody, but especially for those whose gender expression or identity does not fit neatly into one or the other of the categories.
Gender-diverse	We have adopted the term gender "diverse" to signify any biologically male or female child who *persistently* expresses their gender or has a gender identity that is contrary or inconsistent with the expected "binary" configuration. We presume that a child's gender identity (and sexual identity) will become clear to them as they age but this is not always the case. *Gender-diverse* children, therefore, describes for us the full range of trans, cis, or gender-fluid and nonconforming identities that children may express. Gender identity is separate from sexuality (or sexual identity).
Gender Fluid	Someone whose gender identity or expression shifts between man/masculine and woman/feminine or falls somewhere along a spectrum of expression.
Gender Expression	A person's outward gender presentation, usually comprising personal style, clothing, hairstyle, makeup, jewelry, vocal inflections, and body language. Gender expression is typically categorized as masculine, feminine, or androgynous. All people express gender. Gender expression can be congruent or non-congruent to a person's gender identity.
Gender Identity	A person's deep-seated, internal sense of who they are as a gendered being; the gender with which they identify themselves.

(Continued)

Table 2.1 **(Continued)**

Term	Definition
Gender Nonconforming	A person whose gender expression is perceived by others as being inconsistent with cultural norms expected for that gender. Specifically, for boys or men categorized as "not masculine enough" or too feminine . . . or for girls or women as "not feminine enough" or too masculine. Not all transgender people are gender nonconforming, and not all gender-nonconforming people identify as transgender. Cisgender people may also be gender nonconforming. Gender non-conformity is often inaccurately confused with sexual orientation.
LGBT	Lesbian, Gay, Bisexual, and Transgender
Nonbinary	A spectrum of gender identities and expressions, often based on the rejection of the gender binary's assumption that gender is strictly an either/or option of male/masculine/man or female/feminine/woman based upon the sex assigned at birth. Terms include "agender," "bi-gender," "gender queer," "gender fluid," and "pangender."
Sexual Orientation	A person's primary sexual and romantic attraction (attracted to one of the opposite sex, the same sex, both or neither).
Young Children	Usually referring to the age of infancy, preschool, and primary school, commonly from birth to age eight.

Source: Generated by the Authors.

UNDERSTANDING GENDER, UNDERSTANDING SEXUALITY: CHANGING ROLES IN CARE SETTINGS

During a recent conference presentation about this work (Gunn 2023a; Kroeger, Gunn, and Sullivan 2023b), an eager graduate student working on their research proposal asked quickly at the end of the session, "what one or two ideas do you think we really need to take a hold of if we're going to change thinking and practice in education towards the myriad ways genders and sexualities are proliferating today?" It was an excellent question that pushed us closer toward other key un-learnings we are striving for in our work. Alex's reply was along the lines of developing an understanding of the human and scientific production and liberatory disruption of the normative binary configurations of gender (male/female) and sexuality (heterosexual/ and everything else), moves inspired by queer and feminist theorizing and politics. Second, Alex reminded us to continue to disrupt the sense that gender and sexuality, once arrived at, will be fixed and immutable categories of personhood for all time. We think that describing gender and sexuality as continua of experience and expression across a lifetime, which may change, provides a much more useful and accurate way to appreciate the potential diverse expressions and identities of humans.

Our effort to deconstruct Freudian, Piagetian, and Kohlberg's constructs, while maintaining psychoanalytic approaches, with our descriptions of gender diversity today, as well as our attempt at exposing the complicated relation between intersex history and trans-identity development, is posed here as an unlearning of the gender binary. This chapter is our invitation to care workers, educators, and others who are working with young children and families to read, think, and discuss changing values and beliefs about gender and sexuality in the broader world so that when children's emergent identities and expressions differ from what the adults expect, the child's educator can lead conversations and understanding in a sensitive and respectful way. We must educate ourselves if we're going to catch up with the myriad ways youngsters and youth are changing and challenging the norms for gender and sexuality. When educators and care workers bring these topics to the table, they can help their institutions and others develop proactive policy and practice so that settings are equipped and able to welcome everybody.

NOTES

1. We are aware that there are many controversies and questions about the support and treatment of gender-nonconforming youth. Supportive medical professionals question the extensive distribution and efficacy of the treatment of gender-diverse youth when hormonal treatments are supplied without a well-rounded network of medical and psychological follow-ups and supports (commonly labeled as gender-affirming care). See Chang and Chakrabarti 2023.

2. Gender dysphoria is the persistent discontentedness with one's gender assigned at birth and is used as a diagnostic term to classify transgender individuals.

3. For historical examples of arguments about homosexuals as pedophiles made within psychoanalytic or psychiatric perspectives, see Erika Burman 2017, 261–262.

4. In this chapter, we ignore issues of oral (and anal) fixation, but oral fixation is a good example of an earlier construct that Freud interpreted as sexual, which has been supplanted by current interpretation: The movement, sensation, and necessity of a functioning mouth and tongue, promoting oral development and influencing language, is necessary for the integration of body, brain, and a functioning neurosensory system—with a significant portion of the motor cortex devoted to oral sensory capacity of the mouth and tongue. Oral functions ensure feeding and survival (as well as attachment) within sensory motor integration (as vision, hearing, sucking, and tactile

sensations coordinate), laying the foundation for complex neural pathways and ensuring a foundation for adequate cognitive capacities in later life.

REFERENCES

Alcabes, P. 2022. "Sigmund Freud's America." *The Paris Institute for Critical Thinking*. Accessed April 29, 2024. https://parisinstitute.org/depictions-article-sigmund-freuds-america.

Baker, E. K. C., and J. Carlson. 2017. "Kleinian Theory: A Neo-Adlerian Approach?" *The Journal of Individual Psychology* 73 (2): 156–170. https://doi:.org/10.1353/jip.2017.0013.

Blaise, M. 2010. "Gendered Narratives and Sexuality." *Australasian Journal of Early Childhood* 35 (1): 1–9.

Breaux, H. P., and B. A. Thyer. 2021. "Transgender Theory for Contemporary Social Work Practice: A Question of Values and Ethics." *International Journal of Social Work Values & Ethics* 18 (1): 72–89.

Breen, C., and K. Roen. 2023. "The Rights of Intersex Children in Aotearoa New Zealand: What Surgery Is Being Consented to, and Why?" *The International Journal of Children's Rights* 31 (3): 533–567.

Burman, E. 2011. "Desiring Development? Psychoanalytic Contributions to Anti-Developmental Psychology." *International Journal of Qualitative Studies in Education* 26 (1): 56–74. https://doi.org/10.1080/09518398.2011.604650.

Burman, E. 2016. "Knowing Foucault, Knowing You: 'Raced'/Classed and Gendered Subjectivities in the Pedagogical State." *Pedagogy, Culture & Society* 24 (1): 1–25. https://doi.org/10.1080/14681366.2015.1057215.

Burman, E. 2017. *Deconstructing Developmental Psychology*. 3rd ed. Routledge.

Butler, J. 1999. "Revisiting Bodies and Pleasures." *Theory, Culture & Society* 16 (2): 11–20.

Cahill, B., and R. Theilheimer. 1999. "Stonewall in the Housekeeping Area: Gay and Lesbian Issues in the Early Childhood Classroom." In *Queering Elementary Education: Advancing the Dialogue About Sexualities in Schooling*, edited by W. J. Letts IV and J. Sears, 39–48. Rowan & Littlefield.

Carpenter, M. 2018. "Intersex Variations, Human Rights, and the International Classification of Diseases." *Health Human Rights* 20 (2): 205–214.

Chang, J., and M. Chakrabarti. 2023. "Journalist Hannah Barnes on the inside Story of the Collapse of Tavistock's Gender Identity Clinic." *OnPoint Radio Boston*. Retrieved April 4, 2024. www.wbur.org/onpoint/2023/03/09/the-inside-story-of-the-collapse-of-the-tavistock-gender-service-for-children.

Chapman, R. 2023. *Gender Expansion in Early Childhood Education: Building and Supporting Pro-Diversity Spaces*. Palgrave Macmillan.

Cornell University. 2015. "What Does the Scholarly Research Say about the Well-Being of Children with Gay or Lesbian Parents?" *What We Know: The Public Policy Research Project*. Retrieved January 9, 2023. https://whatweknow.inequality

.cornell.edu/topics/lgbt-equality/what-does-the-scholarly-research-say-about-the
-wellbeing-of-children-with-gay-or-lesbian-parents.

Counterman, L., and D. Kirkwood. 2013. "Understanding Healthy Sexuality Development in Young Children." *Voices of Practitioners* 8 (2): 1–13.

Coward, R. 1980. "On the Universality of the Oedipus Complex: Debates on Sexual Divisions." *Critique of Anthropology* 4 (15): 5–28.

Crain, W. 2014. "Freud's Psychoanalytic Theory." In *Theories of Development: Concepts and Applications*, edited by William Crain, 5th Edition, 261–288. Pearson.

Crissman, H. P., M. B. Berger, L. F. Graham, and V. K. Dalton. 2017. "Transgender Demographics: A Household Probability Sample of US Adults, 2014." *American Journal of Public Health* 107 (2): 213–215. Accessed May 6, 2024. https://ajph .aphapublications.org/doi/full/10.2105/AJPH.2016.303571.

Cuadra, M., R. Baruch, M. E. Lamas Amorales, A. Arredondo, and D. Ortega. 2024. "*Normalizing* Intersex Children Through Genital Surgery: The Medical Perspective and the Experience Reported by Intersex Adults." *Sexualities* 27 (3): 533–552. https://dx.doi.org/10.1177/13634607221101142.

deMayo, B. E., A. E. Jordan, and C. A. Olson. 2022. "Gender Development in Gender Diverse Children." *Annual Review of Developmental Psychology* 4: 207–229.

DePalma, R. 2013. "Choosing to Lose Our Gender Expertise." *Sex Education* 13 (1): 1–15. https://dx.doi.org/10.1080/14681811.2011.634145.

DePalma, R., and E. Atkinson. 2010. "The Nature of Institutional Heteronormativity in Primary Schools and Practice-Based Responses." *Teacher and Teacher Education* 26 (8): 1669–1676. https://doi.org/10.1016/j.tate.2010.06.018.

Derman-Sparks, L., J. O. Edwards, and C. M. Goins. 2020. *Anti-Bias Education for Young Children and Ourselves*. 2nd ed. NAEYC.

Ehrensaft, D. 2014. "Found in Transition: Our Littlest Transgender People." *Contemporary Psychoanalysis* 50 (4): 571–592. https://doi.org/10.1080/00107530.2014 .942591.

Ehrensaft, D. 2017. "Gender Nonconforming Youth: Current Perspectives." *Adolescent Health, Medicine and Therapeutics* 8: 57–67. https://doi.org/10.2147.AHMT .S110859.

Field, T. L., and G. Mattson. 2016. "Parenting Transgender Children in PFLAG." *Journal of GLBT Family Studies* 12 (5): 413–429. http://doi.org/10.1080/1550428x .2015.1099492.

Flanagan, P. 2011. "Making Sense of Children's Sexuality: Understanding Sexual Development and Activity in Education Contexts." *Waikato Journal of Education* 16 (3): 69–79.

Flores, D. D., S. P. Meanley, K. T. Bond, M. Agenor, M. V. Relf, and J. V. Barroso. 2012. "Topics for Inclusive Parent-Child Sex Communications by Gay, Bisexual, Queer Youth." *Behavioral Medicine* 47 (3): 175–184.

Foucault, M. 1978. *The History of Sexuality: An Introduction*. Pantheon Books.

Freud, S. 1925a. "The Infantile Sexuality." In *Three Contributions to the Theory of Sex*, translated by A. A. Brill, 36–67. Nervous and Mental Disease Publishing Co.

Freud, S. 1925b. "The Sexual Aberrations." In *Three Contributions to the Theory of Sex*, translated by A. A. Brill, 1–36. Nervous and Mental Disease Publishing Co.

Freud, S. 1925c. *Three Contributions to the Theory of Sex*, translated by A. A. Brill. Nervous and Mental Disease Publishing Co.

Frye, D. 2022. "10 Things Parents of Trans Kids Want to Know." *Psychology Today*, September/October, 32–37.

Gates, G. J. 2011. "How Many People Are Lesbian, Gay, Bisexual, and Transgender?" *The Williams Institute*, April 2011. Accessed April 29, 2024. http://escholarship.org/uc/item/09h684x2.

Gill-Peterson, J. 2018. *Histories of the Transgender Child*. University of Minnesota Press.

Ginsburg, H., and S. Opper. 1969. *Piaget's Theory of Intellectual Development: An Introduction*. Prentice-Hall.

Gross, D. 2024. *Infancy: Development from Birth to Age Three*. 4th ed. Rowan & Littlefield.

Gunn, A. C. 2008. "Heteronormativity and Early Childhood Education: Social Justice and Some Puzzling Queries." Doctoral Thesis University of Waikato, 2008.

Gunn, A. C. 2023a. "Advocacy Perspectives of Early Childhood Teachers of Gender Diverse Children: Early Insights for Professional Learning and Policy Development." Paper presentation *New Zealand Association for Research in Education Annual Meeting and Conference*, Palmerston North, November 20–22, 2023.

Gunn, A. C. 2023b. "Timely Interventions: Queer Activist Early Childhood Teaching in Aotearoa New Zealand." In *Queer Studies and Education*, edited by N. M. Rodriguez, R. C. Mizzi, L. Allen, and R. Cover, 175–194. Oxford University Press.

Gunn, A. C., and J. Kroeger. In press, Fothcoming. Researching Parent and Teacher Advocacy for Genderqueer Children in the Early Years: A Mixed-Methods Approach. *Bloomsbury Handbook for Gender and Sexuality in Early Childhood*, edited by Jessica Prioletta, Adam Davies, and Kylie Smith.

Halberstam, J. 2018. *A Quick and Quirky Account of Gender Variability*. University of California Press.

Heatherington, L., and J. A. Lavner. 2008. "Coming to Terms with Coming Out: Review and Recommendations for Family Systems-Focused Research." *Journal of Family Psychology* 22 (3): 329–343. https://doi.org/10.1037/0893-3200.22.3.329.

Heilman, E. 2008. "Hegemonies and 'Transgressions' of Family: Tales of Pride and Prejudice." In *Other Kinds of Families: Embracing Diversity in Schools*, edited by Turner-Vorbeck and M. Marsh, 7–27. Teachers College.

Hendrick, J. 2001. *The Whole Child: Developmental Education for the Early Years*. 7th ed. Prentice-Hall.

Hodges, Ian. 2011. "Queering Psychoanalysis: Power, Self and Identity in Psychoanalytic Therapy with Sexual Minority Clients." *Psychology & Sexuality* 2 (1): 29–44. https://doi.org/10.1080/19419899.2011.536313.

Honig, A. 2000. "Psychosexual Development in Infants and Young Children." *Young Children* 55 (5): 70–77.

Jackson, E. F., and K. Bussey. 2023. "Broadening Gender Self-Categorization Development to Include Transgender Identities." *Social Development* 32: 17–31. https://doi.org/10.1111/sode.12635.

Kohlberg, L. A. 1966. "A Cognitive-Developmental Analysis of Children's Sex Role Concepts and Attitudes." In *The Development of Sex Differences*, edited by E. E. Maccoby, 82–173. Tavistock Publications.

Kroeger, J. 2023. "Queer Bodies in Early Childhood: Gender and Sexuality Disruption(s) & Impure Feminisms to 'Get Us Free.'" In *Feminisms and the Early Childhood Educator*, edited by R. Langford and B. Richardson, 139–155. Springer.

Kroeger, J., A. Gunn, D. Oleskiewicz, A. Sanchez, and C. Konieczko. 2024, in review. "Complicating Gender: Gender and Education." *Contemporary Issues in Childhood Education.*

Kroeger, J., A. Gunn, and A. Sullivan. 2023. Panel Convener: "Critical Perspectives on Gender & Sexuality and Young Children." *29th Annual Reconceptualizing Early Childhood Education Conference,* Manchester, England.

Kroeger, J., A. E. Recker, and A. Gunn. 2019. "Tate and the Pink Coat: Exploring Gender and Enacting Anti-Bias Principles in Practice." *Young Children* 74 (1): 83–92.

Kroeger, J., and L. Regula. 2017. "Queer Decisions in Early Childhood Teacher Education: Advocating for Gender and Sexual Minority Young Children and Families." *The International Critical Childhood Policy Studies Journal* 6 (1): 106–121.

Li, G., K. T. F. Kung, and M. Hines. 2017. "Childhood Gender-Typed Behavior and Adolescent Sexual Orientation: A Longitudinal Population-Based Study." *Developmental Psychology* 53 (4): 764–777. https://dx.doi.org/10.1037/dev0000281.

Liben, L. S., and R. S. Bigler. 2017. "Understanding and Undermining the Development of Gender Dichotomies: The Legacy of Sandra Lipsitz Bem." *Sex Roles* 76: 544–555.

Martin, C. L., and D. Ruble. 2004. "Children's Search for Gender Cues." *Current Directions in Psychological Science* 13 (2): 67–70. https://doi.org/10.1111/j.0963-7214.2004.00276.x.

Mimica, J. 2008. *Mother's Umbilicus and Father's Spirit: The Dialectics of Selfhood of a Yagwoia Transgendered Person.* Oceania.

Murray, S. 2009. "Within or beyond the Binary/Boundary: Intersex Infants and Parent Decisions." *Australian Feminist Studies* 24 (60): 265–274. https://doi.org/10.1080/08164640902852464.

Murray, S. O. 2009. "The Pre-Freudian Georges Devereux, The Post-Freudian Alfred Kroeber, and Mohave Sexuality." *Histories of Anthropology Annual* 5 (1): 12–27. University of Nebraska Press.

Murray, S. O., and R. Darnell. 2000. "Margaret Mead and Paradigm Shifts within Anthropology during the 1920s." *Journal of Youth and Adolescence* 29 (5): 557–573.

Nagoshi, J. L., C. T. Nagoshi, and V. K. Pillai. 2023. "Transgender Theory Revisited: Current Applications to Transgender Issues." *Current Opinion in Psychology* 49: 101546. https://doi.org/10.1016/j.copsyc.2022.101546.

Noppe, I. C. 2002. "Gender Role Development." In *Child Development*, edited by N. J. Salkind, 161–165. Macmillan.

Nutt, A. E. 2015. *Becoming Nicole: The Transformation of an American Family.* Random House.

Paechter, C. 2017. "Young Children, Gender, and the Heterosexual Matrix." *Discourse Studies in the Cultural Politics of Education* 38 (2): 277–291. https://doi .org/10/1080/01596306.2015.1105785.

Piaget, J. 1965. *The Moral Judgment of the Child*, translated by M. Gabain. Free Press.

Quinn, N., and W. Luttrell. 2008. "Psychodynamic Universals, Cultural Particulars in Feminist Anthropology: Rethinking Hua Gender Beliefs." *Ethos* 32 (4): 493–513.

Rich, A. 1980. "Compulsory Heterosexuality and the Lesbian Existence." *Signs: Journal of Women in Culture and Society* 5 (4): 631–660.

Richardson, D. 2004. "Locating Sexualities: From Here to Normality." *Sexualities* 7 (4): 391–411.

Rosky, C. J. 2013. "No Promo Hetero: Children's Rights to be Queer." (Law brief.) *Cardozo Law Review* 35: 425–510.

Sangren, S. P. 2008. "Psychoanalysis and its Resistances in Michel Foucault's *The History of Sexuality*: Lessons for Anthropology." *Ethos* 32 (1): 110–122. https:// anthrosource.onlinelibrary.wiley.com/doi/abs/10.1525/eth.2004.32.1.110.

Savin-Williams, R. C., and K. M. Cohen. 2015. "Developmental Trajectories and Milestones of Lesbian, Gay, and Bisexual Young People." *International Review of Psychiatry* 27 (5): 357–366. http://dx.doi.org/10.31095402161.2015.1093465.

Schnabel, D., and A. S. Keuroghlian. 2023. "Clinical Considerations for Children of Lesbian, Gay, Bisexual, Transgender, Queer, Intersex, Asexual, and All Sexually and Gender Diverse Families." *LGBT Health*: 1–5. https://doi.org/10.1089/lgbt .2023.0225.

Shankman, P. 2021. *Margaret Mead*. Berghahn Books.

Shulman, M. E. 2021. "What Use Is Freud?" *Journal of the American Psychoanalytic Association* 69 (6): 1093–1113. https://doi.org/10.1177/0003065111059546.

Skolnick, A. 1986. *The Psychology of Human Development*. Harcourt Brace Jovanovich.

Sotevik, L. 2023. "Playing with Straight Lines and Queer Times: Children Engaging with Romantic Love within and beyond Heteronormative Temporalities." *Sexualities*: 1–18. http://doi.org/10.1177/13634607231171323.

Steele, K., and J. Nicholson. 2020. *Radically Listening to Transgender Children: Creating Epistemic Justice through Critical Reflection and Resistant Imaginations.* Lexington Books.

Steinberg, Lawrence. 2017. *Adolescence*. 11th ed. McGraw-Hill Education.

Stryker, S. 2008. "Transgender History, Homonormativity, and Disciplinarity." *Radical History Review* 100: 144–157.

Surtees, N. 2005. "Teacher Talks about and around Sexuality in Early Childhood Education: Deciphering an Unwritten Code." *Contemporary Issues in Early Childhood* 6 (1): 19–29.

Tait, G. 2011. "'No Touch' Policies and the Government of Risk." In *Touchy Subject: Teachers Touching Children*, edited by A. Jones, 39–49. University of Otago Press.

Tasker, F. L., and S. Golombok. 1997. *Growing Up in a Lesbian Family: Effects on Child Development*. Guilford Press.

Taylor, A., and C. Richardson. 2005. "Queering Home Corner." *Contemporary Issues in Early Childhood* 6: 163–73.

Tobin, J. 1997. *Making a Place for Pleasure in Early Childhood Education*. Edwards Brothers.

Trawick-Smith, J. W. 2024. *Early Childhood Development: A Multicultural Perspective*. 7th ed. Pearson.

Turban, J. L., and D. Ehrensaft. 2018. "Research Review: Gender Identity in Youth: Treatment Paradigms and Controversies." *The Journal of Child Psychology and Psychiatry* 59 (12): 1228–1243. https://doi.org/10.111/jcpp.12833.

Wanta, J., W. Tordoff, D. Collin, A. Stepney, C. Taylor, D. Inwards-Breland, and A. Kym. 2021. "Mental Health Outcomes in Transgender and Gender Nonbinary Youth Receiving Gender-Affirming Care." *Journal of the American Academy of Child and Adolescent Psychiatry* 60 (105): 5224–5225.

Wurtele, S. K., and M. C. Kenny. 2011. "Normative Sexuality Development in Childhood: Implications for Developmental Guidance and Prevention of Childhood Sexual Abuse." *Counseling and Human Development* 43 (9): 1–24.

Zhang, Q., M. Goodman, N. Adams, T. Corneil, L. Hashemi, B. Kreukels, J. Motmans, R. Snyder, and E. Coleman. 2020. "Epidemiological Considerations in Transgender Health: A Systematic Review with Focus on Higher Quality Data." *International Journal of Transgender Health* 21 (2): 125–137. http://doi.org/10.1080/26895269.2020.1753136.

Chapter 3

"Reading Is Cheating!"

Children with Learning Disabilities and Their Need to Communicate

Ionas Sapountzis

Brian was a six-year-old boy who would become very frustrated and agitated when presented with tasks like copying letters onto a page or identifying the sounds of different letters. When faced with such tasks, he would put his head on the desk, make growling sounds, and refuse to respond to the teacher's attempts to help him. His frustration would often boil over into full meltdowns that included screaming and kicking the desk in front of him, taking his shoes off, throwing anything that was on his desk to the floor, and attempting to run out of the classroom.

Everyone at Brian's school felt that his intense reactions were the result of the trauma he had experienced earlier on when he witnessed his mother's partner repeatedly assault and threaten her. To escape the abuse, his mother had moved with Brian to New York City the year before. Even though a year had passed since the move, Brian could not fall asleep if his mother was not at home. With his mother's second job ending late in the evening, Brian would stay awake in bed waiting for her return. The next day at school, he would be very tired and moody and would often fall asleep on his desk. Brian was also very sensitive to loud sounds, disliked the cafeteria, and was prone to scream at his classmates if they got too close to him.

Given Brian's history, his emotional dysregulation and low frustration tolerance were understandable. He was a boy who was traumatized by what he had witnessed, and his mind was preoccupied with his mother's and his own safety. Yet, his frustration with simple academic tasks also suggested the possibility of an underlying learning disability that needed to be explored and, if confirmed, addressed. Brian's psychoeducational evaluation confirmed the presence of an underlying phonological deficit, which is the most common type of dyslexia. It also revealed significant delays in early reading skills and in recognizing letters, difficulties that most likely contributed to his negative reactions and his tendency to refuse to engage in tasks he experienced difficulty with. Brian's reactions were consistent with the reactions of children who experience learning difficulties in school. As several researchers have noted (Fletcher et al. 2007; Miller 2010; Pennington 2006), children with learning disabilities often display negative reactions toward school and academic tasks and are prone to give up trying.

Brian's evaluation also revealed how troubled he was by his learning difficulties and how these added to his confusion and negative outlook. His scores on the achievement, cognitive, and executive functioning tests offered a good understanding of the areas he was struggling with, but it was his responses on the Figure Drawing and Sentence Completion projective tests that conveyed how ineffective and helpless he felt. He drew a very tiny figure of a child with no hands or feet and no pupils, as if suspended in the air. Interestingly, he drew his mother the same way, without hands or feet, but at the corner of the sheet, as if she were going away or as if she were literally on edge. He drew two homes that were also suspended in the air, a large one and a tiny one without windows or doors, leaning toward each other.

His sentences for the Sentence Completion test were all about the Super Mario video game and the different levels of that game. At first glance, his responses to the Sentence Completion test could lead one to think that he did not understand the test or that he was avoiding getting engaged in it. The latter hypothesis was confirmed by the sentences he made when presented with the prompts "Reading" and "At school." He looked down and mumbled, "is cheating" when asked to make a sentence that started with the word "reading" and looked down again and mumbled, "I don't want to talk about it" when asked to make a sentence that started with the prompt, "At school." He remained with his head on the desk for a while and shook his head no when the evaluator tried to engage him again with the task. A few moments later, when the evaluator suggested that maybe they could take a short break, Brian quietly nodded yes.

Unlike Brian, Yelena was a seven-year-old girl who did not find school to be a place she did not want to talk about. She had many friends in school and would, according to her teacher, enter the class every day "with a big grin on her face." She responded very well to the teacher's requests, had excellent organization skills, and always participate enthusiastically when the teacher asked students to help with any classroom task, like decorating the classroom for an event. However, she had found it increasingly challenging to do her work and appeared to have a hard time staying focused on tasks that involved reading.

Unlike Brian, Yelena came from an intact family and appeared to have felt very supported at home. Her evaluation confirmed the presence of an underlying reading disability, specifically a phonological-deficit reading disability. As in Brian's evaluation, her drawings and statements also gave a glimpse of how ineffective she felt despite her efforts and her pleasant demeanor. She used many colors in the drawings she made that evoked associations of a happy girl and was very attentive to details, like matching the color of the figure's eyes and hair with hers as well as the color of the figure's clothes and hairband. And yet, despite her attention to details, the figures she drew of herself, much like the figures Brian drew, were at the bottom corner of the sheet and did not have hands and feet. Similarly, she drew a big colorful tree and a big apartment building with light coming out of all windows that were both, like Brian's, suspended in the air. At school, she "had fun," she said, because she had many friends, even though reading was "hard." She did not respond when the evaluator asked what she found hard about reading. Instead, she reached for the crayons on the table and became absorbed in tracing colored lines on a sheet of paper.

The evaluations of Yelena and Brian took place toward the end of the school year, as Brian was completing the first grade and Yelena the second grade. A question that needs to be asked is why these two children were not evaluated for the possibility of an underlying learning disability earlier on since both were experiencing difficulties with reading. This has been a chronic issue in the field, particularly when it involves children who attend schools in economically disadvantaged areas. Early signs of dyslexia often go unnoticed until the children's difficulties and their reactions to these difficulties become more pronounced (Miller 2010; Pennington 2006). The delay in making a learning disability diagnosis is usually longer for children of different ethnic, racial, and socioeconomic backgrounds, who typically attend underserved and understaffed schools (Carpenter-Song et al. 2011; Shim et al. 2017) and whose parents are not as familiar with school policies and regulations that would help them to better advocate for services for their children (Daisy-Etienne et al. 2022; Sapountzis et al. 2023). Neither Yelena's parents nor Brian's mother were likely to contact the school to inquire about their child's progress. Their difficulty with communicating in English was one reason, and their working schedules were another. Additionally, the school's failure to develop initiatives that would make it easier for parents who are facing language and scheduling challenges to become more involved was another reason.

But perhaps the main reason for not recommending psychoeducational evaluations for Brian and Yelena earlier in the school year was their histories and symptom presentations. Brian's difficulties were primarily attributed to his emotional state, to how traumatized he was and how unsafe he felt in life, rather than to the possibility of an underlying learning disability. He was, after all, only six years old. Yelena's difficulties were not seen as that significant or as interfering with her school work and adjustment. Her pleasant and engaging disposition had a reassuring effect on everyone who interacted with her. She was not complaining in class and did not throw tantrums. She was very responsive to the feedback she received, leaving teachers feeling that she was trying and that it was only a matter of time before she caught up with her peers.

Children who come from disorganized households and have developed insecure patterns of attachment are less likely to tolerate demanding tasks and to cope with frustration (Sroufe 1989). Instead, they are more likely to feel distressed when they are unable to perform well and to either act out or withdraw and give up when they feel discouraged or threatened (Sroufe 1989, 1996). Predictably, their behaviors tend to elicit negative reactions from others, making them feel more alone and even disliked in the process. By contrast, children who are securely attached feel more worthy and effective and are better able to use the teacher's help (Sroufe 1989). In school, these children are more enthusiastic and more confident in solving problems and are more likely to persist in their efforts. The behaviors displayed by Yelena and Brian in class were consistent with these findings. Brian, who came from a very conflict-ridden household, was moody and prone to give up, whereas Yelena, who came from an intact and very close-knit family, was very friendly and pleasant and would not let the anxiety and possibly the frustration she felt affect her behavior in class.

A risk in focusing only on the attachment patterns of children who are emotionally dysregulated without considering the possibility of underlying learning disabilities contributing to their dysregulation is that one may end up downplaying the effect of a neurodevelopmental disability on the behavior of these children and their relations with peers and adults. A closer look at some of the cases that are presented in articles about children with a neurobiological disorder points to the effect underlying disabilities can have on the parents and how their inconsistent or ambivalent responses can add to the children's fragility and confusion. Writing about children with an ADHD diagnosis, Salomonsson (2011) pointed out that the parents' ambivalent and often conflicting responses toward their child's behavior and emotional states only confirm the child's feelings of how bad and unmanageable they are. The parents' "faltering containment" (91), Salomonsson wrote, leaves their children without the support and stability they need to face emotions and impulses that confuse and at times overwhelm them.

Containing their child's anxieties and impulsive acts is likely to be negatively affected when the parents' capacity to be mindful of their child's difficulties and to reflect on what is happening is compromised. Moreover, as

Bleiberg (2001) noted, there is a high risk that children with an underlying neurodevelopmental disability who live in disorganized households will generate very negative reactions from their parents. The biological vulnerabilities of children who live in disorganized households can add to the chaos that exists at home (Sapountzis 2020) and to the distress family members may have experienced early in their lives and, in many cases, continue to experience (Music 2009). As Bleiberg (2001) pointed out, to parents who are still struggling with the consequences of their own traumatic histories, their child's distress and intense reactions can remind them of the disorganization they experienced earlier in their lives, making it even more likely that they will respond in an unreflective and punitive manner.

Curiously, an area that has received relatively little attention in the literature is how children with learning disabilities experience themselves and what they see when they look at their parents for support. Children, writes Winnicott (1967), look at their mother and in her gaze see a reflection of themselves. When the mother is preoccupied with other matters, the children register that preoccupation as an absence and are left feeling unsure as to what happened and why their mother is less available and/or attentive to them. It is very possible that Brian was experiencing a similar absence when he looked into his mother's eyes. His mother, after all, was a young woman in her mid-twenties who had herself been traumatized and had no help whatsoever. It is very possible that Brian had registered his mother's depression, her "deadness" (Green 1986), and felt very threatened and alone as a result. But the absence some children with underlying learning disabilities register when they look into their parents' eyes may also be related to the disappointment they see reflected in them. Every child, writes Likierman (1988), longs to feel that they are the "apple" of their parents' eyes, that they mean everything to them. Children who find themselves facing repeated failures and are unable to perform at the level their peers do are less likely to experience pride in their parents' gaze. Instead, they are likely to find concern and sometimes disappointment and disapproval, experiences that leave them feeling empty and like they are falling (Winnicott 1974) inside.

What can children who are aware of their difficulties and can sense that they generate not pride but concern and disappointment in their parents do? Without the affirming and steadying presence of an Other, many of them, in my experience, are left with one option: avoiding that gaze and instead acting as if they are not seeing and are not noticing what is reflected in it. For these children, thoughts and experiences have become bad internal objects that are "fit only for evacuation" (Bion 1962, 112). Some children, especially boys, are prone to act out. Their outbursts and loud complaints are expressions of frustration that serve to deflect blame from themselves and project it onto others (Willock 1987). Like the provocative acts of many children from chaotic households who, Bleiberg (2001) argued, seek to create a sense of predict-ability and to contain the helplessness they experience by eliciting negative reactions from their parents, the disruptive acts of children with underlying disabilities may help to shift the focus from their disability to what they do and what their parents' or teachers' reactions are. Other children, however, like Yelena, tend to hold their emotions in and avoid eliciting reactions that make them feel, to quote Willock again, disliked and unloved. Yet, regardless of how different the reactions of these children might be, deep down they are all likely to feel not good enough, as if something is missing.

Brian and Yelena communicated the sense of something missing by draw-ing themselves without hands. Jeremy, a restless seven-year-old boy with big brown eyes who came from a rather disorganized household and had diffi-culty remaining in his seat during testing, conveyed his view of himself more poignantly. He was a boy who, according to the teacher, was prone to hitting his head when frustrated and when he realized he had made a mistake. Jeremy already had a diagnosis of ADHD and was assessed to determine whether he also had an underlying reading disability that made his adjustment to school even harder. He did not. His scores were all in the average range, which, given how distractible he was during testing and in class, suggested that the obtained scores underestimated his potential. His stories, which were about boys being "whooped" by their mothers, about people appearing and disap-pearing, and about things happening to him without any obvious connection, reflected how disorganized his internal world was and how he experienced himself in the world. Unlike Yelena and Brian, he drew a caricature-like figure that filled the entire page when asked to Draw-A-Person. It was a caricature of a person, a person with a pumpkin head and crazy eyes on a triangle-shaped body with large breasts and with feces and urine falling to the ground. When he finished, he wrote "pippi-caca-doodoo boy" in big letters at the top of the page.

Bleiberg (2001) and Mathelin (1999) pointed to the dread children who evoke negative responses from their parents feel and how destabilizing that feeling can be. To Bleiberg, the parents' negative or punitive reactions, often at the very moment when a child needs their stabilizing and containing pres-ence, leave the child with nothing to hold on to and no one to turn to. In these moments, the child is in effect deprived of the holding environment he or she needs. Mathelin's work adds another dimension to the failure of parents to provide a holding environment for their children. She speaks of the "vertigo of the mother who cannot imagine her child," the mother whose child "evokes no feelings in her" (122). That is a terrifying experience for the child, akin to the experience of falling that Tustin (1986) and Winnicott (1974) described, as the child is left feeling "unheld" at the very moment the child needs to feel held the most. Mathelin was referring to a seven-year-old girl who, faced with her mother's inability to see past her symptoms, felt that she was an "object of horror" (122) to her mother. The little girl could not put words to her fears as her expressions drove her mother further into despair. Instead, she drew forms without eyes, strange-looking creatures that could not see or speak.

The vertigo of a mother who cannot imagine her child can be matched, I suspect, by the vertigo of a child who evokes no feelings or only negative ones in the important people in their life. It can also be matched by the experience of others seeing little in the child and expecting only the negative from that child. Jeremy's drawing, in my view, alluded to a similar vertigo. It was the vertigo of a child from a disorganized household who did not make sense to others and did not evoke any pride in them, the vertigo of a child who depicted himself as a weird boy who could not control any of his functions and deserved to be the object of ridicule.

Jeremy's drawings, like Brian's and Yelena's, communicated a core experience of his that only projective measures can provide. These tests, however, are increasingly ignored in the neuropsychology and school psychology fields and are regarded as not valid or meaningful. The tendency to dismiss the value of these tests coincides with the growing trend in the field to downplay subjective experiences and to focus almost exclusively on data obtained through standardized and norm-referenced tests. As a result, in conducting psychoeducational and neuropsychological evaluations to assess the likelihood of a disability, psychologists rely almost exclusively on behavioral checklists to obtain a measure of children's emotional state and their level of depression, anxiety, and/or sense of hopelessness.

Arguably, a major advantage of using such checklists is that they are norm-referenced and therefore provide a good sense of how elevated a child's score on a particular subscale is and how it compares to that of his or her peers. Elevated scores in the Anxiety and Depression scales of the BASC, for instance, can give a psychologist a good sense of how a child's scores in these areas compared to his or her peers but not much else. Brian's and Jeremy's scores on the Depression and Anxiety subscales were in the areas of significant risk and so were Yelena's. In fact, there was little difference between their scores.

This is precisely the limitation of these tests: the profiles that can be generated from them do not capture how the children experience their difficulties. Statements like "reading is cheating" or "reading is hard" and drawings of silly or tiny figures without hands and feet give a very clear sense of how children view themselves and how they have internalized their failures. They are communications of how these children feel. Treating such information as not valid because it is not obtained through standardized measures (Lilienfeld et al. 2000), and referring to these tests dismissively, as Motta and his colleagues (1993) did, is indicative of an underlying bias, if not ignorance. It is a stance that denies not only the experiences these children convey in their drawings but also the desire, however unconscious, to communicate something about themselves, to present themselves to an Other, and to seek his or her understanding.

From a Winnicottian perspective, the statements and drawings made by Jeremy, Yelena, and Brian were more than just expressions of how they felt about themselves. They were spontaneous gestures that took place in the intimacy of the testing encounter and reflected these children's desire to communicate "on the subject of [their] disability" (Winnicott 1971, 13). They represented a moment when they dared to reveal themselves to an Other and sought to make contact with that person. For Winnicott, these spontaneous moments are expressions of the True Self (1963) and should be regarded as "sacred" (1971, 4), as embedded in them is the hope of being seen by the other. The failure to recognize the wish that is present in these spontaneous gestures is regarded by Winnicott as a "wasted" (1971, 5) opportunity to acknowledge the child's desire to communicate their internal world to an Other and to feel understood.

In his seminal paper, "Fear of Breakdown," Winnicott (1974, 81) speaks about the "primitive agony" children who find themselves without the mother's understanding and facilitating presence experience. The mother's failure to respond to the child's gaze and to recognize the child's need to be acknowledged leaves the child experiencing an emptiness that can bring them to an "unintegrated state" and can evoke the sensations of "falling" (81) and of collapsing inside. Children with histories of learning failures due to underlying disabilities may experience a similar agony at home and in school as they often go on without the understanding and encouraging gaze they need. Instead, when they look at their parents' or teachers' gaze, they often find skepticism, if not disapproval. The literature on children who experience significant learning difficulties points to how prone these children are to develop a very negative view of themselves from early on (Leuzinger-Bohleber et al. 2011; Salomonsson 2011). As tasks and subjects become more demanding and complex, these children tend to increasingly respond by giving up (Migden 2002; Sugarman 2006).

I have seen this pattern in many children with learning disabilities that I have worked with over the years. It was repeatedly confirmed in the neuropsychological evaluations my students and I conducted over the course of several years at a school in the New York City metropolitan area. All thirty-six children who had an underlying learning disability displayed clear signs of how bad they felt about themselves. Much like Brian, they drew tiny figures without feet or hands; some even refused to draw themselves. Several of the older children, who were in the fourth and fifth grades, stated that their biggest fear was being held back in school and not being able to go to college. Regardless of age, all of these children conveyed through their statements, drawings, and acts their awareness of how unlike their peers they felt. The girls, like Yelena, typically made few demands, while the boys, like Brian and Jeremy, were more agitated and reactive.

Jeffrey, for instance, an eight-year-old boy with dyslexia, made very faint, almost imperceptible drawings of a person and of a house and a tree, leading one to think that he was very self-conscious about his drawings. Yet, when asked to make a drawing of any person he wanted to, he drew with sharp lines the face of Jim Brown, a rapper who at the time had made the news for his aggressive outbursts and abusive behaviors. In other words, he could draw his anger as long as he could locate it onto someone else. Like almost every other child who, as a result of their failures, had come to feel, to paraphrase Winnicott (1963), not good enough, he found it difficult to present himself and generate his own symbols.

Jeffrey's almost invisible drawings, despite his visible anger, are reminiscent of the young children described in Mathelin's (2004) paper who cannot write their names. These children were until recently referred to in France as the children who are "born under X" (369). This designation was given in France to children who were put up for adoption at birth, as the names of the father and of the mother on their birth certificate were marked with an X. Surprisingly, many of these children found it hard to learn to write in school, as if they were reluctant to leave a trace. Their writing disability was not derived from an underlying neurological deficit that made learning and the generation of symbols difficult for them, but from the threat they experienced at the prospect of knowing and the possibility of being the agents of their own creation. Adding to the difficulty these children experienced in learning to make a mark was their parents' uncertainty as to how to respond and what to make of their adopted children's acts.

For children with underlying learning disabilities, many of whom are reluctant to write, their difficulty in learning to write reflects, I suspect, a different kind of reluctance than that of creating the possibility of a link with a past that cannot be imagined. It is a reluctance that is rooted in the fear of finding again what they have come to expect about themselves. Although in his writings on the Negative, Green (1999, 2005) does not make any references to young clients with disabilities, one can easily see how his ideas apply to these children as well. They are children whose lives are characterized by multiple negatives—the negative of who they are and who they cannot be, the negative they experience in the responses of others, and the negative of what they see reflected in the gaze of others.

The emptiness that many children who are experiencing these multiple negatives might feel was conveyed very clearly, in my view, by Clara, a seven-year-old girl whose neuropsychological evaluation was sent to me by her mother before the start of family consultation sessions. Clara's neuropsychological evaluation was very detailed, and the lengthy report offered clear evidence of an underlying reading disability. Her profile was also consistent with her ADHD diagnosis. Missing from the report, however, was a sense of who the girl was. The report began with a statement that she was an adorable young girl, but that impression became lost amidst all the scores and the narrative that accompanied them. As I waited for our first consultation, I became aware of how much information I had about her underlying strengths and weaknesses and yet how little I knew about her and what it was like being with her.

Clara was indeed an adorable tornado who ran into the room ahead of her parents for the initial consultation and with extended arms announced, "I'm here!" She was a girl whose incessant movement resulted in being repeatedly corrected and redirected at home and at school. Doing homework and spending ten minutes reading at home, as every child in her grade was expected to, had already become a very frustrating experience for everyone. Yet, despite these almost constant reminders of how difficult she was and how upset others were with her, Clara did not seem to get angry at others. After noticing how she was repeatedly corrected by her parents, I pointed out that one could miss how tolerant she was with everyone and how she took in all criticisms and corrections without getting angry and snapping back. This was a long sentence, and I was not sure what Clara made of it. But when her parents turned toward her and asked her if this was true, it became clear that she had heard and understood everything. She turned to her parents and loudly replied, "Duhhh." When her parents, taken aback by her response, asked her when she felt that way, Clara replied in an even louder voice, while nodding her head, "How about ALL THE TIME?"

Two sessions later, Clara entered the room in a state of distress and quickly began to cry. "I can't take it anymore," she repeated several times while sobbing. When asked what had happened and what it that she could not take anymore, she tapped emphatically at her chest and said, "This, this, my ADHD." On the way to the session, the family had stopped for pizza at a favorite place, but what was supposed to be a pleasant outing quickly devolved into a tense one as Clara kept changing her mind and asking for different slices with many toppings, and her parents became impatient with her. At first glance, Clara's distress seemed to be directly related to what happened on the way to the session and how unsettling her parents' anger and disappointment were for her. But it was more than that. She was a girl who continuously felt that she was coming up short and that she was not like others. These narcissistic injuries became a persecutory internal object for her. And even though the initial impression of her was of an adorable girl, she was aware that others felt that she was "too much" (Bollas 2013) and were often tired of her.

Expecting to find only the negative can explain why a therapist working with children who are impulsive and have experienced many failures may find it hard to connect with them and create meaningful exchanges. These children have given up and find safety in withdrawing from contact and in seeking and expecting less from others. Jeremy and Brian conveyed through their behavior that they expected little from others, and so did Clara despite her initial enthusiastic announcement of her arrival. All three children, in different ways, acted in a manner that was likely to trigger responses from their caretakers that confirmed the absences and/or ruptures they had experienced in their lives and the expectations they had about themselves. The tendency in the field is to attribute the behavior of these children and the difficulties in creating meaningful exchanges with them to their impulsivity and reactivity. These acts, however, may be indicative not only of what their underlying weaknesses might be, or what had been absent in their exchanges with their caretakers, but also of what they are seeking and are hoping to find.

In his paper "Fear of Breakdown," Winnicott (1974) drew attention to this possibility when he remarked that children who have experienced an absence earlier on, a breakdown in their experience of going on being, often seem to "compulsively" (95) seek the very experiences they fear. In Winnicott's view, these children keep searching for a presence in an absence, for the mother's acknowledgment despite her unavailability, in the hope of finding that what they experienced before is not the case anymore. The same may be true with impulsive and reactive children, like Clara, Brian, and Jeremy, whose acts may also be indicative of the wish for a containing response, one that is not focused on their disability but on their potential and what else others can see in them.

Alvarez (1992) speaks of the importance of identificatory introjection, of others seeing more in a child than what the child sees in himself or herself. Holding in mind the potential some children cannot hold onto and imagining for them who they are and who they can be are acts of containment. The deprived or severely depressed children Alvarez presents in her writings may not have the dreams of "glory or nobility" (175) that most children have because they may not be able to imagine or hold on to such dreams. Or their dreams may seem outlandish considering how many obstacles they face. This was the case for a six-year-old boy I saw a few years ago. He had noticeable physical impairments and a significant language delay but kept insisting that he was going to be a professional wrestler and the president of the United States. To Alvarez, such boastful statements may not simply reflect the wish to deny the impotence such a child feels. They may also contain a question as to whether one can see that potential in the child. They contain the seed of a wish to see oneself as someone who can achieve something of importance and to feel that others can entertain that possibility as well. They may represent, as Alvarez suggested, a "tentative trying on of a new identification" (179).

Reaching children like Clara, Jeremy, and Brian, who have very negative views of themselves and expect little from others, requires that one looks for the presence of an underlying disability. Failure to do so may leave these children without the remedial support they need to face experiences that cannot help but become bad internal objects for them. But it also requires looking for their potential, the potential that is often obscured by the children's negative reactions and states of resignation. Children whose statements and acts reflect an absence of imagination and anticipation, and whose present is filled with a sense of what they cannot do and who they have not been, need others to hold onto the possibility of who they can become and to dare to imagine it for them. Recognizing the potential in children who seem to actively seek the absences that mark their lives and for whom being without may bring a temporary relief from the sense of feeling without requires persistence and faith in what can be found. It also requires, as Tuber (2015, 290) pointed out, one to be mindful of the language children use and to use that language to connect with the "affective life" of these children "on an immediate, visceral level."

Present in the drawings and statements of children like Brian, Yelena, Jeremy, and Clara is the desire to feel seen and to communicate (Winnicott 1965). Their statements and drawings are acts of communication (Winnicott 1965) that are easy to miss as the intent to make themselves known is often less direct, and the content of their drawings or statements feels too emotional and at times confusing. But if one perseveres and inquires about their dreams (Winnicott 1971) and fantasies (Salomonsson 2004, 2011), if one attends to the "whatness" or "isness" of their emotional states, what they feel, and how overwhelming that feeling can be for them (Alvarez 2012, 21), and if one insists on creating a bridge between "soul and soul" (Ekstein 1983, 416), then one is likely to find what is often unseen or unrealized in a child. Present in the symbolic representations children make, however incomplete or confusing these may be, are elements of their potential, the potential that enables them to create these representations. That potential emerges any time children seek to make themselves known by an Other and allow themselves, to quote Winnicott (1965) again, to be found. Failure to recognize that potential is more than a wasted opportunity. It is a reminder of the failure they experience when these children turn to Others and a confirmation of how little they evoke in them.

REFERENCES

Alvarez, Anne. 1992. *Live Company: Psychoanalytic Psychotherapy with Autistic, Borderline, Deprived and Abused Children*. London: Routledge.

Alvarez, Anne. 2012. *The Thinking Heart: Three Levels of Psychoanalytic Therapy with Disturbed Children*. London: Routledge.

Bion, Wilfred R. 1967. "A Theory of Thinking." In *Second Thoughts: Selected Papers on Psycho-Analysis*, edited by Wilfred R. Bion, 110–9. Northvale: Jason Aronson.

Bleiberg, Efrain. 2001. *Treating Personality Disorders in Children and Adolescents: A Relational Approach*. New York: Guilford.

Bollas, Christopher. 2013. *Catch Them Before They Fall: The Psychoanalysis of Breakdown*. London: Routledge.

Carpenter-Song, Elizabeth, Rob Whitley, William Lawson, Ernest Quimby, and Robert E. Drake. 2011. "Reducing Disparities in Mental Health Care: Suggestions from the Dartmouth-Howard Collaboration." *Community Mental Health Journal* 47: 1–13. https://doi.org/10.1007/s10597-009-9233-4.

Daisy-Etienne, Nicole, Ionas Sapountzis, Kirkland Vaughans, and Yvette Jones. 2022. "Meeting the Needs of Children from Disadvantaged Households: The Derner-Hempstead Child Clinic." *Journal of Infant, Child and Adolescent Psychotherapy* 21, no. 1: 197–207. https://doi.org/10.1080/15289168.2022.2043060.

DuPlessis Nelson, Justine. 2015. "How Do You Solve a Problem Like Agbon? The Trials and Tribulations of Applying Diagnoses to Children of a Foreign Culture." *Journal of Infant, Child and Adolescent Psychotherapy* 14, no. 4: 423–33. https://doi.org/10.1080/15289168.2015.1059308.

Ekstein, Rudolf. 1983. *Children of Time and Space of Action and Impulse*. Northvale: Jason Aronson.

Fletcher, Jack M., G. Reid Lyon, Lynn S. Fuchs, and Marcia A. Barnes. 2007. *Learning Disabilities: From Identification to Intervention*. New York: Guilford Press.

Green, André. 1986. "The Dead Mother." In *On Private Madness* by André Green, 142–73. London: Karnac.

Green, André. 1999. *The Work of the Negative*. London: Free Association Books.

Green, André. 2005. "The Work of the Negative." In *Key Ideas for a Contemporary Psychoanalysis: Misrecognition and Recognition of the Unconscious*, edited by André Green, 212–26. London: Routledge.

Laezer, Katrin Luise. 2015. "Effectiveness of Psychoanalytic Psychotherapy and Behavioral Therapy Treatment in Children with Attention Deficit Hyperactivity Disorder and Oppositional Defiant Disorder." *Journal of Infant, Child and Adolescent Psychotherapy* 14, no. 2: 111–28. https://doi.org/10.1080/15289168.2015.1014991.

Leuzinger-Bohleber, Marianne, Katrin Luise Laezer, Nicole Pfennig-Meerkoetter, Tamara Fischmann, Angelika Wolff, and Jonathan Green. 2011. "Psychoanalytic Treatment of ADHD Children in the Frame of Two Extraclinical Studies: The Frankfurt Prevention Study and the EVA Study." *Journal of Infant, Child and Adolescent Psychotherapy* 10: 32–50. https://doi.org/10.1080/15289168.2011.575703.

Likierman, Meira. 1988. "Maternal Love and Positive Projective Identification." *Journal of Child Psychotherapy* 14, no. 2: 29–46. https://doi.org/10.1080/00754178808254825.

Lilienfeld, Scott O., James M. Wood, and Howard N. Garb. 2000. "The Scientific Status of Projective Techniques." *Psychological Science in the Public Interest* 1, no. 2: 27–66. https://doi.org/10.1111/1529-1006.002.

Mathelin, Catherine. 1999. *The Broken Piano; Lacanian Psychotherapy with Children.* New York: Other Press.

Mathelin, Catherine. 2004. "What I Hear I Can't Write." *Journal of Infant, Child and Adolescent Psychotherapy* 3, no. 3: 369–83. https://doi.org/10.1080/15289160309348472.

Migden, Stephen. 2002. "Self-Esteem and Depression in Adolescents with Specific Learning Disability." *Journal of Infant, Child and Adolescent Psychotherapy* 2, no. 1: 145–60. https://doi.org/10.1080/15289168.2002.10486390.

Miller, Daniel C. 2010. *Best Practices in School Neuropsychology: Guidelines for Effective Practice, Assessment, and Evidence-based Intervention.* Hoboken: John Wiley & Sons.

Motta, Robert W., Steven G. Little, and Michael I. Tobin. 1993. "The Use and Abuse of Human Figure Drawings." *School Psychology Quarterly* 8, no. 3: 162–9. https://doi.org/10.1037/h0088273.

Music, Graham. 2009. "Neglecting Neglect; Some Thoughts about Children Who Have Lacked Good Input and Are 'Undrawn' and 'Unenjoyed.'" *Journal of Child Psychotherapy* 35, no. 2: 142–56. https://doi.org/10.1080/00754170902996064.

Pennington, Bruce F. 2006. *Diagnosing Learning Disorders: A Neuropsychological Framework*, 2nd ed. New York: Guilford.

Salomonsson, Björn. 2004. "Some Psychoanalytic Viewpoints on Neuropsychiatric Disorders in Children." *International Journal of Psychoanalysis* 85: 117–36. https://doi.org/10.1516/002075704322798978.

Salomonsson, Björn. 2011. "Psychoanalytic Conceptualizations of the Internal Object in an ADHD Child." *Journal of Infant, Child and Adolescent Psychotherapy* 10, no. 1: 87–102. https://doi.org/10.1080/15289168.2011.575711.

Sapountzis, Ionas. 2020. "Can You Help Me Be? Commentary on Mr. Mikulka's Paper 'Surviving Destruction and Finding Connection: Play Therapy with an 11 Year Old Boy'." *Journal of Infant, Child and Adolescent Psychotherapy* 19, no. 2: 170–6. https://doi.org/10.1080/15289168.2020.1755087.

Sapountzis, Ionas, Karen Lombardi, Michael O'Loughlin, Nicole Daisy-Etienne, Kirkland Vaughans, Yvette Jones, Tiffany Narain, and Elzinette Wheeler. 2023. "Creating a School-Based Mental Health Program to Meet the Needs of Children in Underserved Communities and Schools: The Derner Hempstead Child Clinic." *International Journal of Applied Psychoanalytic Studies* 20: 220–9. https://doi.org/10.1002/aps.1811.

Shim, Ruth S., Michael T. Compton, Shun Zhang, Kristin Roberts, George Rust, and Benjamin G. Druss. 2017. "Predictors of Mental Health Treatment Seeking and Engagement in a Community Mental Health Center." *Community Mental Health Journal* 53: 510–4. https://doi.org/10.1007/s10597-016-0062-y.

Sroufe, L. Allen. 1989. "Relationships, Self, and Individual Adaptation." In *Relationship Disturbances in Early Childhood: A Developmental Approach*, edited by Arnold J. Sameroff and Robert N. Emde, 70–94. New York: Basic Books.

Sroufe, L. Allen. 1996. *Emotional Development: The Organization of Emotional Life in the Early Years*. Cambridge: Cambridge University Press.

Sugarman, Alan. 2006. "Attention Deficit Hyperactivity Disorder and Trauma." *International Journal of Psychoanalysis* 87, no. 1: 237–41. https://doi.org/10.1516/F2BD-QXEU-NENX-QL3N.

Tuber, Steve. 2015. "Psychological Mindedness in the Face of a Learning Disability: The Utility of Play." *Journal of Infant, Child and Adolescent Psychotherapy* 14: 288–93. https://doi.org/10.1080/15289168.2015.1064260.

Tustin, Frances. 1986. "Falling." In *Autistic Barriers in Neurotic Patients*, edited by Frances Tustin, 183–96. London: Routledge.

Willock, Brent. 1987. "The Devalued, (Unloved, Repugnant) Self. A Second Facet of Narcissistic Vulnerability in the Aggressive, Conduct-Disordered Child." *Psychoanalytic Psychology* 4, no. 3: 219–40. https://doi.org/10.1037/h0079137.

Winnicott, Donald W. 1963. "Ego Distortions in Terms of True and False Self." In *The Maturational Process and the Facilitating Environment*, by Donald W. Winnicott, 140–52. New York: International Universities Press.

Winnicott, Donald W. 1965. "Communicating and Not Communicating Leading to a Study of certain Opposites." In *The Maturational Processes and the Facilitating Environment* by Donald W. Winnicott, 179–92. New York: International Universities Press. (Originally published 1963).

Winnicott, Donald W. 1967. "Mirror Role of Mother and Family in Child Development." In *The Predicament of the Family: A Psycho-Analytical Symposium*, edited by Peter Lomas, 26–33. New York: Hogarth Press.

Winnicott, Donald W. 1971. *Therapeutic Consultations in Child Psychiatry*. New York: Hogarth Press.

Winnicott, Donald W. 1989. "Fear of Breakdown." In *D. W. Winnicott: Psycho-Analytic Explorations*, edited by Clare Winnicott, Ray Shepherd, and Madeleine Davis, 87–95. Boston: Harvard University Press. (Originally published 1974).

Chapter 4

Projective Identification at Work in the Psychological Assessment of Children

Greta Carlson

A four-year, six-month-old cisgender girl of Puerto Rican and English descent I will call "Hallie" walks into the testing room at an outpatient group practice where I conduct psychological assessments, smiling and holding a small water bottle adorned with colorful stickers of cartoon unicorns. She greets me with an amicable "hi," and looks at the red blocks, organized in a square atop a green sheet of paper on the small table in the room. She takes a seat in front of the blocks and begins separating them from their original square formation. Hallie begins stacking the red blocks taller, one by one, and organizing other blocks at the base of the stacked blocks. "I'm making a building!" she exclaims, points to the structure, and shifts her gaze and attention from the blocks to me, making eye contact. "Yes, I see the building!" I reply. Hallie stacks the red blocks ever taller, now creating a circle around the structure. This time for Hallie to engage in free play with blocks while I, as the assessor, observe her is intentionally built into the administration process for the assessment Hallie is completing this morning—the Gesell Developmental Observation-Revised (GDO-R). After free play, I will observe Hallie as she works to replicate a series of structures with the blocks from a three-dimensional model. Hallie is engaging in this psychological assessment so I can provide detailed recommendations to support her education and learning to her teacher at her new public elementary school. Hallie had been referred to me by her parents, who expressed interest in a psychological assessment to determine if she was performing at an academic level consistent with her chronological age and grade and to learn more about Hallie's general cognitive functioning.

Hallie is a kindergartener at the school, having matriculated from a cooperative nursery school in a suburb of Washington, D.C. She resides with both parents in a single-family home, and while she has been exposed to both

89

English and Spanish languages, her mother, Ms. C., noted her primary language at home and school is English. Hallie has one older sister, Rachel, who is seven years old. The family identifies with the Catholic faith and attends church on a weekly basis. Ms. C. reported an uncomplicated, full-term pregnancy and delivery with Hallie and no major separations from her during infancy or interruptions during breastfeeding. Ms. C. had access to regular prenatal care and maternity leave from her work as a consultant for a marketing firm. Hallie's mother noted that Hallie met her scooting, crawling, walking, and talking developmental milestones within normal time limits, and her toileting developmental milestone slightly later than her similar-aged peers. Hallie does have a medical history of chronic sinus infections, no known trauma history, and a paternal mental health history of generalized anxiety disorder. She has no known hearing, eyesight, speech, fine or gross motor impairments, has had access to routine medical and dental well-checks, and socializes with same-age peers at a weekly ballet dance class. Mr. C., Hallie's father, noted that Hallie enjoys drawing and engaging in pretend play with her older sister.

I sit across from Hallie to begin the structured tasks of the GDO-R. As I consider her behavioral gesture to her "building," I take note of Hallie's ability to initiate "joint attention" (Meindl and Cannella-Malone 2011), an important developmental milestone that typically emerges between the ages of eight and fifteen months (Bakeman and Adamson 1984; Jones et al. 2006). When initiating joint attention, a child invites, either verbally or non-verbally, another person to attend to a third object or event that both may be able to perceive. I also register my own bodily feelings of delight and curiosity in response to Hallie's initial actions and consider her ability to verbally ascribe her concept of "a building" to the stacked red blocks. In essence, in addition to joint attention, she shows evidence of engaging in symbolic play, a skill which develops between the ages of eighteen and twenty-four months in typically developing children, in which a child can view one object as representing another or enact events in play that had occurred during a previous time (Thiemann-Bourque et al. 2019). Before the GDO-R assessment has formally begun, there is already much to be observed in the unique universe (Ferro and Basile 2009) that is created between examiner and examinee during the clinical encounter.

The Gesell Developmental Observation—Revised relies on direct observation of a child's language usage, social-emotional responses, fine and gross motor behavior, and problem-solving ability to make inferences about their cognitive and socio-emotional development. The GDO-R is comprised of five "strands," each of which is designed to assess a core facet of cognitive (language/comprehension; visual/spatial discrimination; letters and numbers; and fine/gross motor skills), social, and emotional development in children ages two and a half to nine years old. Dr. Arnold Gesell (1880–1961) was an American psychologist, academician, and pediatrician who gathered behavioral data from thousands of infants and young children ages zero to nine years old. From these sizeable data sets, Gesell perceived common patterns of problem-solving ability and overt behaviors, including "language behavior," as children progressed in their chronological age. Gesell's direct observations led him to develop the Maturational Theory of Child Development, which posits that most children follow a similar progression in their cognitive and socio-emotional development as time naturally unfolds. Gesell also developed the idea that chronological age differs from developmental age, and that a child who is four years old, chronologically, may exhibit language, fine and gross motor behavior, and problem-solving skills that are consistent with the typical behavior of a child of another chronological age (Weitzman and Harris 2012). Rather than a full-scale *intelligence* quotient (FSIQ), as seen in the Wechsler family of assessments, including the Wechsler Preschool and Primary Scale of Intelligence—4th Edition (WPPSI-IV), after completing the tasks of the GDO-R, the young examinee is provided a qualitative descriptor of their overall development—"Age-Appropriate; Emerging; or Concern," and a "developmental age," which may or may not be aligned with their chronological age. As part of the overall assessment, both the child's parent and teacher are provided with self-report questionnaires to document their impressions of the examinee's behavior in both home and school contexts.

Gesell emphasized the importance of being as objective as possible when documenting and recording the behaviors of infants and children zero to nine years old. He encouraged clinicians assessing and working with children to identify and describe their moment-to-moment overt behaviors, wording and sentence structure, and facial expressions without ascribing meaning or judgment. One might argue that, philosophically, Gesell took a phenomenological approach in his method of understanding a young child's growth over time, chiefly characterized by *describing*, as opposed to *explaining* or *analyzing*. Gesell appeared to believe that it was possible for an assessor or clinician to take an *objective*, rather than *subjective*, perspective when observing a child's behaviors. French phenomenological philosopher Maurice Merleau-Ponty described objectivity as a mode of thought in which an individual detaches from their subjectivity enough to perceive the external world independent of their own experiences *about* and *around* it (Shand 2015). When administering the GDO-R with Hallie, for example, I am careful to record her exact words as I hear them and her behaviors i.e., "sitting, standing up, moving three blocks," as I see and perceive them.

Gesell's maturational theory, supported by decades of documented observations, helped lay the foundation for later stage-theorists in the field of childhood cognitive and emotional development, including Jean Piaget, Lev

Vygotsky, and Erik Erikson. Their theories were organized using the metaphor of a series of stages, or steps, that the developing child "passes through," or "masters," before proceeding to the next stage. Perhaps to better capture the fluidity and changeability inherent to early childhood development, Anna Freud altered this metaphor slightly in her "developmental lines" concept, or the idea that a child can show evidence of both age-appropriate and emerging speech, cognition, motor cognition, reality testing, patterns of defenses, object relations, and adaptability. Anna Freud viewed these domains as existing on multiple continua, with children able to move forward and backward (i.e., regression) on each developmental line, depending on their unique environmental factors, stressors, and circumstances (Neubauer 1984). While Gesell has often been critiqued for diminishing both the role of a child's external environment and the influence of their socio-cultural background on their cognitive, social, and emotional development (Thelen and Adolph 1994), Anna Freud's theory honored the interplay between environment and the individual child. She considered how external stressors in a child's life might catalyze a temporary regression to a previous developmental stage (Freud 1963).

In addition to individual activities that comprise the five strands of the Gesell Developmental Observation, the assessment includes the documented observation of a young examinee in multiple contexts beyond the testing room through questionnaires that are administered to both the child's parents and educators. These questionnaires are designed to capture the social and emotional behaviors of the child and help the assessor develop a holistic picture of their overall developmental age. They contain items designed to gauge a child's level of self-control in structured and unstructured situations, independence with activities of daily living, and ability to cooperate with others (Gesell Program 2021). This element of the GDO-R differs considerably from the Wechsler Preschool and Primary Scale of Intelligence—Fifth Edition (WPPSI-IV), an assessment of cognitive functioning for children ages two years, six months through seven years, six months. After Hallie's assessment, I gather both questionnaires from her parents and preschool teacher and look for consistencies and discrepancies in their observations of her in each environment.

Arnold Gesell published the Gesell Developmental Schedules, the first version of the Gesell Developmental Observation, in 1925. Approximately fifteen years after this assessment was published, in 1939, Romanian American psychologist Dr. David Wechsler published the Wechsler-Bellevue Intelligence Scale for adults. Wechsler based his scales for adults on a theory of intelligence that included both verbal comprehension and concept knowledge *and* nonverbal (performance) intelligence, or one's ability to identify patterns in visually presented data and solve novel nonverbal problems with inductive and deductive reasoning[1] (Gibbons and Warne 2019). A student of mathematician Karl Pearson and statistician Charles Spearman, Wechsler arrived at his own model of intelligence following his administration of the Stanford-Binet to recruits for the Army. Wechsler believed that the current definition of human intelligence was too narrow and relied heavily on one's acquisition of and facility with language and verbally encoded concept formation. In his pivotal article published in *The Psychological Bulletin*, Wechsler defined human intelligence as "the aggregate, or global capacity of the individual to act purposefully, to think rationally and to deal effectively with his environment" (Wechsler 1940, 7).

Wechsler's view, perhaps more than Gesell's maturational model and emphasis on observation, considers the interplay between one's mental processes and their environment. The Wechsler-Bellevue Intelligence Scale for adults (WBIS) eventually evolved into the Wechsler Adult Intelligence Scale (WAIS), published in 1955. The WAIS is now in its fourth revision, published in 2008. The Wechsler family of assessments quickly expanded to include the Wechsler Intelligence Scale for Children (WISC), published in 1949, and the Wechsler Preschool and Primary Scale of Intelligence (WPPSI), published in 1967. The WISC is now in its fifth edition, which was released in 2014, and the WPPSI is in its fourth edition, released in 2012. The WISC and the WPPSI, adapted from Wechsler adult intelligence scales, grew out of a need for cognitive assessments for children and adolescents that offered a glimpse beyond language expression and command of verbal knowledge and into their nonverbal reasoning, visual-spatial reasoning, and processing speed abilities (Kaplan and Saccuzzo 2005). Unlike the Gesell Developmental Observation—Revised, which provides a qualitative description of a child's developmental level and is based largely on the examiner's observations of their language usage and behavior patterns, the WPPSI-IV yields a full-scale intelligence quotient, derived from the examinee's performance on indices designed to assess their verbal comprehension abilities, visual-spatial and motor integration skills, nonverbal/fluid reasoning, working memory, and processing speed (Raiford and Coalson 2014). Compared to the GDO-R, the WPPSI-IV contains more subtests that rely on a child's nonverbal problem-solving and pattern recognition abilities. Similar in format and content to the WISC-V and the WAIS-IV, Wechsler's assessment for preschool-aged children is clearly derived from his original Wechsler-Bellevue scales of adult intelligence and, unlike Arnold Gesell's assessment, does not seem to reflect an underlying theory that cognitive functioning in young children is a multi-faceted developmental process that ebbs and flows over time.

Hallie completes the GDO-R and returns for testing administration day two to complete the WPPSI-IV the following week on time with her mother, Jen. This time, she enters the testing room quickly, without hesitation, sits down at the small table in the testing room, and begins to fill the space with a narrative of a friend's birthday party she attended over the past weekend, after glancing at a few small decorative pumpkins in the office. "You've got pumpkins! I got to go to a pumpkin patch for my friend's birthday party and picked out my own pumpkin. We went on a hayride after. The hayride was bumpy, but fun. And I got to take my pumpkin home." I take note of Hallie's ability to recall a memory from a prior time, and her apparent connection from the pumpkins she sees in the testing room to pumpkins in her memory of the birthday party. Hallie settles into the testing situation to begin the Block Design subtest on the WPPSI-IV. Unlike the GDO-R, there is no time structured in during the WPPSI-IV for an examinee to play freely with the testing materials at the beginning of the assessment, but that doesn't stop four-year-old Hallie from eyeing the half-red, half-white colored blocks placed on the testing table. Pointing to the blocks, she notes, "those look like flags!" Consistent with Hallie's identifying the structure she built at the beginning of the GDO-R as "a building," she quickly assigns meaning to the color and shape of the blocks in the WPPSI-IV. In a sense, in addition to subjective meaning-making, there may be an element of projection. Hermann Rorschach, the first developer of the Rorschach Inkblot Test, or "form interpretation test," believed that when presented with an ambiguous stimulus, or one that has no readily apparent meaning, a person will perceive and *project* his or her unconscious psycho-logical processes onto it (Rorschach 1942). When taking a psychodynamic approach to conducting a psychological assessment, an examiner can be curi-ous not only about a young examinee's cognitive and academic functioning but also the interplay between elements of their socio-emotional world.

Although Hallie's family sought a psychological assessment to inform and guide her learning process at school, the interplay between Hallie's cogni-tive ability, emotional, and interpersonal life is apparent during the testing administration. As Hallie works through the Block Design subtest, in which she is asked to create a three-dimensional object from a two-dimensional picture, more meanings emerge. Like perceiving characters and objects in clouds and landscapes, or items in a Rorschach inkblot, Hallie describes that she sees "robots" and "baby foxes," as she assembles blocks from the pictures she is presented with. When she arrives at a complex design which requires more blocks to create, Hallie pauses and begins to fidget with the blocks, turning them around on the table. She frowns and begins kicking her legs under her chair. "This one is hard," she exclaims. Hallie tries two more times to turn and position the blocks to match the picture in front of her, her eyebrows furrowed. Correspondingly, I notice a bodily pang of anxiety which feels to me like a tightness in my chest in response to Hallie, and a sense of an *impasse*, or blockage, as though perhaps she is approaching the limits of her visual-spatial ability. Although Hallie is now working past the time constraints allotted during this assessment item, I wait to see if Hallie will eventually be able to create the design. She turns the blocks around slowly a couple more times and sighs, appearing frustrated. I take this as a sign to move on to the next item. "That's a tough one—let's try another," I note, and Hallie's expression eases and brightens slightly. She replies, "Okay, yeah." I encourage Hallie to take a deep, five-second breath and stretch, and then I administer the next item in the sequence. After pausing and regulating her anxiety and frustration, Hallie can complete the next two items on the Block Design subtest within the time constraints before reaching her limit, or the point at which she no longer shows that she is able to solve the task.

Beyond her cognitive scores on the WPPSI-IV indices and her developmental age and description on the GDO-R, Hallie has provided additional data that cannot easily be captured or measured with quantitative analysis. This vital information can be gleaned through the *transference/countertransference*[2] matrix of the testing situation, or the unconscious emotional communication from examinee to examiner and vice versa. Through this channel of understanding, an examiner can gain important clues into the feelings, or affective states, experienced by an examinee during the completion of a cognitive task. Although the theory of *transference/countertransference* dynamics has long been central to a psychodynamic or psychoanalytic perspective in therapeutic intervention with young children, I posit that these dynamics are just as present and alive in the testing room and can be harnessed to arrive at a deeper understanding of a young examinee's problem-solving process. In turn, this understanding can be used to create detailed and specific recommendations for intervention within the academic setting.

Countertransference, a concept which appeared early in the psychoanalytic literature (Freud 1910) refers to the unconscious and conscious feelings, thoughts, attitudes, and perceptions the therapist or analyst has in response to the patient. Otto Kernberg, a psychoanalyst, noted that historically, two approaches to countertransference can be observed: the first "classical" proposition by Sigmund Freud that the analyst's countertransference is the unconscious reaction to the patient's transference and needs to be "worked through" and overcome by the analyst, and the second "totalistic" view of countertransference as the total emotional reaction of the analyst to the patient in the treatment situation. Kernberg notes that in the "totalistic" approach, rather than a potential barrier to understanding to be resolved, the analyst's countertransference is a useful means of understanding aspects of the patient's experience (Kernberg 1965). Within this totalistic view, an analyst's countertransference may consist of both dissociated and projected material from the patient's inner world into the analyst's psyche and the analyst's own clearly idiosyncratic views of the patient that may be more relevant to the analyst's history, sense of relationships, and internal conflicts.

Projective identification, a clinical concept first introduced by Melanie Klein in 1946, was an elaboration of Sigmund Freud's initial theory of projection, a process wherein "internal states influence the perception of the outer world" (Lindzey 1961, 27). In Klein's projective identification, one person unconsciously experiences a feeling that cannot be consciously thought of in words or verbalized, which leads to intense anxiety. That person then uses their feeling to describe the character or affective state of the other person, in a sense, evacuating the feeling that led to intolerable anxiety, and locating it in the other person to relieve themselves of anxiety. Klein also noted that projective identification need not only involve evacuating unpleasant (bad) affects like shame, rage, and envy, but also pleasant (good) ones like love and attraction. Projective identification may also include the first person subtly treating or regarding the second person in such a way that they evoke the unwanted or split-off feeling in the second person. Klein expanded upon the concept to include *introjection*, to include a complex phenomenon in which a person "enters into" the mind of another person to obtain coveted characteristics of that person (Routledge 2011).

Later Kleinian theorists explored projective identification both as an early defense against certain feelings and as a powerful and nonverbal way of communicating feelings to another person, to be better understood by them. Thomas Ogden summarized his views on projective identification not only as a psychological defense and mode of communication but also as a potential avenue for change within the individual, wherein a receptive therapist or analyst helps the patient to understand, think about their intolerable feelings, and communicate them in a more direct way. This process then allows for re-internalization and integration into the patient's sense of self. Ogden describes the developmental origins of projective identification when he theorizes, "each of these functions of projective identification evolves in the context of the infant's early attempts to perceive, organize, and manage his internal and external experience and to communicate with his environment" (Ogden 1979, 5). Herbert Rosenfeld emphasized the importance of differentiating between projective identification as a defense, mode of communication, and "an infantile type of object relationship" often observed in a psychotic process, wherein a patient believes he has "forced himself omnipotently into the analyst, which results in a fusion or confusion with the analyst and anxieties related to the loss of the self" (Rosenfeld 1983, 263).

Kleinian thinkers emphasize the unconscious, non-verbal nature of projective identification in the clinical situation, and the importance of working to become aware of one's own feelings in response to patients, as they contain clues as to what might be happening in the relationship between patient and analyst. Kleinian thinkers consider how these happenings can be used to help the patient come to know his, her, or their own psychological and emotional processes. Betty Joseph framed a patient's transference as a

> living relationship in which there is constant movement and change . . . the patient's psychic organization based on his early and habitual ways of functioning, his fantasies, impulses, defenses, and conflicts will be lived out in some way in the transference. (Joseph 1985, 453)

According to Joseph's perspective, the patient's past is very much alive in the present *here-and-now* way of relating (or not relating or partial relating) to the therapist or analyst, and the work of therapy involves trying to understand how the patient's mind works in relation to the analyst. Joseph also notes, "the way in which our patients communicate their problems to us is frequently beyond their individual associations and beyond their words and can often only be gauged by means of the countertransference" (Joseph 1985, 453). For Joseph, ideas about the patient's unconscious life, defenses, and past relationships can be gleaned not only through their spoken narratives, illustrations, and play, but also through the analyst's own feelings and thoughts while in the room with the patient.

Klein posited that a child or adult might use projective identification more often when they are in the *paranoid-schizoid* position. Rather than construct an underlying framework of a series of stages one passes through, as seen in the writings of the developmental stage-theorists, Klein used the metaphor of "positions" to describe an individual's different manner of relating to themselves and others. Klein put forth that when a person is in the paranoid-schizoid position, which first begins from birth through the first six months of life, they perceive their world (and, in the infant's case, the mother's breast, during feeding) in solely good or bad ways. According to Klein's theory, when in this position, a person may project their own aggressive, "bad, hated" feelings onto an external other, and then experience intense fears of persecution. The infant may experience the breast as entirely frustrating, dissatisfying, withholding, and delivering "bad" contents, or as entirely good, nourishing, and satisfying. The person in the paranoid-schizoid position will be unable to integrate both "bad" and "good" parts of their experience of themselves and external objects together into a complex and multifaceted whole. Klein believed that one could "work through" the paranoid-schizoid position toward the *depressive* position, through being able to tolerate their frustration and the reality that the Other will not be able to consistently provide "good" nourishment and mourn the loss of the idealized external object. Klein thought that the infant's ability to tolerate their frustration in the absence of the breast, gradually develop, and hold onto the idea that their mother would eventually return for more feeding was also central to achieving the depressive position.

When in the depressive position, a person can hold in mind and integrate both "good" and "bad" feelings, and perceptions of self and other. Rather than projecting out and identifying with certain discrete feelings in the other, for safekeeping or as a complex defense, a person in the depressive position can accept and hold a range of feelings and perceptions, both pleasant and unpleasant. For Klein, a person's ability to achieve the depressive position in their emotional/relational repertoire is an important maturational step, and an individual can shift fluidly between the paranoid-schizoid and depressive positions from moment to moment (Routledge 2011).

Although the testing situation has a different frame compared to psychodynamic psychotherapy or psychoanalysis, in that testing constitutes a temporary relationship between examiner and examinee and is limited to approximately three meetings and a feedback session, the psychoanalytic concepts of projective identification, attending to the moment-to-moment transference/countertransference dynamics, and the paranoid-schizoid and depressive positions are useful for being curious about the emotional lives of children as they engage in a psychological assessment. There is a vast and growing literature which provides support for the theory that one's emotional life is instrumental to the motivation needed to learn and complete cognitive tasks. Emotion is thought to have a particularly strong impact on attention and plays a crucial role in determining which set of stimuli one attends to in their physical surround, in addition to being a powerful motivating force toward behavior (Tyung et al. 2017). Emotion is also believed to facilitate or interfere with a young learner's ability to encode verbal information in their long-term memory, depending on a range of factors, including which feelings are experienced when a child is learning, and how the child is able to modulate these feelings when they are attending to (Vuillehemier 2005) information, memorizing new information (Phelps 2004), and reasoning (Jung et al. 2014) with information.

When a young examinee experiences unpleasant feelings, like frustration, anxiety, shame, or embarrassment in a dysregulated manner, their ability to think flexibly and work through a given novel problem becomes hindered. They may lose motivation to solve the task altogether and begin to worry about how the examiner or educator will perceive them. Older children may start to compare themselves unfavorably to their peers or "check out" and drift off into a daydream, describing an experience of their minds "going blank." In moments of intense dysregulation, a child may experience themselves as a "bad" student or learner and perceive the educator as punitive, demanding, or even shaming. The testing situation allows a psychodynamically oriented clinician a glimpse into a young child's attentional, cognitive, *and* intra/interpersonal processes. An attuned clinician can then formulate hypotheses about which kinds of cognitive or academic tasks elicit frustration, anxiety, apathy, hopelessness, or avoidance in young examinees and communicate these ideas to their teachers, tutors, and allied professionals. Teachers, then, may add to their frameworks for understanding the feelings and thoughts underneath fidgety behavior, tantrums, and avoidance of certain tasks in the academic setting, knowing when to intervene with five-minute breaks, the child's preferred affect regulation skills, and helping the child to "name and tame" (Siegel and Bryson 2016) their feelings of distress. Further, a teacher or tutor may be better able to scaffold a child's learning of skills that are naturally more challenging for them, and understand where their limits are, in addition to helping them expand on their cognitive strengths.

Hallie engages with the Picture Concepts subtest of the WPPSI-IV with a smile. In this activity, a young examinee is asked to look at two, and then three rows of objects, and choose the objects from each row that share a trait with each other. The subtest measures an examinee's ability to discern underlying conceptual relationships between seemingly unrelated objects, a part of abstract reasoning ability (Raiford et al. 2014). I watch as her eyes dart from one object to the next in each row, pointing to the objects she sees as related. "This is easy!" she exclaims. I notice and welcome physical/bodily feelings of contentedness, clarity, and calm in response to Hallie as she works, and wonder if I might be experiencing a *concordant countertransference* (Racker 1957), or a feeling that is closely aligned with what Hallie might be experiencing at this moment, as she successfully solves the problems put forth in the subtest. Racker theorized that in a concordant countertransference, a therapist identifies, or partially identifies, with an aspect of the patient's mind and emotional experience. This understanding of countertransference differs from other writers' ideas that patients "put feelings into" therapists during the clinical encounter. Although Racker put forth that a concordant countertransference may lead to empathy for a patient's experience, clinicians have cautioned not to "over-identify" with aspects of a patient's verbalizations, demeanor, or overall presentation in the therapy or testing room (P. Gedo, personal communication, March 2016). Furthermore, analysts have emphasized the importance of continually working to become aware of one's own mind (as much as is possible), personal history, and "baseline" of emotional experience, so as to mitigate the risk of projecting aspects of their experience into the clinical situation or harboring a fixed perception of the patient. Indeed, countertransference is co-created, with "relative and varying contributions from the analyst and the analysand" (Carveth 2012, 4).

As her testing process unfolds, Hallie reaches the Zoo Locations subtest. This subtest requires Hallie to hold the arrangement of pictures with animals in her short-term visual memory and then re-create these arrangements immediately after seeing them. The number of cards and positions of cards an examinee must recall increases throughout the subtest. The activity is designed to assess an examinee's working memory ability. Hallie appears to experience more of a challenge during this subtest compared to other activities in the WPPSI-IV. She begins to place the cards on the table quickly and with more force than how she has handled previous testing materials. She shows a frown on her face, looks up at me, makes eye contact, and notes, "I forget where they were." She then directs her gaze back to the cards, fiddling with them in her hands. She sighs deeply. In response, I think of the word *defeated*, to describe her demeanor and experience an emerging sense of anxiety. I decide to simply comment on her behavior without ascribing any meaning. "You're holding the cards in your hands." Hallie lifts her shoulders in a shrug, looks down, and replies, "I don't know where to put them now. I don't remember." I notice my own feelings of uncertainty and confusion and feel a slight impulse to "fix" Hallie's dilemma as she struggles to "get the right answer" on the subtest, a potential transference/countertransference dimension. Hallie quickly shifts her gaze back to the pumpkins on the window and brightly states, "those pumpkins are still there. The ones that were like the one I got at Mandy's birthday party."

When I continue to reflect, I wonder about the unconscious expectations Hallie may place on herself to complete the assessment in a "perfect" way and how that might serve to alleviate anxiety and, potentially, feelings of shame. Perhaps she drifted back into her memory of her friend's birthday party to distance herself from these emotions. I wonder, too, if I have identified with this aspect of Hallie's process in my impulse to solve the problem that has elicited Hallie's distress. I keep these ideas in mind as hypotheses about Hallie in the testing encounter and sit with the uncertainty inherent in not having a completely "objective" view of Hallie. In considering a clinician's own subjectivity, Warren Poland highlights,

> our earliest views of the world are always shaped by a viewpoint with ourselves at the center. With experience and with learning, we come to understandings more complex and more subtle, more modest regarding our own centrality. But the new, elegant edifice of sophistication is shaped by the naive self-centeredness around which it grew. It is so in our individual lives, and it is so in our science. (Poland 1992, 381)

Thinking back to the data within the testing session—how Hallie was able to regulate herself and complete more items in sequence during the Block Design subtest—I decide to "test the limits" of Hallie's performance on Zoo Locations and offer her the space to still make a choice of where to put the cards, before moving on to the next activity. "Would you like to make your best guess?" I ask, hoping to open a space for Hallie to freely provide her response and to offer a chance for her to potentially earn more points within this activity. Testing the limits in assessment with children may mean the examiner needs to deviate slightly from the provided testing administration script to ensure a young patient is not answering an item incorrectly due to interfering performance anxiety or frustration but rather because they do not know the correct answer. Hallie nods and places the animal cards in new locations as we discontinue Zoo Locations and smoothly transition to the next subtest.

Following Hallie's assessment, release of the report, and feedback session with her parents, I provided the results to her kindergarten teacher, Ms. Dennett. On the GDO-R, Hallie has shown "age-appropriate" skills in the general developmental, letters/numbers, language/comprehension, adaptive skills, and social-emotional development strands, and "emerging" skills within the visual/spatial discrimination strand. On the WPPSI-IV, Hallie earned a full-scale intelligence quotient above 95% of her similar-aged peers, showing relative strengths in her verbal comprehension skills and fluid reasoning skills, while showing relative weaknesses in her working memory and visual-spatial abilities. The purpose of the current assessment was to identify any significant impairments in Hallie's cognitive and socio-emotional functioning early on in her development and to provide a comprehensive profile to Ms. Dennett so she can become aware of which cognitive domains Hallie shows great facility in, and which domains pose more of a challenge for her. One uses their visual-spatial skills, for example, when understanding and solving problems within the science, technology, engineering, and mathematics (STEM) fields (Anderson 2014). The assessment can support and help guide Ms. Dennett as she plans instruction and adjusts curricula. If Hallie were to show significant impairment in one or more areas of her development and cognitive functioning, the assessment could help Hallie and her family obtain an intervention early in her academic trajectory.

The projective processes at work in Hallie's assessment also provided clues into when she is likely to become anxious and overwhelmed during her learning process in the academic setting. While each educator Hallie works with will inevitably have their own ways of experiencing and understanding her, unconsciously tapping into different aspects of her psychological and emotional life, there are likely to be consistencies in her learning style across time. A psychodynamically or psychoanalytically trained psychological assessor can work to be receptive to different feelings, defenses, and conflicts evoked by their examinees, and tune into their countertransference to engage in the process of understanding an examinee in a more holistic way—beyond their cognitive and academic capacities to include their intra- and inter-personal life. In turn, they can provide their moment-to-moment observations of an examinee during an assessment to educators and paraprofessionals, providing insight into when and how a teacher can intervene. Intervention might include supporting a child in identifying and regulating their feelings when they become frustrated, overwhelmed, anxious, or unfocused during academic work. Over time, a child may be able to internalize an attuned educator's ability to accurately observe, contain, and reflect on their emotional experience and begin to reflect on their inner life independently, even when enduring chaotic and stormy feelings.

I communicated to Ms. Dennett that her new student, Hallie, may excel at activities that rely on a command of language, verbal comprehension, and abstract reasoning, and that she may benefit from visual aids and written reminders to complete tasks and follow directions in the academic environment due to some relative challenge within her working memory. I noted that Hallie may also require some extra support when learning about two-dimensional and three-dimensional shapes, given her present relative weakness in visual-spatial skills. Reflecting on the transference/countertransference dimensions of Hallie's assessment, I also described my sense that Hallie may tend to exert pressure on herself to perform at a high level to allay her anxieties and may show subtle signs of these anxieties through fidgeting and inattention when she typically attends well to tasks. A playful and social little girl, Hallie may turn her attention to positive memories of interacting with friends when experiencing worry around her academic performance. Ms. Dennett provided me with a detailed description of the curricula the class will be covering this year, and we brainstormed ways for Hallie to further develop her visual-spatial skills through playing with tangrams and using construction toys. She replied that she would keep in mind my hypothesis about Hallie's tendency to pressure herself and check in with Hallie if she appears unusually restless and fidgety in class. Ms. Dennett described that she has a colorful feelings identification wheel posted in the classroom for students to learn about and practice identifying their primary emotions, alongside their academic learning.

During a psychological assessment and in the classroom, clinician and examinee and student and teacher have an undeniable and remarkable influence on each other. Young children under the age of eight must project their complex feelings onto a receptive and mature other who, in turn, can contain and safely metabolize these nonverbal feelings, providing back a way to help the child symbolize them with words or pictures to better understand them. Academic work can undoubtedly elicit intense affects, anxiety, and emotional defenses in young learners as they navigate each new lesson plan and homework assignment. Psychodynamic psychological assessment in early childhood and collegial collaboration between clinician and educator can help to scaffold a child's learning while providing an opportunity for them to feel affectively contained and confident when approaching new tasks and challenges in the academic environment. Over time, as a child progresses in the academic endeavor, they may be able to begin to reflect realistically on *both* their strengths and growth areas, without becoming overwhelmed by intense shame, fear, or negative self-appraisals.

NOTES

1. The term "inductive reasoning" is used to describe reasoning that involves using specific observations, such as observed patterns, to make a general conclusion. Deductive reasoning is used to describe starting from a set of general premises and then drawing a specific conclusion that contains no more information than the premises themselves (Merriam-Webster 2023).

2. While these concepts have varied in their definition depending on the theorist and psychoanalytic school, I define transference here as the total set of feelings, thoughts, perceptions, and attitudes the patient has toward the therapist/analyst, and countertransference as the total set of thoughts, feelings, and perceptions the therapist/analyst has toward the patient in the clinical situation. The transference/countertransference *matrix* refers to the context and ever-changing, dynamic process of the therapeutic relationship.

REFERENCES

Andersen, Lori. 2014. "Visual–Spatial Ability: Important in STEM, Ignored in Gifted Education." *Roeper Review* 36, no. 2: 114–121.

Bakeman, Roger, and Lauren B. Adamson. 1984. "Coordinating Attention to People and Objects in Mother-Infant and Peer-Infant Interaction." *Child Development* 55, no. 4: 1278–1289.

Bradley, Margaret M., and Peter J. Lang. 2000. "Emotion and Motivation." *Handbook of Psychophysiology* 2: 602–642.

Carveth, Donald L. 2012. "Concordant and Complementary Counter-Transference: A Clarification." *Canadian Journal of Psychoanalysis* 20, no. 1: 70.

"Deductive Reasoning." 2023. *Merriam-Webster.Com.* Retrieved November 20, 2023 from https://www.merriam-webster.com/dictionary/deductivereasoning.

Ferro, Antonio, and Roberto Basile. 2009. *The Analytic Field: A Clinical Concept.* London: Karnac Books Ltd.

Freud, Anna. 1963. "The Concept of Developmental Lines." *The Psychoanalytic Study of the Child* 18, no. 1: 245–265.

Freud, Sigmund. 1912. "The Dynamics of Transference." *Classics in Psychoanalytic Techniques* 12: 97–108.

Gibbons, Aisa, and Russell T. Warne. 2019. "First Publication of Subtests in the Stanford-Binet 5, WAIS-IV, WISC-V, and WPPSI-IV." *Intelligence* 75: 9–18.

"Inductive Reasoning." 2023. *Merriam-Webster.Com.* Retrieved November 20, 2023, from https://www.merriam-webster.com/dictionary/inductivereasoning.

Jones, Emily A., Edward G. Carr, and Kathleen M. Feeley. 2006. "Multiple Effects of Joint Attention Intervention for Children with Autism." *Behavior Modification* 30, no. 6: 782–834.

Joseph, Betty. 1985. "Transference: The Total Situation." *International Journal of Psycho-Analysis* 66: 447–454.

Jung, Nadine, Christina Wranke, Kai Hamburger, and Markus Knauff. 2014. "How Emotions Affect Logical Reasoning: Evidence from Experiments with Mood-Manipulated Participants, Spider Phobics, and People with Exam Anxiety." *Frontiers in Psychology* 5: 570.

Kaplan, Robert Malcom, and Dennis P. Saccuzzo. 2005. *Psychological Testing: Principles, Applications, and Issues.* Belmont: Thomson Wadsworth.

Kernberg, Otto. 1965. "Notes on Countertransference." *Journal of the American Psychoanalytic Association* 13, no. 1: 38–56.

Klein, Melanie. 1946. "Notes on Some Schizoid Mechanisms 1." *International Journal of Psycho-Analysis* 27: 99–110.

Meindl, James A., and Helen I. Cannella-Malone. 2011. "Initiating and Responding to Joint Attention Bids in Children with Autism: A Review of the Literature." *Research in Developmental Disabilities* 32, no. 5: 1441–1454.

Neubauer, Peter B. 1984. "Anna Freud's Concept of Developmental Lines." *The Psychoanalytic Study of the Child* 39: 15–27.

Ogden, Thomas H. 1979. "On Projective Identification." *International Journal of Psychoanalysis* 60, no. 3: 357–373.

Ogden, Thomas H. 1991. "Analyzing the Matrix of Transference." *The International Journal of Psycho-Analysis* 72, no. 4: 593.

Phelps, Elizabeth. A. 2004. "Human Emotion and Memory: Interactions of the Amygdala and Hippocampal Complex." *Current Opinion in Neurobiology* 14: 198–202. 10.1016/j.Conb.2004.03.015.

Poland, Warren S. 1992. "From Analytic Surface to Analytic Space." *Journal of the American Psychoanalytic Association* 40, no. 2: 381–404.

Racker, Heinrich. 1957. "The Meaning and Uses of Countertransference." *Psychoanalytic Quarterly* 26: 303–357.

Raiford, Susan Enji, and Diane L. Coalson. 2014. *Essentials of WPPSI-IV Assessment.* Hoboken: John Wiley & Sons.

Rorschach, Hermann. 1942. *Psychodiagnostics: A Diagnostic Test Based on Perception.* New York: Grune & Stratton.

Rosenfeld, Herbert. 1983. "Primitive Object Relations and Mechanisms." *The International Journal of Psycho-Analysis* 64: 261.

Shepard, Lorrie A., Sharon Lynn Kagan, and Emily Wurtz (eds). 1998. *Principles and Recommendations for Early Childhood Assessments.* Washington: The Panel.

Siegel, Dan, and Tina Payne Bryson. 2016. *No-Drama Discipline: The Whole-Brain Way to Calm the Chaos and Nurture Your Child's Developing Mind.* New York: Bantam.

Spillius, Elizabeth Bott, Jane Milton, Penelope Garvey, Cyril Couve, and Deborah Steiner. 2011. *The New Dictionary of Kleinian Thought.* Hoboken: Taylor & Francis.

Thelen, Esther, and Karen E. Adolph. 1994. "Arnold L. Gesell: The Paradox of Nature and Nurture." In R. D. Parke, P. A. Ornstein, J. J. Rieser, and C. Zahn-Waxler

(Eds.), *A Century of Developmental Psychology. American Psychological Association.* https://doi.org/10.1037/10155-027.

Thiemann-Bourque, Kathy, Lynette K. Johnson, and Nancy C. Brady. 2019. "Similarities in Functional Play and Differences in Symbolic Play of Children with Autism Spectrum Disorder." *American Journal on Intellectual and Developmental Disabilities* 124, no. 1: 77–91.

Tower, Lucia E. "Countertransference." *Journal of the American Psychoanalytic Association* 4, no. 2: 224–255.

Tyng, Chai M., Hafeez U. Amin, Mohamad N. M. Saad, and Aamir S. Malik. 2017. "The Influences of Emotion on Learning and Memory." *Frontiers in Psychology* 8: 1454.

Vuilleumier, Patrik. 2005. "How Brains Beware: Neural Mechanisms of Emotional Attention." *Trends Cognitive Science* 9: 585–594. 10.1016/j.Tics.2005.10.011.

Waska, Robert T. 1999. "Projective Identification, Self-Disclosure, and the Patient's View of the Object: The Need for Flexibility." *The Journal of Psychotherapy Practice and Research* 8, no. 3: 225–233.

Wechsler, David. 1940. "Non-Intellective Factors in General Intelligence." *Psychological Bulletin* 37: 444–445.

Weizmann, Fredric, and Ben Harris. 2012. "Arnold Gesell: The Maturationist." In W. E. Pickren, D. A. Dewsbury, and M. Wertheimer (Eds.), *Portraits of Pioneers in Developmental Psychology*, 1–20. New York: Psychology Press.

Part II

PSYCHOANALYTIC APPROACHES TO EARLY CHILDHOOD EDUCATION SETTINGS

Chapter 5

Is There a Place for Psychoanalytic Theory in the Classroom?

Michael Trout

Freud hasn't exactly been a go-to guy among educators for some time. Psychoanalytic teachings have often been seen as irrelevant in the classroom. Deservedly, a bit of credibility was lost when Freud changed his mind; he first believed the stories of sexual abuse told by his patients (Trout 1988), and then reversed himself, inventing a set of developmental theories about young children (Masson 1984, 1985) that just didn't hold water, from the perspective of many.

So, it's not altogether illogical that educators are dismissive of psychoanalytic theory as impractical—or, worse, unscientific and laughably out of date. But psychoanalytic teachings have matured and, for the most part, stepped away from some of the rigidity—especially regarding the focus on infant and early childhood sexuality. Research applications have been made regarding the lasting effects of trauma, how memory is retained, how internal working models are created and sustained (even when the child's actual current experience would suggest that what he imagines and predicts about his world is inaccurate), and how early narratives are created and brought into subsequent relationships (including those with authority figures, teachers, and other children). Clinical applications, based on this research, have expanded into the development of the new, trans-disciplinary and relationship-based field of infant mental health[1], which has a great deal to teach us about why a particular child behaves as he does and what he needs to be able to manage himself and to learn.

In the face of enormous pressure in the classroom to conform to standardized curricula; warnings about touching or becoming "too attached" to students; increasing behavior problems in the halls, on the playground, and in classrooms; and declines in teachers' felt sense of efficacy, demands for practical and rapid problem-solving strategies have soared. Expulsions have also soared (Zinsser 2022), as have the number of districts around the United States that have turned to having police roam the halls (Snow 2012; Turner 2019). It's hardly a surprise that teachers (as well as the administrators and consultants who back them up) have retained trust only in concrete strategies for managing student behavior that aim to "get everybody back in line." That some of these "evidence-based" methods have not really worked is a frustration to educators; oddly, this frustration has caused many educators to just dig in, looking ever more desperately for concrete ways of eradicating problem behavior and keeping order in their schools, rather than trying on new perspectives. Meanwhile, we have abandoned many of the relationship-based models of teaching and responding to behavioral challenges that were once at the very heart of teaching.

This chapter aims not to introduce psychoanalytic teachings into the classroom but to suggest where they might be useful in day-to-day interactions, in responses to behavior, and in gaining clarity about why certain children behave as they do. Underlying these ideas will be a suggestion that teachers have many of the same opportunities and characteristics as psychotherapists and parents. They are not psychotherapists, and it is not the intention of this chapter to suggest that they should be. And they are not parents, which may turn out to be as much a blessing as a limitation.

Educators are something else, entirely. It will be proposed in this chapter that many of the capabilities and characteristics of educators—some of which come from training, some from experience, some from personal traits—are supported by psychoanalytic theory. They come "naturally" to many teachers, even as they are overlooked, undervalued, and underused when administrators and teachers talk about classroom management, best practices, and the guiding principles they struggle to remember. Strikingly, many of these capabilities and characteristics are found in psychodynamic accountings of what hurt children need: of what all children need, in fact. These include:

- Teachers are containers, holding the affect of a single child or holding the spiraling chaos of an entire room, meanwhile showing children that their behavior can be managed and will not overtake the grownups.
- Teachers are observer-scientists, not only persistently accumulating data but synthesizing it to create ideas about certain children and, sometimes, their parents—ideas that lead to optimal approaches and even solutions.
- Teachers are absolute masters at one of the core child development principles arising from psychoanalytic theory: that behavior has meaning. Behavior is a child speaking. Often the meaning arises out of lived (or felt) experience; in this way, it reflects the child's history. In spite of our protestations to the contrary, behavior almost never comes out of the blue. There's always an important chance that the child has been here before—or,

at least, it feels to the child as if they have, as if the current situation is just like other situations that seemed the same, that smelled the same, that sounded the same. Teachers intuitively grasp this idea—often overlooked in the literature and in Individualized Family Service Plans (IFSP), and it guides them in building their responses to the children.

The beauty of these capabilities and characteristics is that they offer hope. They lead to understanding what's really wrong. Understanding what's really wrong often leads to intuitive and principled solutions—a promise not made when we settle merely for a diagnosis. Concluding that a child has ADHD is often comforting to parents and teachers alike, which is why IFSPs often focus their attention on "discovering" an applicable diagnostic category. But the label does not help us know what it was like for this child to be inside the uterus of a drug-addicted mom, to feel "frazzled" (the word one child used, years later, to describe his brain to me). At age four, I diagnosed him with "a broken heart" from maternal rejection and subsequent maternal loss, rather than ADHD. My assessment led to waves of empathy from the adoptive parents and his understandably bedraggled preschool teacher, who were now equipped to respond to his climbing the walls by asking him if he was feeling "frazzled," and offering to contain him with a weighted blanket or a hug (both of which had previously been rejected by the child), thereby challenging his internal working model that he was unsafe and uncontrollable. The ADHD diagnosis made previously by the family's doctor led only to one predictably concrete outcome: medication.

The point of this chapter is not to get teachers to send children to therapy or to become psychoanalysts-in-the-classroom. The point is also not to give teachers more to do in their already crowded, high-pressure rooms. The point is to take note of the marvelous capacities and capabilities already extant in each teacher's room, in each teacher's heart. The point is to support consciousness of what the mindful teacher already knows. The point is to encourage teacher self-confidence (arising from their growing sense of self-efficacy). The point is to look again at a literature often ignored and to make it both accessible and practical in everyday places, to teachers and administrators sitting in IFSPs together but afraid to speak from the soul of what led them to this room in the first place.

TEACHERS ARE CONTAINERS

John could not be contained, which is probably why, after his third expulsion from a preschool, I was called in. His adoptive parents were at their wits' end, as was his latest teacher. He flailed, he screamed, he assaulted other children, and he rejected all efforts at intimacy. He was small (tenth percentile for height, zero for weight). He took way too many risks with his body, yet was terrified of falling.

A little nosing around on my part led to a description of the words his first mother spoke about him, on the day of his birth. The adoptive mother had already arrived at the hospital. The birthmother pointed to him: "There he is. Do you want him?" My guess was that this same attitude persisted throughout the pregnancy, so that even before birth John knew he was not contained. He was not someplace where he was safe, much less loved.

His new adoptive parents were eager to have him and poured all their energies into caring for him. They had been infertile for some time, but I was unaware, at first, that John was not the first child they had tried to adopt. In fact, he was named for a child they were planning to adopt, but whose birthmother changed her mind at the last moment. They were heartbroken and were on the defensive about any possibility of losing another child. Part of their coping involved declining to buy a crib for John, so he slept in a car seat on the dining room table for his first five months. I began to understand not only his fear of falling but his sense that he was not contained, that maybe he was uncontainable.

Prior to the school calling me, the adoptive parents had taken him to endless specialists. John had acquired multiple diagnoses and was already on Paxil and Risperdal. Nothing seemed to change his core rage and terror; tucked away, of course, was the feeling he would never be able to acknowledge: that he belonged to nobody, that he was not contained.

None of this should have been the preschool teacher's problem. Yet, of course, it was. John took up way too much "space" in her classroom, and he exhausted her. It was too much to ask that she somehow help this tiny child to feel contained. Yet she came to know that he had to feel safe in her room, or he would blow it up.

The safety of a typically developing five-year-old is often rooted in the adequacy of his introjects: a clever identification with—and then taking in of—another (Bowlby 1969; Erikson 1950; Klein 1948; Sandler and Freud 1985). It is one of those psychoanalytic developmental notions that sounds mysterious but is actually entirely practical and incredibly necessary in the normal development of every child. As the infant becomes attached to a reliable and available primary caregiver during pregnancy and in the first year of postpartum life, and then begins the clumsy work of individuating from that very attachment figure (Mahler et al. 1975; Ruskin and Turrini 1981), he plays a little mental trick: taking the "other" with him, even as he "leaves" (psychologically and only partially). This introject of the attachment figure provides comfort while not demanding either proximity or constant dependence. What a joy for the kindergartner to momentarily feel as if he cannot possibly cross the threshold of the school, all alone, and then to "discover" that he can take his primary attachment figure "with" him, mentally. This does not mean he will feel completely confident at every moment of the day. He will miss his mother, for example, but if the defensive strategy we are calling "introjection" works, he will be able to soothe himself and return to whatever he was doing. He sort of "remembers" his mother. He is not necessarily conscious of this episodic mental return to her, nor does he know he has "taken her in" to himself, so that she is actually "with him" all day long.

But what about a child like John, who likely had no attachment whatsoever to his first mother, and whose attachment to his adoptive parents was contaminated—or, at least, delayed—by the parents' anxiety about loss? He would have to deny all connection, something the adoptive mother experienced with him every day as he resisted all physical contact with her and eventually began to demean and berate her. But the complexity of his inner life with respect to attachment was driven home one night when—upon discovering she had left the house for a few minutes—he went to her side table in the master bedroom and carved deep gouges with a knife he had brought from the kitchen. He had expressed not a word of regret or worry that she was gone, but did find an alternative means of expressing his rage that an "object" (a psychoanalytic term for someone with whom one has established a connection) he pretended had no value to him had stepped away, just as his first mother had.

And so, as this little boy faced crossing the threshold of kindergarten, he had no object to take with him, no introject of a safe, containing "other" to whom he could turn mentally while away from her. All he could do was flail.

How could we help him? How could we help his teacher, both flummoxed and overwhelmed by a child who presented as no other child she had ever seen? By the time I entered her classroom to talk things over, John was on the verge of getting his walking papers from school for the third time.

We couldn't make up for John's losses. Reassurance was useless, of course; he was way too damaged, and his defenses too sophisticated for grownup words or pats to have any effect. Absent an introject, he was a frightened, wild animal in that room.

We began with the obvious things, each pathetically inadequate on their own. His desk should be moved near the teacher, of course, and it should be away from the windows (through which he could see all sorts of triggering "threats": a woman walking to her car that he could imagine was familiar and would leave him or hurt him; trash collectors who made sudden noise; even a child on the playground). We would need to lower the lighting a bit, as there was evidence he was hearing the fluorescent "hum" and turning it into a threat.

But the most important interventions were the human ones. This was a hard "sell" for the teacher, who had already been made to feel impotent in the face of John's pattern of ignoring, rejecting, and even belittling her. We understood he would resist all human outreach, even as he desperately needed to be contained—and, ironically, wished to be. We limited his hours at the school and engaged the services of a home tutor, whom I coached about how to be with John. We just couldn't afford another loss, and we knew John would quickly set his sights on running her out of the house. She would need to be firm, kind, hyper-attuned to his movements and rapidly changing affects, and organized.

Little could be asked of an already suspicious and stressed classroom teacher who truly wanted to help but didn't see how she could, while attending to twenty-eight other children. We made sure to ask nothing of her that would amount to more expenditure of time or energy, but only slight reorganizations of things she was already doing: the greeting in the morning, the persistence of her outreach with her eyes and maybe a modest touch on the shoulder as she passed by. Perhaps most importantly, we counted on the conversation about his loneliness and his desperate need for containment to make him seem less frightening and more worthy of her empathy.

The principal agreed to assign an aide to the room and to situate him right next to John's desk. We lucked out. The aide we found was an upper-level student from the university, and John was interesting to him. He needed nothing from John, and this little boy didn't scare him (as he did most everyone else). The aide was a burly fellow but calm and tender. For the two hours per day that John was in the classroom, the aide did nothing more than give John something to push against, a force that was bigger than he was (physically and metaphorically), and something quieter and more accepting than the uterus in which John began life. This aide made himself a container.

John didn't get all better because of our little classroom intervention. But he didn't get expelled again, either, and he began to tolerate more and more hours of school each day. The teacher passed on her wisdom about containment to the first-grade teacher, and she to the next one. John is now grown up, and while he is not all better, he did make it all the way through the public school system. It didn't take more time or more energy from his wise teacher, but only different time and different energy. My sense was that this educator merely called on capacities that had always been in her but that had wasted away a bit in the face of feeling overwhelmed by the challenge of managing so many kids with so many needs and with so little encouragement to remember what she once knew.

My belief has always been that Freud changed the world not because he invented theories, schemes, and structures, but because he made some of his first patients feel held. He saw them in ways others did not. He "mirrored" them (Winnicott 1971/2005, 160), in much the way a parent does, while exchanging gaze with his or her newborn.

John's teacher did the same. In the process, she not only increased his felt sense of safety, but she challenged John's "negative internal working model of adults as incapable of effectively empathizing with, and responding to, their dysregulated affect" (Goldsmith 2007, 210).

TEACHERS ARE OBSERVER-SCIENTISTS

The very best educators are full of wonder. This does not suggest they are pie-eyed or naïve, but that they are everlastingly curious and driven. They are scientists, probably without ever noticing that they have earned this title.

They know they don't know all the answers ("Why was my classroom in pandemonium this morning?" "What has gotten into Bobby this week?" "How in the world am I going to get through to Ruth?"), which only causes them to look more, to imagine more, to be yet more curious. They know the danger of reaching conclusions too early. If pressed, they would likely acknowledge the psychoanalytic principle that the answer to why a child is having trouble lies somewhere inside the child. The classroom becomes, then, a place to consider possibilities, to try out responses—not just to implement behavioral programs (which takes little scientific rigor).

It probably helps that many teachers are equipped with the legendary "third ear." Perhaps related to the literal "eyes in the back of her head" many children imagine about their mothers' anatomy, the third ear has been alluded to in the psychoanalytic literature from the beginning. Freud was explicit that a unique kind of listening was critical to his clinical work; only the analyst who truly has "ears to hear," he asserted, has the capacity to make "conscious the most hidden recesses of the mind" (Freud 1901/1905, 77–78).

It was his student, Theodor Reik, who implied that this kind of listening—with what he called "the third ear" (a phrase he borrowed from Nietzsche, in *Beyond Good and Evil, Part VIII,* p. 246) (Reik 1948)—catches not only what people say but also what they do not say, but only feel and think (Reik 1948).

So the observer-scientist in the classroom attends not only to students' words, but to how they are spoken. She attends to feelings, including those that are expressed in words and those denied but expressed in behavior. She notices patterns in the classroom, changing affects, interactions among students, and shifting individual moods. Most teachers have been collecting data in these ways regarding each group of students all year long without ever thinking about it, and it has influenced what they say next, what they do next, and how they respond to the next challenge. In so doing, this sort of teacher sets herself apart from many. She is neither parent nor psychotherapist, but she uses her own remarkably similar capacities as an observer-scientist every day as she goes about running an orderly classroom and helping her children learn.

I was asked to evaluate a four-year-old who was mute; her mom, indeed, claimed that she had never spoken. She was, of course, slipping behind other kids in the first grade. She presented few behavioral challenges; in fact, her teacher acknowledged it would have been easy to treat her as if she were not even there. But something in this teacher resisted letting Alice become invisible. She imagined the child had something to say. And she was right, though she found little support for her scientific curiosity in the several IFSPs that, so far, had focused only on "getting Alice to talk." Two years of speech therapy had produced little insight and zero change.

I thought the teacher was onto something. She had no psychoanalytic training, of course, but she persistently expressed a core psychoanalytic idea, if only in her attitude toward her children: If you want to know what's going on with a young child, ask them. This didn't mean, to her, that she should pose dumb, closed-ended questions and expect the child to cough up a coherent response. But it did mean she was moved to look carefully, to wonder without presuppositions, to imagine possibilities, and to not be seduced by easy "answers" or comforting diagnoses.

On the day Mom arrived with Alice for my little evaluation, Alice diverted her mom to the bathroom, where she collected two paper towels, folded them into tiny squares, wetted them, and carried them into my office. Neither Mom nor I had any idea what she was up to. She sat quietly at the little table I had arranged with some props to be used in the evaluation. Evidently, Alice had her own plan.

She used the wet paper towel squares to slowly and methodically wipe at her mouth. The strokes were slow, right-to-left, then left-to-right, then back again. All the while, she stared into my face. Mom sat quietly. I knew the teacher was right; Alice had something to say. I had no idea why she decided to tell me her story on this particular day, but science always respects the emergence of data, however and whenever it happens.

After a few moments, I moved a few feet away, beckoning Alice to join me for some gross motor tests. Paper towels still in hand, she stood but did not move toward me. I invited her again. Mom, evidently meaning to encourage her daughter's cooperation, asked, "What's the matter, Alice? Why won't you go be with the man?"

Whereupon Alice screeched. I didn't sense that she was acutely afraid; rather, it seemed as if the noise was part of some sort of story, some sort of answer to my implied question: "Tell us, Alice. Why don't you talk?" It was as if this noise was essential in her communicating what she needed to tell us.

She accompanied the screeching with hand gestures, pointing her index finger to her throat, and then to her mouth.

I was staggered, as I suspect, was Mom. We all sat quietly for a bit, whereupon I asked Mom if it would be OK for Alice to play with my secretary for a few moments so mom and I could talk in private. The moment Alice was out of the room, Mom said with indignation and defensiveness, "I know what you're thinking, but I'm telling you he could never have done that. He just couldn't; he knows how it feels." She then told the story of her husband's sexual molestation as a little boy.

It was true, it turned out. Dad was taken into custody and admitted that he had orally penetrated Alice's precious mouth for some months when she was younger. His pathetic defense: "It was a long time ago, when she was one or so. I know she can't remember it because I quit by the time she was two."

Alice had done what very young children often do when faced with trauma: they defend themselves with whatever tools they have at their disposal. In Alice's case, all she could do was take back control of the orifice that had been invaded by her father. She couldn't stop an unwanted thing from going into her mouth, but she could stop things from going out of her mouth. She could cease babbling, and she could stop herself from learning to speak. Even when the immediate danger had passed (assuming Dad was telling the truth about stopping the abuse), Alice—like so many kids who have faced trauma—kept up the defense long after it did any good.

Now, what is our point? Merely that educators often do something that other childhood specialists—speech therapists, family doctors, clinicians untrained in the psychoanalytic principles that help us link bits of data about a child's life in a way that will make present behavior coherent—don't do: They watch. They look, every day, noticing patterns and behavioral shifts that (the teacher notes) follow slight environmental changes. Without ever particularly focusing on her scientific posture, the teacher collects and synthesizes data, day after day. If she's very lucky, and very persistent, an answer begins to emerge.

Everyone else just wanted Alice to knock it off, to talk, for goodness' sake! The teacher, meanwhile, wanted to know her student, and she imagined that her student might have something to say. I was lucky enough to be there on the day Alice decided to let us in on the secret, but the teacher and I shared the noble and patient role of observer-scientist. Psychoanalytic teachings helped us to interpret the data—including Alice's profoundly sad screech while pointing to her throat and her mouth—but the teacher didn't have to be a psychoanalyst to imagine that the precious, silent child in her room might actually have something to say.

TEACHERS KNOW THAT BEHAVIOR HAS BOTH
MEANING AND HISTORY

It's a core psychoanalytic principle known intuitively by good teachers: If a child's behavior is irrational, there's a pretty fair chance he's carrying into the situation expectations pieced together from other, earlier experiences in his life—maybe the day before, or maybe when he was very small. If, for example, he treats his teacher as if she were a monster—or conversely, as weak and ineffectual—it's just possible this has nothing whatsoever to do with the teacher. It may have to do with someone who came before her—a parent, or another teacher, perhaps—and the child is defensively projecting expectations developed in that relationship onto this teacher, in this moment, in this present situation. Without such understanding, we would be in a constant state of taking personally the misbehaviors or the taunts of the children in our classrooms. Believe it or not, early childhood educators are some of the few folks walking this earth who, along with psychoanalysts, have long caught on to this basic principle.

Modern neuroanatomy, trauma theory, and clinical infant mental health have built on the core of Freud's ideas about the erection, use, and maintenance of defenses in ways Freud—who saw himself first as a neuroscientist, and only secondarily as a therapist—would have loved. Scientists trying to understand the brain at rest—a presumed passive baseline state, or "default mode" (Conaby 2022, 92)—have come to see that this state "is not a do-little default system at all. It plays a key role in our internal life, in how we recall memories about ourselves and use them to build an ongoing autobiography, to solve problems . . . and to simulate alternate outcomes and future needs" (Conaboy 2022, 93). Even a child sitting quietly should not be mistaken for an empty vessel. He may "go from zero to 60 in a heartbeat," giving rise to the mistaken belief that a child's behavior "came out of nowhere." But his brain was always full of narratives—giving rise to predictions about what things mean and what's going to happen next—that would help him to anticipate, and then to create behavior in line with that anticipation, even when those narratives were mistaken.

A child melts down when another student in his preschool classroom turns his carefully aligned row of toy trucks topsy-turvy. He yells at the other student and is about to hurl one of the metal trucks at the perpetrator of the upset to his controlled world when the teacher intervenes: "Bobby! You must share your trucks!"

Bobby not only fails to see the logic of his teacher's scolding and rein in his behavior, but he skyrockets. He acts as if his world is falling apart because, to him, it is.

Which is our cue.

Two things have just happened:

1. Bobby was not just playing with trucks. He was organizing his world, which must mean that his world—unbeknownst to the rest of us—must have been in desperate need of organizing, lest chaos be allowed to reign. His reaction was full of panic and rage, so the stakes must have been high. Until someone imagines this—perhaps by empathizing, "Oh, my! You had made such a perfect row of trucks, and now they're all messed up. I wonder if you and I will be able to make them neat again?"—he will go on raging. And he will go on feeling unseen and not understood, which puts him on edge for the rest of the day, if not the rest of the year. Because the stakes are so high—because chaos threatens, mysteriously—he will be wary of the little boy who messed with his trucks, and on high alert for other "assaults."

2. Bobby has expectations that his teacher cannot, or will not, protect him. This is irrational, as the teacher is kind, and the teacher is big. So his expectations were likely formed somewhere else, and it's even possible there are good reasons for him to have them. As attachment researcher Douglas Goldsmith put it, certain children have experiences with caregivers who have been "unresponsive to their inner turmoil," and "ineffective in calming their affective storms and restoring their emotional equilibrium" (Goldsmith 2007, 208). The result: the child (resorting to a defense known to psychoanalysts as "projection") then "assumes the teacher will be equally ineffective" (Goldsmith 2007, 208). The child has built an "internal working model of adults as ineffective and unavailable" (Goldsmith 2007, 208). Too bad for the teacher, who may well be oblivious to the fact that the child's treatment of her has little to do with her; he is reacting to her as if she is someone else, someone who has repeatedly let him down.

If you're a teacher who has had just such an experience with just such a child, you may well be wondering what difference it makes to use such a complex psychoanalytic paradigm to ponder the child's meltdown and to reconsider what you should do about it. After all, he does need to learn to share, doesn't he? And he does need to learn to calm himself, even if he won't let you help him with it!

Unhappily, as a dear colleague of mine puts it, "That, plus $5, will get you a cup of coffee." In other words, the assertions are true, but they don't help. They don't get you anywhere, at least with this particular child, on this particular day. The child's overwhelming fear of chaos—something he evidently knows way too much about—will cause him to blow up when his lineup of toy trucks is disturbed, every time, irrespective of classroom mores. And his internal working models relative to caregiving will cause him to mistrust his perfectly well-intentioned teacher—or, at least, remain convinced of her lack of reliability as a protector. We need something else. And he needs this "something else" to be repeated, consistently and reliably. He needs evidence that someone "gets it" about his fearfulness, while making certain to never shame or embarrass him about it. He needs someone to go toe-to-toe with him—not with words, which are useless to him, but with consistent and repeated behavior—about one of his closely-held internal working models: that caregivers will not look after him, and that they are weak. It's a huge mental leap we're asking him to make: that his teacher is different. She is not them. She is big and strong and will not give up and will neither go away nor throw him away.

It's not necessary that the teacher become a psychoanalyst. In fact, it's not even necessary that she grasp—or appreciate—psychoanalytic principles. What is necessary is that she:

- Be practical. Failing to take note—or, at least, to be curious about—the history and meaning of classroom behavior is to insist on ignoring a powerful reality. Sometimes, what we're doing just doesn't work. We need another tool. And I find that teachers often have that tool right there, in their minds, in their empathy, in their love of scientific inquiry, in their devotion to restoring order by discovering what is causing it to be upset.
- Avoid the seduction of shallow and categorical thinking: "He comes from a bad family" (without going further into musing on what, precisely, that might mean for this particular child, on this particular day); or "He's just ADHD, and his mom must not have given him his meds this morning" (without going further into musing just what might have so frazzled his brain that experts have given him a label that most expect will end any further scientific inquiry into what really happened).
- Avoid the silly trap of assuming that behavior "just came out of the blue", and replace it with the far more noble, practical and fundamental notion that behavior has meaning, and it has history.

Sometimes, there is little the teacher can do except to organize and calm herself with the principle ("This is not me he's striking out against; it's the ghost of someone else who hurt him.") just long enough to come up with some empathy and some sturdy holding. We don't have to have the answers in the moment; we only need to wonder about them for a couple of seconds, long enough to cut short our labeling, long enough to calm ourselves, long enough to remember why we went into teaching in the first place.

A five-year-old punches another kid on the playground, reportedly unprovoked. He's been a problem all day. The principal is outraged and makes sure the first grader knows it. It never occurs to anyone that the principal's behavior may make him appear weak, unavailable, and ineffectual to the child. The child dismisses him. The principal calls the mom (whom he disparages, in a conversation with me, by referencing her work as a stripper), threatening to call child welfare if the mom does not "Get that kid on medication."

The power that this principal has—shared by the boy's teacher—is that he knows behavior never comes from nowhere. There is a story. There is meaning, and it probably goes beyond whatever label everyone is tempted to use to categorize the first grader who blew up. It's absolutely the only power I had when Mom came to me a day or two later, desperate to avoid making her son into a zombie (which, as it would turn out, Mom knew a great deal about) by putting him on medication. She offered no alternative explanation for his behavior, but it just didn't fit that her boy was hyperactive. "He's always been quiet."

But that changed one night at dinner. Noticing the lesions on his dad's face were getting worse, the boy blurted out, right over the mashed potatoes: "If you die, I won't be able to stand it."

Everyone froze. Things like this were just not talked about in this family. Mom and Dad somehow imagined their children did not know Dad was HIV+. But the boy, at least, did know, and he was anticipating an unimaginable loss. No one spoke. No one affirmed the boy's fears or showed empathy for his worries. He fell back into silence. Until the next day, on the playground, that is.

Were the teacher and the principal expected to know all of this? Of course not! But might it be reasonable to expect them to hit the "pause" button when outrageous behavior erupted, at least long enough to remind themselves that behavior always has meaning? There is always history, even when we don't know what it is. And then we can imagine, for just the moment or two we have at our disposal, what a child such as this child could need. "Oh, my! Your insides must be spinning around! You and I are going to sit here for a moment." We say such things, and do such things, even when they are rebuffed (because the psychoanalytic principles we've learned in this chapter teach us why they would be rebuffed); even when they seem to have no effect (because the psychoanalytic principles we've been discussing show us that the forces pushing the behavior are powerful, indeed—and, anyway, we're mature enough in our profession by now, to see that the other behavior-management strategies we've tried also don't work reliably, either).

Perhaps an example from the earliest years of child psychoanalysis will help. At the time (mid-1950s), it was thought that nearly all blind babies and young children "had" hyperactivity—often mixed with aggression—as part of the clinical picture. Most parents, in those days, were encouraged to institutionalize their blind children, since the emergence of awful behavior was thought to be inevitable.

And then along came Selma Fraiberg (later my teacher), who was not only psychoanalytically trained but who embodied the characteristics of scientific inquiry built on intense curiosity, with a foundation of determination to take nothing for granted, that we've talked about in this chapter.

Peter, blind from birth, exhibited the behavioral characteristics thought to be part and parcel of "blindness syndrome" at the time. Fraiberg, though, did what I'm asking you to consider doing. As she got to know Peter during early home visits, Fraiberg was taken aback when, she said, he "seized me and clawed me" (Fraiberg 1977, 33). She responded to these painful assaults by moving away, maintaining contact only with her voice. Peter would then appear lost, his affect would flatten, and he would begin swaying and rocking. Mother watched the strange sequence, which was most familiar to her; it turned out that Peter often bit her and clawed at her, too, particularly when she was about to put him down. She imagined only that it was aggression. Perhaps he hated her.

Most teachers understand object constancy—that customary developmental milestone that usually shows up in the last part of the first year of life—and the role it plays not only in overall mental development but in the child's sense of security. With object constancy, a new thought or internal idea arrives: things do not go away. They can be counted on to be where last seen.

But what if they have never been seen? How is a child to hold an idea of an object—a toy, a mother, a teacher—if the child has never experienced the object with his eyes? It turns out—for reasons that should have been obvious to us—that blind babies are often sluggish in developing this mental capacity. They need lots of extra help to catch on about the permanence of things "out there," even when they can't be seen. So Fraiberg took one of those empathic leaps into the unknown that educators are challenged to take if they are tired of resting on diagnostic labels and easy answers, and they really seek to understand: She said to Peter, as he was biting and clawing at her, "You don't have to be afraid. I won't go away." Peter released his "death grip" at once (Fraiberg 1977, 33).

Mom, who was watching, was startled, looking anew at a behavior "she had always interpreted as aggressive and now began to understand as a kind of inarticulate terror" (Fraiberg 1977, 33).

A few minutes later, as Mom began to set Peter on the floor, after a period of lap-sitting, Peter dug at her neck and bit her on the shoulder. Professor Fraiberg spoke to him: "You don't have to be afraid. Mother will not go away" (Fraiberg 1977, 33). Peter stopped again. Mom was flabbergasted, not only at the strange new understanding of her baby's behavior she had just acquired, but by the rush of maternal feelings that had so long been dormant. It was "like magic," the mother said.

I'm guessing nearly every educator reading this story could now lay out a plan for Mom that would significantly enhance her relationship with Peter and improve his behavior: a lesson plan, really. Mom will need to begin helping Peter find new ways to locate objects (including her) and then to develop means to "acquire" them. (A little-known fact about blind children, before Fraiberg's studies were published: they were often slow to crawl, sometimes remaining prone on the floor for years. And then it dawned on the world of early childhood educators of the era: If objects cannot be held in the mind, they do not exist. If there are no objects "out there" to find, there is no reason to crawl to them.) (Burlingham 1961; Freedman 1971; Fraiberg 1970, 1977). If Mom's new "lesson plan" is successful, Peter will show new eagerness to find and play with toys; he will begin to crawl to find them, and he will stop "eating" Mom, since he will now have new means to find her and hold on to her.

CLOSING

The best teachers hold their students, even when they're not allowed to touch them. They contain the feelings and the behavior of their students with voice and eyes; their lucky students are, as a result, better able to manage their affects and their impulses. They see their students, allowing little ones not only to feel seen but to be mirrored, allowing the children to see themselves. These teachers notice patterns in the classroom not detected by anyone else. They catch on to possible meanings of classroom behavior as part of their never-ending search for a way to understand those in their care. They listen patiently as others put their children into diagnostic categories, but they take pride in a certain knowledge that they know the little ones they see every day far more richly than most diagnoses could capture.

It's unimportant to give credit where credit is due in this discussion. But I close with a gift and a reminder to those who have made it all the way to the end of this chapter: Really smart people have been working for more than a century on the things that burden you, confound you, and keep you up at night. Sometimes they have turned out to be wrong or preoccupied with one idea while overlooking another one they inadvertently just uncovered. Freud was a man, a father, and a husband before he was the first psychoanalyst, and he undoubtedly stumbled in each of those roles. He tried to make sense of the symptoms both children and adults lay before him. He reflected his medical training and the culture of his era when he built theories that might shed light. The result was (at least from my perspective) that he made mistakes and—by later standards, at least—said some downright goofy things. But he also gave us ways to think about how we humans integrate what happens to us and how we display our internal responses to those things in our daily behavior, often for years, as we try to look after ourselves and avoid getting hurt again.

That's what kids still do. I, for one, feel intensely grateful for the gifts of insight and imagination he gave us, and I easily forgive him his missteps. Because to this day, it gives me hope to know that behavior makes sense.

NOTE

1. The trans-disciplinary field known as "infant mental health" grew out of Fraiberg's studies with blind children such as Peter and her application of such "lesson plans" to enhance the development of sighted children as well. Her accidental use of interpretation-in-the-moment with Peter and his mother produced such affective and relational change that such carefully measured interpretations made while sitting in a kitchen with a parent and infant or young child became part of the very definition of the new clinical field.

REFERENCES

Bowlby, John. 1969. *Attachment and Loss. Volume I: Attachment*. New York: Basic Books.

Burlingham, Dorothy. 1961. "Some Notes on the Development of the Blind." *Psychoanalytic Study of the Child* 19, no. 95: 121–145.

Conaboy, Chelsea. 2022. *Mother Brain: How Neuroscience Is Rewriting the Story of Parenthood*. New York: Henry Holt and Company.

Edward, Joyce, Nathene Ruskin, and Patsy Turini. 1981. *Separation-Individuation: Theory and Application*. New York: Gardner Press.

Erikson, Erik. 1950. *Childhood and Society*. New York: Norton.

Fraiberg, Selma. 1970. "Parallel and Divergent Patterns in Blind and Sighted Infants." *Psychoanalytic Study of the Child* 23: 265–300.

Fraiberg, Selma. 1977. *Insights from the Blind: Comparative Studies of Blind and Sighted Infants*. New York: Basic Books.

Freedman, D.

Freedman, David A., and Cay A. B. Cannady. 1971. "Delayed Emergence of Prone Locomotion." *Journal of Nervous and Mental Diseases* 153, no. 2: 108–117.

Freud, Sigmund. 1905. "Fragment of an Analysis of a Case of Hysteria." In *The Standard Edition of the Complete Psychological Works of Sigmund Freud, Vol 7*, edited and translated by James Strachey, 1–122. London: Hogarth Press.

Gold, Claudia M. 2017. *The Developmental Science of Early Childhood*. New York: W. W. Norton.

Goldsmith, Douglas. 2007. "Challenging Children's Negative Internal Working Models." In *Attachment Theory in Clinical Work with Children*, edited by David Oppenheim and Douglas Goldsmith, 203–225. New York: The Guilford Press.

Klein, Melanie. 1948. *Contributions to Psycho-Analysis, 1921–1945*. London: Hogarth.

Koren-Karie, Nina, David Oppenheim, and Douglas F. Goldsmith. 2007. "Keeping the Inner World of the Child in Mind." In *Attachment Theory in Clinical Work With Children*, edited by David Oppenheim and Douglas Goldsmith, 31–57. New York: The Guilford Press.

Mahler, Margaret S., Fred Pine, and Anni Bergman. 1975. *The Psychological Birth of the Human Infant: Symbiosis and Individuation*. New York: Basic Books.

Masson, Jeffrey M. 1984. "Freud and the Seduction Theory." *Atlantic Monthly* February 1984: 33–60.

Masson, Jeffrey M. 1985. *The Complete Letters of Sigmund Freud to Wilhelm Fliess, 1887–1904*. Cambridge: The Belknap Press.

Reik, Theodor. 1948. *Listening with the Third Ear: The Inner Experience of a Psychoanalyst*. New York: Farrar, Straus and Giroux.

Sandler, Joseph, and Anna Freud. 1985. *The Analysis of Defense: The Ego and the Mechanisms of Defense Revisited*. New York: International Universities Press.

Snow, Mark D., Lindsay C. Malloy, and Naomi E. S. Goldstein. 2021. "Information Gathering in School Contexts: A National Survey of School Resource Officers." *Law and Human Behavior* 45, no. 4: 356–369.

Trout, Michael. 1988. "Infant Mental Health: Monitoring Our Movement into the Twenty-First Century." *Infant Mental Health Journal* 9, no. 3: 191–200.

Turner, Erica, and Abigail J. Beneke. 2019. "Softening' School Resource Officers: The Extension of Police Presence in Schools in an Era of Black Lives Matter, School Shootings, and Rising Inequality." *Race Ethnicity and Education* 23, no. 2: 221–240.

Winnicott, Donald. 1971. *Playing and Reality*. London: Tavistock Publications Ltd. Re-published in 2005, Oxford: Routledge Classics.

Zinsser, Katherine M. 2022. *No Longer Welcome: The Epidemic of Expulsion from Early Childhood Education*. New York: Oxford University Press.

Chapter 6

Winnicott Comes to School

Using Transitional Objects in Classroom Life

Lesley Koplow

Whether children start school at two years old or at seven years old, they often bring unresolved early developmental issues into the early childhood classroom setting. Whether in toddler care or second grade, children also bring all of their life experiences into the classroom milieu. When children attend an early childhood setting every day, the setting itself becomes a shared environment that must accommodate both the developmental processes of the children in the group and the variety of their life experiences that enter the space. Without interacting with these two essential forces that weave into the social fabric of the classroom, teachers may feel powerless to promote emotional well-being and engaged learning during difficult times. In this chapter, we will apply D. W. Winnicott's concept of *the holding environment* to the early childhood classroom and will use some of Winnicott's theories to support the application of emotionally responsive techniques that have been used in hundreds of urban classrooms over a twenty-five-year period as part of the work of the Center for Emotionally Responsive Practice at Bank Street College. There will be particular emphasis on the application of intentional transitional object use in early childhood and early grades educational settings.

FROM "GOOD ENOUGH MOTHER" TO "GOOD ENOUGH TEACHER"

Winnicott's writings contain many references to the importance of the supportive mother-infant relationship. To Winnicott, the "good enough mother"[1] was a parent who was able to create a holding environment for her infant, allowing the child to feel safe within her care, meeting her dependency needs reliably, and empathizing with her infant's emotional states (Winnicott 1971). As a pediatrician, adult analyst and child and family psychotherapist, Winnicott drew a parallel between the mother-infant relationship and the therapist-patient relationship. He saw the therapeutic relationship as a metaphorical holding environment that became strong enough to foster and hold both the patient's loving feelings and rageful feelings. In this chapter, we explore the benefits of considering the definition of the "good enough teacher" as one who can create a holding environment for the children in her care within the classroom setting.

Psychologically informed classroom practice is not a new idea. Anna Freud worked to open the first therapeutic nursery for young war-affected children in 1941, informed by psychoanalytic and developmental understandings (Midgley 2007). She and her colleagues learned about the impact of war on children by observing the children in their care. Being a teacher before becoming a psychoanalyst, Anna Freud firmly believed that there was a unique potential in the teacher-child relationship, because it included the potential to know a child well within a shared social milieu, as well as acknowledging and integrating the reality demands inherent in classroom life. Anna Freud applied psychoanalytic understanding to the teacher-child relationship, noting how both the child's past and the teacher's past created transference and impacted teacher-child interaction (Britzman and Pitt 1996).

Winnicott was even more devoted to the therapeutic value of *being with* children in the here and now, and creating a shared environment that acknowledged life experiences and invited play as a form of emotional integration. For Winnicott, affirming children's emotional experience was a path to facilitating the developmental process. While his work was primarily with children and families who were part of his clinical practice, he shared his ideas with teachers through his writing and lectures. Students of Winnicott took his theories and practices into the classroom. The earliest classroom-based work by Winnicott's protégés was primarily focused on the application of teacher observation and acknowledgment of children's thoughts and feelings in facilitating an authentic writing process in elementary school-aged children (Briton et al. 1975).

Winnicott's own work may have been primarily in the clinical consulting room, but his well-known books and lectures centered on the value of play and creativity as essential to both child and adult mental health. Rather than follow the prevalent drive-based psychoanalytic theories of his time, Winnicott worked to build nurturing relationships with both child and adult patients that were strong enough to hold their stories as well as their positive and negative feelings. He believed in the reparative nature of the therapeutic relationship, providing patients with a therapeutic environment that could facilitate emotional integration and healing, using the nurturing maternal relationship as a model. Moving from Winnicott's concept of "good enough mother" to "good enough psychotherapist" to "good enough teacher" can provide developmentally informed programs with a sound foundation for building bridges between early childhood and early grades classroom practice and the mission of fostering emotional wellbeing in schoolchildren.

TEACHER-CHILD RELATIONSHIPS

Indeed, we know from more recent research that a supportive teacher-child relationship is a significant variable in both learning and social/emotional outcomes for children. Hamre and Pianta found that warmth within the teacher-child relationship in early childhood has the capacity to positively affect social, emotional, and cognitive outcomes throughout the school years (Hamre and Pianta 2001). Highly sensitive teaching has also been shown to be related to closing achievement gaps for such young students at risk of poor performance (Hamre and Pianta 2005). Sabol and Pianta remind us that a sensitive teacher can serve as a safe emotional base, offering a relationship context of closeness, especially useful for children at risk (Sabol and Pianta 2012).

We have also seen that negative behaviors diminish when teacher sensitivity and responsiveness are high (Birch and Ladd 1998; Wentzel, Barry, and Caldwell 2004). In addition, when monitoring children's cortisol levels as a marker of their stress levels in the classroom, studies found teacher-child closeness and positive relationships with peers to promote lower cortisol levels and a higher incidence of pro-social behavior (Ladd and Burgess 2001). Furthermore, research on child care outcomes for children at risk found that high-quality childcare environments, characterized by high levels of teacher support, buffered a significant number of preschool children from a secondary increase in afternoon cortisol levels (Badanes et al. 2012).

The Center for Emotionally Responsive Practice at Bank Street has noted that young schoolchildren impacted by poverty, adverse circumstances, and traumatic stress are often those children for whom traditional mental health resources are least likely to be accessible. Therefore, enhancing the capacity of public sector early childhood teachers and public school teachers to use developmentally informed, relationship-based practice has the potential to promote equity for millions of young children who are in need of emotional and social support.

FROM THERAPEUTIC NURSERY TO PUBLIC SCHOOL

In the decade of the late 1980s–mid-1990s, twelve children per year attended a small, therapeutic nursery in New York City. The children who attended had psychiatric diagnoses including Pervasive Developmental Disorder NOS (now Autism Spectrum Disorder), Reactive Attachment Disorder, and Post Traumatic Stress Disorder, among the most prevalent. Psychosocial histories revealed abuse, neglect, multiple caregiver changes, loss, trauma, and time in foster care for approximately two-thirds of the children who attended.

Essentially, in this therapeutic nursery, the therapeutic teachers embraced their role as "good enough teachers" by creating a holding environment that could hold both the emotional lives and complex experiences of these young fragile children. They expressed empathy for negative emotions and acknowledged the difficult experiences that children carried into the room. Over time, the director of the nursery (who is also the author of this chapter) noticed that those children who brought stuffed animals or other soft comfort objects from home seemed to feel less fragile in the group setting and were more able to tolerate the adverse moments that occur in all early childhood settings.

The children who brought a consistent stuffed toy to school every day were primarily those children with psychosocial histories revealing the fewest disruptions in primary attachment relationships. Always looking for ways to support connection for every child present, the director decided to purchase a classroom Teddy Bear for each child who didn't bring a comfort object from home. The Teddy Bears and the other stuffed animals became members of the therapeutic classroom. When the children came to morning meetings, the stuffed animals attended as well. When the teachers read to the children and talked about the story afterwards, the stuffed animals "listened" as well and were invited to be part of the conversation. When the children were offered the use of feeling charts to let teachers know how they were feeling, the stuffed animals were also asked to have a voice. Over time, the Teddy Bears became transitional objects born of the facilitative environment of the classroom. For many children, the Teddy Bears supported and came to *symbolize* the teacher-child attachment, as well as becoming a symbol of the child's own emergent self (Koplow 2009).

While psychotherapists also worked individually with children and parents, in the nursery, and dyadic work with parent-child pairs or whole families, the power of supporting attachment relationships within the containing structure of the classroom was central to the approach. The therapeutic classroom had predictable routines and promoted play as a healing force, allowing the classroom to become a version of Winnicott's "holding environment." The classroom used the power of play to bridge inner life and external experience and integrate the two in meaningful and developmentally salient ways. This mission was always uppermost in the minds of teachers and therapists in the program. The Teddy Bears and other stuffed animals helped children to self-comfort, communicate, create, and develop the capacity for symbolic play needed to integrate difficult experience.

At the time, our assumption was that the children who attended the nursery had unique needs and required therapeutic approaches that most other children in regular early childhood settings would not require. Yet, when nursery staff visited other mainstream early childhood and early grade classrooms, it seemed that there were more than a few children present who would have been well served by these same approaches. Eventually, outreach to the public-school system's early childhood community about these approaches was successful, and the techniques were slowly integrated into teacher practice in receptive New York City schools. *Teddy Bears in Classroom Practice*, the same process as implemented in the therapeutic nursery, became the norm for those schools and classrooms that embraced it.

WINNICOTT AND THE USES OF TRANSITIONAL OBJECT

Winnicott was fascinated by the baby's evolving attachment to certain preferred objects within the intimate environment of home. After seeing this phenomenon in many of the babies and toddlers that he observed over time, he developed a theory about the developmental meaning of such objects. Winnicott saw the use of a transitional object as a child's "first use of symbol and first experience of play" (Winnicott 1971, 130). He saw the transitional object as "symbolizing the union of the baby and mother, at the point in time and space of the initiation of their state of separateness" (Winnicott 1971, 130). In order for a child to find and invent a transitional object, and to use it to feel secure when apart from the attachment figure, the child's actual dependency needs had to be met reliably within a relationship, supported by a consistent, nurturing, and trustworthy caregiving environment.

Indeed, Winnicott noted that children who were relationship disrupted, deprived of an environment to explore, and/or experienced primary loss or frequent discontinuity in care were less able to play symbolically. He found that children in these circumstances were often hampered in the development of an authentic, integrated self as they grew older (Winnicott 1971). Winnicott pointed to the baby's creation of a transitional object as an example of a fundamental developmental process being dependent on the existence of a facilitating environment. While most child analysts of his time focused solely on the inner lives of children, without acknowledging the interaction/

connection between inner life and the child's actual real-world environment, Winnicott was fascinated by the ways that the attuned environment facilitated the evolution of play as a path to emotional wellbeing in the child.

In his original paper "Transitional Objects and Transitional Phenomenon: A Study of the First Not-Me Possession," later included as the first chapter in *Play and Reality*, Winnicott describes, "staking a claim for an intermediate state between a baby's inability and growing ability to recognize and accept reality" (Winnicott 1971, 3). He goes on to refer to the transitional objects and transitional phenomena "belonging to the realm of illusion (play), made possible by the mother's special capacity for making adaption to the needs of her infant, thus allowing the infant the illusion that what the infant creates really exists" (Winnicott 1971, 19). His conclusion was that the process of symbolic play was essentially relationship-based and was an essential element that allowed children to master and integrate real-life challenges. He found that this held true even through the adversity of wartime when parent-child relationships remained intact.

BRINGING WINNICOTT TO SCHOOL IN THE
TWENTY-FIRST CENTURY

Fast forwarding to the present, in the post–pandemic world, child mental health issues in preschool children, school-aged children, and adolescents are overwhelming school communities across the nation. The years away from school have resulted in younger developmental levels of social interaction, disrupted relationships with teachers and peers, heightened exposure to domestic violence, and a high incidence of loss among young children. This has resulted in pressing emotional and developmental needs in mainstream preschools, kindergarten, and early grades classrooms. While there is acknowledgment of an unprecedented increase in demand for child mental health services at younger and younger ages, often connected to the disruption and traumatic loss of COVID times, in most schools, there has been a narrow focus on post–pandemic "learning loss" without considering how social, emotional, and developmental issues are hindering the learning process.

Those schools committed to the well-being of their children often have to fight for funds necessary for professional development and support to make Emotionally Responsive Practices come to life in their classrooms. It is important to share stories from those early childhood and early grade communities that *have* managed to integrate these therapeutic approaches in the wake of COVID, when trauma comes to school every day. These stories come from public schools and public sector programs that now routinely make room for and "hold" the emotional lives of their children. Many have done so using either *Teddy Bears in Classroom Practice* as a baseline or a version of *Teddy Bears in Traumatic Times*, an approach taught by the Center for Emotionally Responsive Practice at Bank Street College[2].

TEDDY BEARS COME TO SCHOOL

The vignettes included here will be from early childhood and elementary school teachers who have integrated Emotionally Responsive Practice into classroom life, focusing on the benefits of using transitional objects in classroom practice. The early childhood and elementary grade teachers who did the work referenced here did so initially in collaboration with the Center for Emotionally Responsive Practice at Bank Street College.

The teacher's stories included here do not describe the implementation process of the approach but rather highlight individual group and child responses to the work. These stories were shared during interviews with the author or as a result of surveys requiring narratives describing responses to classroom Teddy Bear use. The stories selected came from schools with high percentages of children who qualified for free lunch, lived in stressed neighborhoods, experienced trauma, and served children with identified special needs. While working within challenging demographics, the teachers included here were devoted to being "good enough teachers," providing an environment that facilitated attachment, connection, and play as a tool for emotional integration and communication.

Annie's Stories

Annie taught children between the ages of five and seven years old who had been classified as having special needs in an urban public school setting. She had used ERP's model for integrating Teddy Bears into classroom practice prior to COVID-19, and the Teddy Bears were part of the day-to-day classroom social and learning routines. This included time to draw or write in Teddy Bear Journals, which invited children to represent what might be worrying their Teddy Bears. Annie had noticed that the children's writing and dictation in their Teddy Bear Journals were more elaborate and more thoughtful than any of their other writing or dictation samples. One day, B, a kindergarten child, brought her journal to show her teacher. B explained what she had drawn, and dictated the narrative for her teacher to write. "My bear is worried that when she goes home there might be no food." Annie reflected how difficult it must be for her Teddy Bear to worry about not having food. She reminded the little girl that she could cook some food for her bear in pretend play or share some of her snack with her bear. Now that Annie had reason to believe that food insecurity was an issue for at least one of the children in her classroom, she decided to change the classroom snack routine, making healthy food available for children who wanted it throughout the day, instead of only at prescribed snack times.

After a few days' absence, the office informed Annie that T, one of the children in her class, had been taken from his home by Child Protective Services and was now in foster care far away from the school. Annie gathered the children together on the rug to talk about T, each with their Teddy Bear in their laps. The children were distraught when they learned that their classmate might not be returning. Some of the children knew that the police had been at their classmate's home. They wondered if the little boy had been sent to jail. Annie read a children's book about foster care to the children and their Teddy Bears. She asked if children or bears had any questions or worries. One child raised his hand. "Can we find where T lives now and send him his Teddy Bear in the mail so he won't be so scared?" The rest of the class agreed that sending the bear would be helpful to T. Annie was able to find a mailing address to use by reaching out to the CPS worker. The children drew and wrote notes to send along with T's Teddy Bear.

C, a first grader who was not very verbal, seemed especially withdrawn and preoccupied for a few days. During choice time, C got his Teddy Bear and lay him down in a shoebox. Silently, he gathered other bears around the box. Annie approached the child. He looked up at her. "It's the funeral," he said quietly. "For his uncle. They did this." C pointed to the toys that he had arranged. Annie acknowledged how sad it must have been to lose his uncle. She wondered aloud how they could help the bears who were sad about losing their uncle. No one had told Annie about a loss in C's family. She was glad the play allowed her to bear witness to the event and join C as he tried to process the experience of attending a funeral as a step toward processing a loss. With Annie joining him in the mourning process, C was able to move from having his bear represent his lost uncle to sitting with his bear for comfort while he continued to process the loss by drawing and writing in his Teddy Bear journal. Annie observed that children who had a history of abuse or neglect were caring for their bears in attuned and empathic ways. She felt that the play depicted the way these children *wished* to be cared for. Other teachers using bears had reported seeing the same kind of attentive nurturing play in children who had traumatic histories resulting in placement in foster care.

Randi's Story

Randi taught and cared for three- and four-year-olds in an Emotionally Responsive Practice-informed early childhood community in a low-income rural area.

Jay was a three-year-old child with a traumatic history in Randi's early care classroom. Randi recalled that when the fire bell rang to announce a fire drill in her setting, Jay ran to get his bear before he would agree to leave the room. He said repeatedly that he didn't want his bear to get hurt. He took it outside and kept it safe in his arms, holding it like a baby throughout the fire drill.

Maria's Story

Maria teaches in a K-1 classroom in a public school with a socioeconomically diverse, bilingual student population. Maria's school practices looping allowed for greater relationship continuity in school. If children enter Maria's classroom in kindergarten, they remain in the classroom community in first grade as well.

D's pre-K year was disrupted by the sudden threat of COVID-19, causing schools to function remotely for the rest of the school year and the beginning of the following year. When D re-entered the school building in the middle of his kindergarten year, he rarely interacted with his peers. Throughout the kindergarten year, D seemed quite emotionally distant from both Maria and the other children. While most of his peers were overjoyed to be in the presence of other children after a very long period of being isolated at home, D seemed hesitant to interact. Neither did D show interest in his Teddy Bear. He didn't name it, hold it, or play with it during his kindergarten year, in contrast to every other child.

When D returned to the classroom as a first grader, he promptly looked for and found his Teddy Bear and gave it a name. He made bracelets for his Teddy to wear. D's Teddy Bear then became a bridge to pretend play with other Teddy Bears and with other children in the classroom. After a few weeks, D became an active and well-integrated member of the classroom community.

Maria recalls that a similar relationship evolution had happened with another child when she moved from kindergarten to first grade the following year. Similar to D, R had limited interaction with both her Teddy Bear, her teachers, and her peers in kindergarten, but in first grade became interactive with both, using her Bear as a bridge to the peer community.

TEDDY BEARS AS TRANSITIONAL OBJECTS IN SCHOOL: LOOKING AT EMERGENT THEMES

These few vignettes demonstrate the value of offering transitional objects to children in early childhood and elementary classrooms and provide a sample of emergent themes invited by this classroom-friendly technique.

All of the children referenced had been provided with a Teddy Bear to name, dress, identify likes and dislikes, attribute affects, play with, and become attached to. All of the children were encouraged to hold their bears when they needed comfort, were being read to, were resting, were addressing social and emotional issues, and during expressive drawing and writing. All of the children referenced attended classrooms where transitional object use was the norm.

Annie's children were able to use Teddy Bear work and play to convey their experiences of loss and deprivation that might otherwise have remained unknown to Annie. (B's journal reference to her Teddy Bear's fear of not having any food; D's funeral play.) Annie's awareness allowed her to bear witness to these children's experiences, reflect with empathy and, at times, take action on their behalf. Most important, the facilitative environment of Annie's classroom allowed her to promote communication via symbolic play, drawing, and dictation, thus diminishing social and emotional isolation for the children in her group, and lowering the mental health risk factors that are heightened by ongoing isolation in children.

When T is placed in foster care far from the school and abruptly leaves the community, the children suggest sending T his Teddy Bear, showing that they have internalized the use of traditional objects as a form of comfort and connection during separation.

Randi's little boy insisted on bringing his Teddy Bear outside to keep him safe during a fire drill. His relationship with his transitional object held both the source of comfort that he experienced with his teachers at school, as well as an emerging capacity to provide comfort to a symbol of his "baby self," his Teddy Bear.

Maria's stories focused on the rejection of a transitional object running parallel to the rejection of teacher and peer interactions post–COVID time disruption, and the subsequent eventual embracing of the transitional object as a bridge to peer interaction after returning to the classroom for a second year. Many schools felt unable to allow children to recover from disruption and loss at their own pace, assuming that those who did not recover quickly were unresponsive due to learning issues. In Maria's case, a facilitative looping environment offered the tools for developmental progress within an ongoing open invitation for teacher-child attachment. The schools' use of looping became sustaining for children who required an extended period of contact to allow attachments to form after COVID time disruption. The children's use of transitional objects paralleled their ability to trust in the safety and continuity of relationships with teachers and peers after an extended period of separation.

SUMMARY

This chapter explores applying Winnicott's theory of the power of the nurturing facilitative environment to the early childhood and early grade classroom. It offers a conceptually sound and highly implementable process to translate the supportive value of the "good enough mother" to the teacher-child relationship. References to research on the impact of warm teacher-child relationships on child well-being are provided to affirm the impact of supportive classroom environments on child outcomes. Stories from teachers, and school-based clinicians documenting the emergent themes of transitional object use in classroom practice with vulnerable children during traumatic times are included, and emergent themes are analyzed for common ground meaning and content.

While Winnicott emphasizes the baby's choice in the creation of a home-based transitional object, this version of school-based transitional object use does not feature the element of choice of object. However, the process gives children the opportunity to create the image and identity of their own Teddy Bear, and to bring this image to life in the shared space of the classroom community. Teachers invite expressive opportunities for children and their Teddies, while children determine the evolution of the relationship and its symbolic value according to individual developmental and relationship factors.

Winnicott's core beliefs in using relationship-based holding at any age to promote symbolic processing and emotional integration of life experience are central to the work referenced in this chapter. In order for transitional objects to be a meaningful technique for classroom use, the teacher must be able to create a holding environment in the classroom, where strong and supportive relationships with children can grow. Indeed, no matter the age or grade level of the child, empathy for their "little selves" can be demonstrated via the use of the Teddy Bears, resulting in a therapeutic classroom environment for children who lacked a prior empathic voice. When Winnicott comes to school, the school's holding capacity expands to embrace its student body.

NOTES

1. In Winnicott's time, the nurture of infants and young children was considered primarily a maternal role. His references to "good enough mother" may be more accurately described as "good enough parent" when the primary nurturer is a father, grandparent, or other caregiver.
2. See Appendix B for sample pages from "Teddy Bears in Traumatic Times" taught by the Center for Emotionally Responsive Practice at Bank Street College.

REFERENCES

Badanes, Lisa S., Julia Dmitrieva, and Sarah Enos Watamura. 2012. "Understanding Cortisol Reactivity Across the Day at Child Care: The Potential Buffering Role of Secure Attachments to Caregivers." *Early Childhood Research Quarterly* 27, no. 1: 156–165.

Birch, Sondra H., and Gary W. Ladd. 1998. "Children's Interpersonal Behaviors and the Teacher–Child Relationship." *Developmental Psychology* 34, no. 5: 934.

Briton, James, Tony Burgess, Nancey Martin, A. McLeod, and H. Rosen. 1975. *The Development of Writing Abilities*. London: Macmillan.

Britzman, Deborah P., and Alice J. Pitt. 1996. "Pedagogy and Transference: Casting the Past of Learning into the Presence of Teaching." *Theory Into Practice* 35, no. 2: 117–123.

Burchinal, Margaret, Nathan Vandergrift, Robert Pianta, and Andrew Mashburn. 2010. "Threshold Analysis of Association Between Child Care Quality and Child Outcomes for Low-Income Children in Pre-Kindergarten Programs." *Early Childhood Research Quarterly* 25, no. 2: 166–176.

Connor, Carol McDonald, Seung-Hee Son, Annemarie H. Hindman, and Frederick J. Morrison. 2005. "Teacher Qualifications, Classroom Practices, Family Characteristics, and Preschool Experience: Complex Effects on First Graders' Vocabulary and Early Reading Outcomes." *Journal of school Psychology* 43, no. 4: 343–375.

Dyson, Anne Haas. 2020. "'This Isn't My Real Writing': The Fate of Children's Agency in Too- Tight Curricula." *Theory Into Practice* 59, no. 2: 119–127.

Hamre, Bridget K., and Robert C. Pianta. 2001. "Early Teacher–Child Relationships and the Trajectory of Children's School Outcomes Through Eighth Grade." *Child Development* 72, no. 2: 625–638.

Hamre, B. K., and R. C. Pianta. 2005. "Can Instructional and Emotional Support in the First- Grade Classroom Make a Difference for Children at Risk of School Failure?" *Child Development* 76, no. 5: 949–967.

Hamre, Bridget K., and Robert C. Pianta. 2010. "Classroom Environments and Developmental Processes: Conceptualization and Measurement." In *Handbook of Research on Schools, Schooling and Human Development*, edited by Judith L. Meece and Jacquelynne S. Eccles, 25–41. New York: Routledge.

Jeon, Lieny, Cynthia K. Buettner, and Anastasia R. Snyder. 2014. "Pathways from Teacher Depression and Child-Care Quality to Child Behavioral Problems." *Journal of Consulting and Clinical Psychology* 82, no. 2: 225.

Koplow, Lesley. 2008. *Bears, Bears Everywhere!: Supporting Children's Emotional Health in the Classroom*. New York: Teachers College Press.

Ladd, Gary W., and Kim B. Burgess. 2001. "Do Relational Risks and Protective Factors Moderate the Linkages Between Childhood Aggression and Early Psychological and School Adjustment?" *Child Development* 72, no. 5: 1579–1601.

Midgley, Nick. 2007. "Anna Freud: The Hampstead War Nurseries and the Role of the Direct Observation of Children for Psychoanalysis." *The International Journal of Psychoanalysis* 88, no. 4: 939–959.

Sabol, Terri J., and Robert C. Pianta. 2012. "Patterns of School Readiness Forecast Achievement and Socioemotional Development at the End of Elementary School." *Child Development* 83, no. 1: 282–299.

Suntheimer, Noelle M., and Sharon Wolf. 2020. "Cumulative Risk, Teacher- Child Closeness, Executive Function and Early Academic Skills in Kindergarten Children." *Journal of School Psychology* 78: 23–37.

Wentzel, Kathryn R., Carolyn McNamara Barry, and Kathryn A. Caldwell. 2004. "Friendships in Middle School: Influences on Motivation and School Adjustment." *Journal of Educational Psychology* 96, no. 2: 195.

Winnicott, Donald. 1971. *Playing and Reality*. London: Tavistock Publications Ltd. Re-published in 2005, Oxford: Routledge Classics.

Chapter 7

The Narcissism of Curriculum

The Importance of Listening to Children

Eileen Johnson

It is lunchtime. I am standing at the counter along with three other teachers, while a classroom of children, ages two to three years old, are eating lunch. Our role at this time of the schedule is to warm lunches, help with badly designed lunchboxes, supply water, intervene if a child feels annoyed by another child's actions, or any other things teachers of young children feel called upon to do to make lunchtime go smoothly.

A three-year-old girl who is sitting close to where I am standing, let's call her Lucy, lifts her metal water bottle and, despite the fact that it is quite large for her little hands, drinks expertly from it. She says out loud to no one in particular, as young children do: "The water in this bottle is really cold!"

I respond, pointing to the water jug we keep for children who may not have a personal water bottle: "Oh, there's water in this jug, it's not cold, do you want some?"

She says: "The water in this bottle is really cold!"

I use a slower voice and try to speak more clearly: "This jug here has water in it. It's not that cold. Do you want some?"

She says, in the same exact tone with the same volume as she has previously used: "The water in this bottle is really cold!"

The other teachers giggle a little. I assume they think—as I do—that she is not really listening, or she's having a hard time processing what I am saying, but perhaps they are amused at the disconnect between us. I try again, pointing to the jug and speaking even more slowly and clearly: "Lucy, this jug here has water in it. This water is not cold. I can give you some of this water. Would you like that?"

She says: "The water in this bottle is really cold!"

Finally, I get it. I say, using the same tone she used: "The water in your bottle is really cold!" She nods and, satisfied, returns to her lunch.

I have learned a very important lesson. Or should I say I am once again reminded that this is a lesson I have to constantly relearn. It is something therapists endeavor to keep in mind, as should teachers: Listening is the most important thing you can do. It must precede instruction, feedback, or guidance. Real listening benefits the child, and the teacher, and is essential to the learning process. For very young children, being listened to is central to the development of their sense of self. Evelyn Albright Schwaber (2005) quotes from M. R. Montgomery's (1989) memoir:

> If you are very small, you actually understand that there is no point in jumping into the swimming pool unless they see you do it. The child crying: "Watch me, watch me," is not begging for attention; he is pleading for existence itself. (Schwaber 2005, 35)

Salman Akhtar (2005) refers to the primary importance of listening and empathic attunement in the therapeutic process: "Credulous listening must precede skeptical listening. Consolidation must come before deconstruction, empathy before insight, affirmation before interpretation and containment-holding before transformative looking" (5). Winnicott speaks of the importance of reflecting the self to the child: "This to which I have referred in terms of the mother's role of giving back to the baby the baby's own self continues to have importance in terms of the child and the family" (2005, 155).

The importance of listening to children does not stop in the family. Teachers, in loco parentis for the largest part of the child's day, need to continue this work and allow the child's self to enter the room and be accepted. My attempt to switch Lucy from communication of her feelings to the solution of her "problem" was an example of what Herzog (1984) calls "disruptive attunement." What Lucy wanted was to be understood. She wanted someone to "get" her, to understand *from the inside* what it felt like to be a small child experiencing a very large water bottle filled with very cold water. What, in fact, it feels like to be a child experiencing the world. What I wanted was to fix her "problem." While my behavior was fundamentally benevolent, it was also narcissistic in that I wanted to actuate my own vision: a comfortable child, a happy classroom, and me playing the role of benevolent teacher. The term narcissism has been much used and misused, and I believe there are different levels of narcissism, but a good definition might be from Stolorow (1975): "Mental activity is narcissistic to the degree that its function is to maintain the structural cohesiveness, temporal stability and positive affective colouring of the self-representation" (56). Pajak (2011) speaks about the different kinds and levels of narcissism: "Consensus among scholars and researchers currently holds that narcissism includes a range of behaviors and a spectrum of severity, including normal adult narcissism that is important for regulating self-esteem (Kernberg 2004; Ronningstem 2005). Indeed, "Healthy narcissism plays a crucial role in the human capacity to manage challenges. . . ." (2024).

Most, if not all, teachers feel they need to play a role. Being attached to that role can enable a type of narcissism, a desire to maintain for oneself the image of a person who is knowledgeable and in control, dedicated to achieving the school's goals. Many teachers were "good" students who followed the rules. This "teacher" role has been well-defined over the many years in which society has had schools. The teacher follows the curriculum, and the students follow the teacher. Curriculum is the word that describes both the goal of school and also the map by which the goal is reached. Different schools use different maps and value different kinds of curricula, depending on where they are located, what the prevailing social philosophy is, and what pressures or directives come from outside.

Schools have become such an integral part of our culture that we tend to think that they have always been there. However, school is a relatively new institution, one that came about to serve particular cultural goals. Although most people subscribe to the idea that school is a necessary institution, very few analyze what the role of school is, wonder where school came from, or question why we need schools at all. In her paper "What is Education for?" Pamela Mang (2005) looks at the role of education in society. She writes: "For much of human history, education has enabled acculturation and socialization aimed at maintaining the health of the broader community. Education of the individual was shaped by what it meant to the welfare of the whole" (15).

Enculturation, the passing on of communal values, was originally a process conducted within the family or tribal system through rituals or experiential lessons. In the Middle Ages, young people apprenticed with skilled workers to learn their craft. This apprenticeship system was not an organized system but relied on the personal relationship between teacher and pupils to transmit social values. Padraic Pearse, better known for his role as the leader of the 1916 Irish Insurrection against Britain, was also a poet and educator who founded Scoil Eanna, a school that would be considered very progressive even today. His treatise "The Murder Machine" (1905) was originally a speech to the Irish Parliament decrying the British system of education in Ireland at that time. In it, he describes the "fosterage" system of education in ancient Ireland:

> In the Middle Ages there were everywhere little groups of persons clustering round some beloved teacher, and thus it was that men learned not only the

humanities but all gracious and useful crafts. [. . .] It was always the individual inspiring, guiding, fostering other individuals; never the State usurping the place of father or fosterer, dispensing education like a universal provider of ready-mades, aiming at turning out all men and women according to regulation patterns [. . .]. And this, remember, was not the education system of an aristocracy, but the education system of a people. It was more democratic than any education system in the world to-day. Our very divisions into primary, secondary, and university crystallise a snobbishness partly intellectual and partly social [. . .]. Always it was the personality of the teacher that drew them there. (Pearse 1916, 9)

Fosterage and apprenticeship gave way to enforced schooling. It was during the nineteenth century that many European countries began to institute formal education in settings outside the home. In the United States, institutionalized schooling was introduced shortly after independence from Great Britain. The purpose of this new systematized education was to achieve certain social aims of the new republic. As Richard Quantz (2003) points out, "Civic education became a central aim to those, such as Jefferson, committed to the development of democracy and republicanism" (99). Quantz goes on to say that the development of universal education served the ends of diverse forces which were operating within American culture at that time:

The social elite feared youthful idleness and the unions disliked the exploitation of their children through cheap and dangerous child labor practices. This unlikely coalition between society's most and least privileged pushed through the first compulsory education laws [. . .] By the end of the nineteenth century, all the important cultural forces in America had identified schooling as one important tool to advance their interest. (2003, 100)

According to Quantz, schools quickly became methods of enculturation and, more specifically, ways of preparing children to be hardworking citizens.

At the turn of the twentieth century, kindergarten schools based on "Prussian" models became widespread. These schools, which owed their beginnings to the writings of educational philosophers such as Froebel and Pestalozzi, took hold more rapidly in the United States than in Germany. Meike Sophia Baader (2004) attributes this social development to the particular social and economic conditions in the United States. She indicates that those conditions were a specific result of the combination of industrialization and immigration:

According to Allen, the reasons for the absolutely different acceptance of the kindergarten lie in fundamental differences in policies on the relation between public and private worlds . . . In the immigration society of the United States, it was important to integrate children with various language and cultural backgrounds into society. (437)

Schooling became compulsory throughout the United States in the mid-1800s, according to Bernadette Baker, because of the need to maintain control.

> A place began to "look like a nation" to the extent that it could be demonstrated that a set area had a population with some kind of essence, which could then be schooled, counted, subdivided statistically, and grouped into assemblages amenable to administration, management and taming under the auspices of a welfare reasoning. (2004, 34)

She goes on to say that compulsory education quickly led to "a focus on mind-as-ability" (35) and to the institutionalization of normative values in classrooms. The relationship between child and school became one in which the school took over the community's role of teaching the child and of defining what the child should learn. The young nation became involved in the process of preparing children to be workers in society. The three Rs achieved status as central figures in school curricula since they were deemed necessary to this function.

The selection of curriculum and creation of school texts can be powerful tools for reinforcing cultural values. Since children are impressionable and schooling universally enforced, in certain cultures, schools have managed to extend their influence over young minds in ways that can be described as manipulative and ultimately narcissistic. In times of change or conflict, as William Marsden (2000) points out, schools can be used to promote or reinforce political or religious movements:

> There was indeed a general assumption in Victorian times that battles would loom large in the history textbooks. In the boys' public schools, where it was presumed many pupils would be considering the armed forces as a career, military and political history was granted some priority. (29)

He gives the example of how these kinds of values were inculcated, citing songs sung by young pupils on Empire Day in England during World War I:

> Even the babies' class had a contribution to make in setting an example, as illustrated in verse, song and play: "I want to be a soldier,/With bayonet and gun,/I want to cross the Channel,/And fight this cruel Hun./I'm much too old for playthings,/Like whips and tops and bricks,/I want to be a soldier,/For, listen! I am six!" (Marsden 2000, 29)

Regime change often brings with it the need to ensure the populace is in sync with the goals of the state and to ensure that they will work as agents of the new vision. Schools can be used as an essential part of that process. Under Hitler, German education became part of a movement of social reform:

> The geopolitical focus of education was exemplified in The Nazi Primer, the official handbook for the schooling of Hitler Youth, intent on saving German civilization from Jews, Communists and democracy . . . children were caught young and "drilled to become fanatical preachers of the gospel." (Marsden 2000, 29)

Japan's compulsory education system began in 1868, and one of its primary purposes was moral education. Children had to recite daily the various virtues which they were expected to incorporate, such as filial piety, thriftiness, and subservience to the emperor. When World War II began, the Japanese government turned to schools as a means of indoctrination. Textbooks were refined, and there was a mandatory daily recitation of virtues: According to Hoffman (1999):

> To ensure that this policy was enforced, the Bureau of Thought Supervision, now incorporated in a new institution known as the Institute of National Training (Kokumin Renseijo), was charged with "intensifying thought regimentation for the prosecution of the war effort." (87)

In order to achieve political and societal goals, schools can work to subvert the individuating intent of the child and replace it with the imperative of loyalty to a set of values, along with a mandate of spreading these ideals. In these instances, the child must represent the group. This kind of indoctrination is akin to how a narcissistic parent convinces a child of the parent's grandiose identity and secures the child's allegiance to that greatness—the child being used as a self-object, a vehicle for broadcasting the parent's good image to the world.

These narcissistic impositions happen not only on large scales, such as during great political upheavals, but on micro levels on a day-to-day basis. When I attended school in Ireland, I obtained a scholarship to a private high school, which was considered very desirable and "high class,"—the pupils came from economically advantaged homes, unlike mine. As a scholarship pupil, I was debriefed at the beginning of my enrollment. I was told that now I was a member of an important organization that was respected in the community. My task, even when I was outside school, while wearing the uniform, was to be cognizant of how I behaved—almost as if I was an advertisement for the school. While traveling on the bus, walking along the street, or interacting with shopkeepers, my demeanor and conduct should reflect the school and its values. In this way, I was expected not to be an individual as much as a representative.

School can put the good of the institution, or of society at large, at the forefront of its goals and neglect the individuality of the child. Heinz Kohut (1988), in *The Search for the Self*, speaks about the danger of prioritizing the goals of the group over the need for individual self-awareness and self-actualization:

> If humans are to survive in a way that has any similarity to what we have prized up till now as being the essence of human life. . . . Each individual must refine and work out a new kind of psychological life, a new kind of meaningful existence, by expanding his inner skills and his inner powers. (775)

He goes on to speak about the "group self":

> Group pressure diminishes individuality; it leads to a primitivization of the mental processes, in particular to a partial paralysis of the ego and to a lowering of resistances. The diminution of the influence of the ego is then followed by the cathartic expression of archaic (or at any rate undisguised) impulses, emotions, and ideation. (Kohut 1988, 839)

Group pressure in school can come from the expectations imposed on children to achieve certain standards which are designated as not only desirable but socially mandated. These standards are often limited by cultural factors, and they may be unattainable, unsuitable, or irrelevant to many students. Failure to pass exams can lead to alienation and a sense of shame due to exclusion from the mainstream. In many schools, the methodology the teacher employs is dictated by the need to "drill" subjects into the child which have importance to the teacher but not necessarily to the child, under the assumption that the teacher knows what the child needs to know.

This methodology is described by Richard Quantz (2003) who has written about rituals in society, and specifically about schools. He was struck during his observations in various schools by the pervasiveness of what he calls the "puzzlemaster" ritual. By this, he means that in most classrooms, teachers set themselves up as keepers of knowledge. During the lesson, the teacher will try to elicit the "right" answer from the pupils, who will be duly rewarded if they guess correctly. Quantz points to this quizzing ritual as an indication of the decline of democracy within the school system, a lack of child-centeredness, and a focus on the goals of the organization and its representative, the teacher. Children, he believes, are inculcated into the belief that the teacher is an expert who holds all the answers, and they themselves are passive recipients of learning: "While we might theoretically advance the idea that schools are arenas of democratic struggle, the day-to-day reality of the high schools that I visited found such discourse not only nonexistent, but meaningless" (Quantz 2003, 113). One problem with this kind of focus on "rightness," that Quantz saw in his school observations, is that teachers are tacitly encouraged to be narcissistic—to think that they are always right, that they cannot make mistakes. Any sign of doubt or confusion may be likely to damage the teacher's self-image or the image of the school. Teachers are trained to believe that this is their role, to not show weakness or vulnerability. Varying from that standard may not be comfortable for teachers. Pajak (2011) says: "Pinar speculated that the narcissism of adult egos often has difficulty tolerating the inevitable errors, fantasies, and accidents of immature learners because such imperfections remind adults of who they once were and of their present failings" (20). Another problem with the "puzzlemaster" culture is the assumption that all children are well served by having them follow a curriculum designed for the average student. However, one size shoe does not fit all feet. Howard Gardner is an educator who made a large impact on educational theory beginning in the 1980s when he developed the concept of "multiple intelligences" and his view is often referred to as "MI" theory. Daniel Goleman, author of Emotional Intelligence (2006) explains:

> Gardner's influential 1983 book Frames of Mind was a manifesto refuting the IQ view; It proposed that there was not just one, monolithic kind of intelligence that was crucial for life success, but rather a wide spectrum of intelligence, with seven key varieties. His list includes the two standard academic kinds, verbal and mathematical-logical alacrity, but goes on to include the spatial capacity seen in, say, an outstanding artist or architect; the kinesthetic genius displayed in the physical fluidity and grace of a Martha Graham or Magic Johnson; and the musical gifts of a Mozart or YoYo Ma. Rounding out the list are two faces of what Gardner calls "the personal intelligences": interpersonal skills, like those of a great therapist such as Carl Rogers or a world class leader such as Martin Luther King Jr., and the intra-psychic capacity that could emerge, on the one hand, in the brilliant insights of Sigmund Freud, or with less fanfare in the inner contentment that arises from attuning one's life to be in keeping with one's true feelings. (38)

Gardner contends that these kinds of intelligence can be present in any combination within any individual. Since all intelligences are valuable contributors to society, none should be considered more important than another. Intelligence, in other words, is different in different people, and IQ tests are not always a good indication of success in life. The ability to do mathematical calculations is not better or more important than being able to get a group of people to work together. Setting strict curriculum goals for a group of diverse children with multiple kinds of intelligences indicates a lack of awareness of the importance of individual differences, abilities, and work styles. Another quote from Padraic Pearse, written almost a hundred years prior, illustrates Gardner's theory well:

> I knew one boy who passed through several schools a dunce and a laughing-stock; the National Board and the Intermediate Board had sat in judgment upon him and had damned him as a failure before men and angels. Yet a friend and fellow-worker of mine discovered that he was gifted with a wondrous sympathy for nature, that he loved and understood the ways of plants, that he had a strange minuteness and subtlety of observation—that, in short, he was the sort of boy likely to become an accomplished botanist. I knew another boy of whom his father said to me: "He is no good at books, he is no good at work; he is good at nothing but playing a tin whistle. What am I to do with him?" I shocked the worthy man by replying (though really it was the obvious thing to reply): "Buy a tin whistle for him." (Pearse 1905, 9)

Ivan Illich, in his book *Deschooling Society*, maintained that: "most people gain most of their knowledge outside school, and in school only insofar as school, in a few rich countries, has become their place of confinement during an increasing part of their lives" (2002, 12). It is true that interest and motivation are key elements in the learning process, and learning can and does occur outside school. It is also true that schools can deprive children of the opportunity to follow their own interests, replacing their individual goals with the goals of the organization. However, what Illich is overlooking is the importance of relationships in the learning process. Particularly in early childhood, but also throughout a child's journey through the school system, attachment to a benevolent adult enhances the child's development and encourages learning. This can be especially true when the child's home or social circumstances are adverse. School can be transformative. There are countless examples of famous people who credit one teacher for spotting their talents and encouraging them. In order for a teacher-pupil relationship to be effective, the adult must be able to understand what the child is thinking and where the child is developmentally.

The reverse is true: if educators do not know what a child is hearing and internalizing, then they don't know whether their teaching is effective. Many teachers carry on, regardless of the children who don't seem to be getting it, focusing on the children who do, gratified that someone "gets" them. A teacher who is not able to let go of the need to be "successful" may tend to overlook failures. Ignoring failure increases the likelihood of failure. Paying attention to lapses, errors, failures, enables us to improve. If teachers do not lean in to the "mistakes" children make, and wonder why their teaching is not working, then they do not give themselves the opportunity to improve their methodology.

Jean Piaget is considered one of the greatest contributors to our knowledge of the development of children's cognitive processes. Every teacher during their training learns about Piaget's theories of cognitive development in children. Piaget came to understand these processes through his interest in "mistakes." Piaget first trained as a scientist and later began to work with psychologists in the emerging field of child psychology. While he was employed to work on standardizing the results of children's tests, he became more interested in the reason why children fail than why they succeed. The regular occurrence of "mistakes" made him wonder what the child was thinking that led to the error, and he began to study error patterns. Through examining these patterns, he developed his theories on the stages of childhood cognitive development which are now recognized by educators: sensorimotor (birth until one and a half years), preoperational (one and a half years until seven years), concrete operations (seven years until eleven years), and formal operations (eleven years onward). By listening to children and observing them, he made deductions about their developing powers of reasoning.

> It is interesting to study how children spontaneously learn to measure. One of my collaborators, Dr. Bärbel Inhelder, and I have made the following experiment: we show the child a tower of blocks on a table and ask him to build a second tower of the same height on another table (lower or higher than the first) with blocks of a different size. He begins to look around for a measuring standard. Interestingly enough, the first measuring tool that comes to his mind is his own body. He puts one hand on top of this tower and the other at its base, and then, trying to keep his hands the same distance apart, he moves over to the other tower to compare it. Children of about the age of six often carry out this work in a most assured manner, as if their hand could not change position on the way! (Piaget 2003, 16).

Piaget's studies of children proved that children cannot process certain tasks unless they have reached the appropriate cognitive stage. One of the best-known experiments Piaget conducted revealed interesting results on "conservation" which probably all teachers now study at teacher training college. At a certain age, he discovered, children believe that a quantity of liquid in a tall, thin glass is greater than the same quantity in a short, wide glass. Although they see the truth of this for themselves as they pour the liquid back and forth between the two glasses, they continue to believe that the amount is greater in the tall glass than in the short one. Until they reach a certain age or level of brain development, they cannot grasp the notion that the liquid conserves its quantity no matter where it is placed. If a teacher tries to convince them otherwise, they cannot internalize that concept. By listening to children and understanding how they think, teachers can better support them in their growth toward the next stage. As Voneche (2003) succinctly puts it:

"Children pay attention to what they understand or, in other words, for its existence and growth, knowledge requires internal structures in which to put it" (7). Had Piaget overlooked the "errors" and insisted that children should be made to learn what schools wanted them to learn, stick to the curriculum at all costs, he would not have discovered these cognitive processes, which now inform good educational policies. Thus, it is important for teachers to overlook their own narcissistic goals, or the goals of the school, and to pay attention to the child, especially when things are not going according to plan.

Bettelheim and Zelan (1981) point to the need to understand what the child is thinking or feeling, since the child's feelings impact learning. They, too, were interested in the errors children make—particularly those in which they are learning to read. They tell about an incident they observed when some kindergarten children were reading a story about a monkey who tries to sell a shell. They point out that the textbook is designed to teach the children the difference between "s" and "sh." One girl read the word "sell" a number of times correctly, then the word "shell" also without error. However, when she came to read the line, "I will sell the shell," she misread the line and substituted the word "sheet" for "shell." Since it was clear that the little girl could read the words correctly, they surmise:

> She had probably taken in the sentence and for some reason decided that selling the shell was not acceptable, at least not in the form the sentence demanded, which required her to say that it was she who would sell the shell . . . This speculative explanation of the misreading was supported by a discussion that had taken place earlier in the reading lesson. Several children, including the little girl, objected to the monkey's intention of selling the shell . . . They all preferred a pretty shell to any remuneration it could possibly bring. So while they comprehended what the story said, they didn't agree with it. (Bettelheim and Zelan 1981, 189)

They go on to explain the substitution of the word "sheet" by relating it to another story they had just read a short while before they read this story. In this instance, observation of the girl's emotional life helped illustrate the way in which she was learning to read. Had the word been simply corrected, the rich interconnections between the child and the story would have been missed. The assumption would have been that the child was not understanding, or was not able to read well, and perhaps the teacher would have corrected the child for her lack of progress in the curriculum, as many teachers would do. Instead, showing sensitivity toward the child's emotional response allowed her to feel understood and more likely to be forthcoming in the future.

If teachers can be allowed freedom from absolute compliance with the external goals of the curriculum and be permitted to spend more time listening and lingering in the "mistakes" they can have a richer, deeper interaction and will learn more about the child's mind. This freedom from the oppression of the curriculum can enable teachers to detach from their own narcissistic defenses. Teachers should be liberated from the role of all-knowing expert and the need to engage constantly in presenting a positive self-image. They should be able to tolerate self-doubt and model vulnerability and self-reflection to pupils. Eleanor Duckworth (1996) conducted workshops with teachers, the main goal of which was to encourage them to embrace children's mistakes as well as their own uncertainties. Of her course of study with the group of teachers, she concludes:

> The virtues involved in not knowing are the ones that really count in the long run . . . accepting surprise, puzzlement, excitement, patience, caution, honest attempts, and wrong outcomes as legitimate and important elements of learning, easily leads to their further development. (Duckworth 1996, 69)

Honesty with the self can help teachers expand their own knowledge base, since they will be comfortable with not-knowing. Sitting in the discomfort of uncertainty is a skill that teachers should be permitted to develop. Very often teachers assume they fully understand things that they are teaching, ignoring the mystery that lies at the heart of many subjects. When children keep asking questions as they naturally do, such as, "why? why? why?" and adults lean into these questions and answer to the best of their knowledge, they often come to the endpoint of their knowledge and arrive at the beginning point of wonder and curiosity. This is where learning happens. Duckworth found that teachers who learned not to be afraid of their own lack of perfect knowledge were able to be open to grow:

> After some months, we asked the teachers to take note of instances in their classrooms where a child said or did something that puzzled them—something indicating that the child's understanding was not the same as theirs. They were by then relatively free about acknowledging when they themselves did not understand something about the moon or about mathematics or whatever we had been working on together, and they had developed a level of confidence in each other that really was an essential element of this work . . . For a teacher looking honestly at what a child really understands can be a self-evaluative act; it can be seen as a measure of the teacher's own competence as a teacher (Duckworth 1996, 85).

Being able to stay in the moment, accept what the child is bringing into the classroom, and validate the child's worldview are important skills, particularly in the early childhood setting. Graue, Whyte, and Karabon (2015) studied the teaching methods in early childhood classrooms, observing that though

Early childhood education in the United States has traditionally been distinct from elementary and secondary education in its focus on child-centered practice . . . early childhood programs across the globe are increasingly standardized, with a curriculum dictated by academic standards, limited play and an assessment heavy schedule. (13)

In their paper, they maintain that the interaction between teacher and child in early childhood settings is of primary importance, and that learning occurs best when teachers utilize the "improvisational teaching" approach. Improvisation, in theatrical terms, is interactive performance characterized by spontaneity, openness to the other, the validation of the other's expression, and an invariably positive response. It is often called the "yes, and . . ." rather than the "yes, but . . ." style of interaction. The listener must really hear the intent of the speaker and validate that intent. They must be aware of what the child brings into the classroom and relate to their worldview:

Children's resources from their outside-of-school lives should also inform how teachers respond to children. Children's FoK (funds of knowledge) can often be seen bubbling up into classrooms, but knowing what to do to build on such knowledge can be difficult for teachers. (Graue, Whyte, and Karabon 2015, 17)

The difficulties teachers face in accepting the child's world rather than imposing their own cultural and acquired values are illustrated by examples of the teaching styles of two teachers, one of whom, Mrs. C., is comfortable improvising with children, and the other, Mrs. A., whose approach is dictated by an agenda:

Gary, Tommy, Charlie and Carson were playing on the carpet. They used the bristle blocks to make "battery chargers" that were flying in the air. Tommy said, "Your vitamin D is out." Charlie replied, "All of my battery is out." The boys flew the structures around and made blasting sounds. When Mrs. A approached and asked, "Tommy, what is vitamin D?" Tommy said, "Nothing." Mrs. A walked away. The boys continued to play on the carpet. Tommy added two large yellow cubes onto his structure and said, "I now have 2 vitamin D bombs." When Charlie says, "I don't have any vitamin D" he drops his structure to the floor and makes an explosion sound . . . In this example, we see a lack of connection between Mrs. A and the children. Mrs. A made a bid to enter the boys' play, the bid fell flat. Why? The children are not used to involving Mrs. A in their play—she presented them with an unexpected script. The way that she tried to enter play is by using a known response question—an informal test of child knowledge. (Graue, Whyte, and Karabon 2015, 119)

By comparison, Mrs. C. incorporates the children's thoughts and imaginings into her interactions:

"What does your name start with?" Ryan answered timidly, "An R?" Mrs. C agreed and watched while he wrote his name. "Okay Ryan, go put this in your Batcave and then people will know that you made it and if they want to add something to it that they have to ask you." Ryan ran off to the block area, smiling, but quickly returned, asking if Mrs. C would help him write the word 'Batman.' . . . Mrs. C makes a considered decision to make Batman and his Batcave a part of the classroom because Ryan is a Batman expert. She considers popular culture like superheroes to be one aspect of children's FoK and therefore a tool for teaching and learning . . . She does not hammer away at children's play pounding content into it. (Graue, Whyte, and Karabon 2015, 19)

In these instances, Mrs. C. was able to let go of her attachment to curriculum and orthodoxy. She was able to teach the child from the inside, so to speak. Mrs. A. is unable to see how a child might envision Vitamin D as a source of power, like a battery, instead being compelled to impart her own knowledge. Akhtar (2013) points to Nosek's description of the problems with adherence to acquired knowledge, describing it as "violence":

If we are prepared to forego the violence of knowledge, if we are not incited by the urgency of ontology and the power of positivism, we encounter the territory of hospitality: this means receiving the foreigner as such, allowing him his own existence . . . For us psychoanalysts, this is a radical hierarchical reflection: psychoanalysis is no longer a talking cure but a listening cure. (145)

The "violence of knowledge" refers to the defense mechanism that teachers may use in protecting against the transference and countertransference that occur in the classroom, as in all human situations.

According to Sherry, Warner, and Kitchenham (2021): "Freud popularly referred to teaching as the 'impossible profession,' thus acknowledging the complicated unconscious emotional dynamics present in the teacher-student relationship and anxiety felt by teachers to effect change in their students" (136). Negative feelings such as anger and hatred can present as dangerous to a teacher, whose traditional role dictates a supportive, benevolent approach. West, eds. (2012), points out that unconscious negative feelings, or countertransference, when not acknowledged by the teacher, can negatively impact the classroom:

When Winnicott (1949) writes about countertransference, he takes hatred into consideration. He claims that a real relationship cannot exist unless it includes hate and love simultaneously. However, people usually consider hatred as a dangerous feeling, capable of ruining everything; therefore, it needs to be disavowed. However, as Winnicott points out, when hatred is denied, it is enacted in a variety of forms. As in the case of these schools, where the teachers cannot accept the existence of feelings of hatred and are, therefore, stuck. (114)

Instruction in the meaning of transference and countertransference would be a very important aspect of teacher training. Teachers need to understand that they are allowed to be human with a wide range of emotions and to be open to the child's feelings as well. As Bainbridge and West, eds., (2012) say:

> once the teacher is aware of the dimension of a dynamic unconscious, such as countertransference, they will be able to adjust their attitudes towards their students. The teacher's view of the student's behaviour will be less dependent simply on the transferential relationship and include a consideration of their feelings and responses. (106)

Fortunately, there are many teachers who, though not trained in psychoanalysis, are naturally able to use their negative experiences to connect on a deeper level with children. These teachers can overcome the pressures to conform to an imperfect system. Through resilience, they manage to incorporate their own negative experiences and use them to benefit others. Sherry, Warner, and Kitchenham (2001) conducted studies in which they interviewed teachers about their experiences of transference and countertransference in the classroom. Some teachers had a hard time understanding their own reactions, but others were very insightful:

> Another teacher discussed both triggers and her own schooling in relation to countertransference: "School was hell; nobody had the right to treat a child the way I was treated, humiliated, and I didn't want that to happen to anybody else. [. . .] It was things like that, the humiliation, the denigration, the physical punishment that nobody had the right to treat another person that way and I knew I was smart, I just couldn't get it out. [. . .] And there are things that I have experienced over my lifetime . . . that make me sensitive to what they are thinking and what they are feeling." (147)

As Kohut (1988) says, teachers can in fact: "refine and work out a new kind of psychological life" (175). Using self-reflection, the teacher can avoid the temptation to be a transmitter of approved norms, an enforcer of the curriculum, an instrument of the system. Teachers like the one mentioned above, who prioritize the thoughts and emotions of the student over the orthodoxy of the system, can embrace their own individual experiences and, through empathic attunement, enable school to be an embracing and transformative space for the child.

REFERENCES

Akhtar, Salman, ed. 2007. *Listening to Others: Developmental and Clinical Aspects of Empathy and Attunement.* Lanham: Jason Aronson.

Baker, Bernadette. 2004. "The Functional Liminality of the Not-Dead-Yet-Students, or, How Public Schooling Became Compulsory: A Glancing History." *Rethinking History* 8, no. 1: 5–49.

Bettelheim, Bruno, and Karen Zelan. 1981. *On Learning to Read: The Child's Fascination with Meaning.* New York: Knopf

Duckworth, Eleanor. 1972. "The Having of Wonderful Ideas." *Harvard Educational Review* 42, no. 2: 217–231.

Goleman, Daniel. 2006. *Emotional Intelligence.* New York: Bantam Books.

Graue, M. Elizabeth, Kristin Lyn Whyte, and Anne Elizabeth Karabon. 2015. "The Power of Improvisational Teaching." *Teaching and Teacher Education* 48: 13–21.

Herzog, James. 1984. "Fathers and Young Children: Fathering Daughters and Fathering Sons." *Foundations of Infant Psychiatry* 2: 335–343.

Hoffman, Stuart D. 1999. "School Texts, the Written Word, and Political Indoctrination: A Review of Moral Education Curricula in Modern Japan (1886–1997)." *History of Education* 28, no. 1: 87–96.

Illich, Ivan. 2002. *Deschooling Society.* London: Marion Boyars.

Mang, Pamela. 2005. "What is Education for?" *Independent School* 64, no. 3: 14–18.

Marsden, William E. 2000. "'Poisoned History': A Comparative Study of Nationalism, Propaganda and the Treatment of War and Peace in the Late Nineteenth and Early Twentieth Century School Curriculum." *History of Education* 29, no. 1: 29–47.

Montgomery, M. R. 1989. *Saying Goodbye: A Memoir for Two Fathers.* New York: Alfred A. Knopf.

Ornstein, Paul H. 1978. *The Search for the Self: Selected Writings of Heinz Kohut: 1950–1978.* Madison, Connecticut: International Universities Press, 1988.

Pajak, Edward. 2011. "Cultural Narcissism and Education Reform." *Teachers College Record* 113, no. 9: 2018–2046.

Pearse, Patrick H. 1916. *The Murder Machine: The Bodenstown Series No. 2.* Dublin: Irish Freedom Press.

Piaget, Jean. 2003. "50, 100 & 150 Years Ago." *Scientific American* 289, no. 5: 16.

Quantz, Richard A. 2003. "The Puzzlemasters: Performing the Mundane, Searching for Intellect, and Living in the Belly of the Corporation." *The Review of Education, Pedagogy & Cultural Studies* 25, no. 2: 95–137.

Sahin, Alper. 2012. "Psychoanalysis and Education: Minding a Gap." In *Psychoanalysis and Education*, edited by Alan Bainbridge and Linden West, 103–116. New York: Taylor & Francis Group.

Schwaber, Evelyne Albrecht. 2017. "The Unending Struggle to Listen: Locating Oneself within the Other." In *Listening to Others: Developmental and Clinical Aspects of Empathy and Attunement*, edited by Salman Akhtar, 17–39. Lanham: Jason Aronson.

Shearer, Branton. 2004. "Multiple Intelligences Theory After 20 Years." *Teachers College Record* 106, no. 1: 2–16.

Sherry, John, Leslie Warner, and Andrew Kitchenham. 2021. "What's Bred in the Bone: Transference and Countertransference in Teachers." *Brock Education: A Journal of Educational Research and Practice* 30, no. 1: 136–154.

Sophia Baader, Meika. 2004. "Froebel and the Rise of Educational Theory in the United States." *Studies in Philosophy and Education* 23, no. 5: 427–444.

Stolorow, Robert D. 1975. "Toward a Functional Definition of Narcissism." *The International Journal of Psycho-Analysis* 56: 179.

Voneche, Jacques. 2003. "The Changing Structure of Piaget's Thinking: Invariance and Transformations." *Creativity Research Journal* 15, no. 1: 3–9.

Winnicott, Donald. 1971. *Playing and Reality*. London: Tavistock Publications Ltd. Re-published in 2005, Oxford: Routledge Classics.

Chapter 8

Psychotherapeutic Practices Are for Everyone

Alex Collopy

All that we do in the classroom is shaped by ideas and assumptions about children, human development, and learning. Educators continuously construct and revise their theories about children throughout their training and in-service experiences in relationship with children and families. Each of us "see" children through multiple, rich, and valuable lenses. Glenda MacNaughton (2003) called these lenses our "Model of the Learner." By confronting the extent to which our ideas adhere to and depart from classical theories, we may better "build an informed position on children as learners on which to base" our teaching, as our interpretations of any theory carry implications for curriculum and instruction (MacNaughton 2003, 11). As a preschool teacher, studying psychoanalysis informed my "Model of the Learner" and in turn shook up my ideas about the purposes of early childhood education, which MacNaughton (2003) termed our "Curriculum Position." Our "Curriculum Position" includes our perceived role as educators as well as our hopes for children and society, which shape how and what we teach in formal curriculum as much as incidental learning through, for example, classroom rules and expectations.

PSYCHOANALYSIS AS A MODEL OF THE LEARNER?

To some, if not most, educators and parents, "psychoanalysis" and "psychotherapeutic" are loaded, scary words. These worries make sense. Colloquially, people misappropriate the word "psychoanalyze" as interpreting what is "wrong" with someone, often making hasty, problematic conclusions about parents and their perceived failures. So, let's get this out of the way: by that (sorely misinformed) pop definition, as a psychoanalytically oriented educator, I am not here to "psychoanalyze" children, nor am I recommending that other teachers "psychoanalyze" children. Another common public misconception is that psychoanalytic theories are only relevant to children with psychiatric diagnoses. It may surprise some to learn that psychoanalytic approaches beyond the clinic have nothing to do with diagnosis. Psychotherapeutic practices benefit everyone—not just those with identified disabilities, though it is often those children for whom everyday classroom practices have particularly urgent consequences.

Psychoanalytic theorists generally share Freud's belief that our earliest relationships shape the development of the self, and that each person has a subjective, never entirely conscious experience of the world. Psychoanalytic education scholars argue for a critical examination of how *relationships* in classrooms, and our inherently subjective experience of those relationships, might both help and hinder how we come to understand and facilitate learning (Bibby 2010; O'Loughlin 2013). I began to gravitate toward psychoanalytic theories as they offer both a lens for understanding products of those relationships and a process for navigating them, less afforded and even stifled by other theoretical orientations. Psychoanalysis provides me not only a developmental theory of mind but also a method for understanding the ways in which lifelong lived experiences newly emerge through classroom relationships, as a generative process. The ways in which we experience this process are reflected, created, and ripe for examination in the ways we choose to engage with children's emotions and behaviors. I gained insight into not only how children's inner worlds develop but also everyday psychotherapeutic approaches to supporting that development. Further, psychoanalysis provides an indispensable reflexive method for navigating the psychic and emotional labor of teaching and learning fundamentally inseparable from the ways that teachers understand and engage with children.

Misconceptions about psychoanalysis also indicate widespread lack of awareness around psychoanalytic theories and practices generated over the last century in response to anthropological and clinical critiques of Freudian theory, described earlier in this volume. Graduate courses at Penn State that privileged cross-cultural perspectives in anthropology, Reconceptualizing Early Childhood Education (RECE) (Bloch 2013; Canella 1997; Burman 2008; Farley 2018), and social-psychoanalytic Disability Studies (Goodley 2011) prepared me well to apply theories with greater caution, knowing their significant consequences for in/equity in research and school practices (MacNaughton 2003). Developmental theories, including but not limited to psychoanalysis, have been applied in ways that pathologize children's bodies and minds that fall beyond the bounds of a culturally desired norm, providing justification for the disproportionate punishment and exclusion of children with disabilities and other intersecting differences from schools. Individuals' subjective understandings and experiences may be shaped and constrained by dominant discourses about normalcy: normal bodies, normal children, and normal ways of knowing and being. Sapon-Shevin (2007) explains that a major focus of scholarship in both RECE and DSE has been flipping the script by turning the so-called "gaze" away from individual difference to instead attend to "disabling" practices in classrooms and schools, with the end goals of looking for ways to "widen the circle" of normalcy and to be inclusive of all differences. I gained greater understanding into development as a complex product of nature and nurture but also the ways in which the "normal" child is environmentally constructed, driving my curiosity about the ways in which those constructions might be disrupted and transformed through creative pedagogical practice. As my dear mentor Linda Ware highlighted, "schools typically orchestrate our earliest experiences with disability, and thus, by default, these sites manage the meaning that is made of disability through the everyday mechanisms of schooling" (2011, 255). Ware and other DSE scholars argue that disability is a difference that emerges within groups; psychoanalytic theories similarly encourage us to consider the complexity of group dynamics. Together, these theoretical orientations toward individuality, subjectivity, disability, and difference have implications for defining the "therapeutic." To the inclusive educator, individual children or disabilities are not the "problem" in need of fixing; upholding this norm would be inherently exclusionary. We might instead consider group relations as a space for reimagining disability and as a therapeutic vehicle for attending to the needs of all children. If difference is not inherent to an individual, inclusion depends on group experiences, not only on the presence of children with disabilities, on the success of intervention services, or those equally critical universally designed supports for children to succeed in mainstream classrooms.

I came to understand the nature and meaning of disability as an always dynamic difference that emerges within groups, and an inclusive community as one that is therapeutic. I define the therapeutic experience as one in which an individual has opportunities to experience themselves otherwise (O'Loughlin 2019). An inclusive classroom provides children multiple, flexible opportunities to "show up," emerge, and participate as each of their full, ever-changing selves, where everyone in the classroom values individual and shared differences and needs (Koplow 2008). In line with my "Model of the Learner," a psychotherapeutic approach to inclusion demands both "healing work" with individuals and groups of children (O'Loughlin 2019), as well as intentional and incidental opportunities to imagine and experience *difference* in new and mutable ways. But what might a psychotherapeutic approach to inclusion look like? In what follows, I reconstruct from my personal teaching journals a story about Emily, a child with an identified disability, whose emotions and behaviors I sometimes found really challenging. As an impassioned though highly anxious novice teacher, I faced multiple, competing opinions about how I ought to engage with Emily. Everyday encounters with children, and discussing those with others, made me realize incongruities between my "Model of the Learner," "Curriculum Position," and what I was actually feeling and doing in the classroom. I ultimately rejected taken-for-granted, prescriptive approaches to managing children's behavior. For me, this changed entirely what it meant to teach and to be a good, inclusive preschool teacher, leaving me with a far more challenging task.

WELCOME TO ROOM 102

On the first day of school, three-year-old Emily entered our classroom like a cyclone. Wriggling with excitement, Emily ran and hugged me with such force that I fell onto the floor. She began speed-walking through the room, knocking puzzles and trays of crayons off tables and skittering across the floor in her wake. I felt encouraged by Emily's enthusiasm and excited about the movement and messiness that brought life to a previously empty classroom.

As the morning wore on, I watched Emily's joyfulness run thin. "HEY!" she snarled angrily, as she yanked a blue car from three-year-old Ben's hands and shoved him to the ground. As Emily fled the scene, Ben sputtered, through tears, "that girl punched my arm." As I attempted to console him, I watched in my periphery as Emily ran to the book corner and sunk into a heap on the floor, sobbing. "Can we go talk to Emily together?" I asked Ben. He composed himself, shook his head stoically, and returned to playing with the toy cars.

I approached Emily, who clutched a picture book against her heaving chest. I sat down cross-legged a few feet away. Emily crawled into my lap, nuzzling my forearm and gazing up at me.

"I saw you push Ben," I told her calmly.

"Mhm," Emily nodded, "I wanted the blue car. Blue is my favorite." Her words were at first difficult for me to discern, between her tears and apparent speech impediment.

"Did you ask Ben for the car?" I asked.

"I said please! But he didn't give it to me," Emily justified.

"I wonder whether Ben also likes blue," I proposed. "Do you think he wasn't done playing with it?"

"But I wanted it," she reminded me.

I wasn't sure it would be productive to coach Emily in turn-taking or apologizing when she was so upset. Moreover, it was clear to me that Emily knew she shouldn't hit other children; she did it anyway. Emily wasn't sorry, at least not yet.

"I know you love blue. We might need to get more blue cars. Until then, we have to share," I told her.

"Please read this to me, Miss Alex," she said, abruptly changing the conversation. As I read, Emily traced the edges of the pages with her finger. Occasionally, she interrupted to tell me about books she enjoys with her grandmother. By the time we finished reading, Emily's crying had subsided, and she excitedly returned to join the growing group playing with cars.

Such peer conflicts weren't at all unusual in my previous experience as a nanny and teacher. I reassured myself knowing Emily was an only child, on her first day of preschool—surely an adjustment period. I didn't imagine that day how Emily's emotions would escalate. Most mornings, my assistant teacher Jill and I moved throughout the room, following Emily's desperate shouts and consoling children she battled in pursuit of each blue toy. We attempted to facilitate turn-taking and considered how we might be more proactive in supporting Emily, whose behaviors we found difficult to anticipate. Emily seemed to operate in two extremes, with little middle ground. When Emily wasn't angry or devastated, she was profusely affectionate. She hugged other children so roughly that they often sought shelter by my side.

At pick-up time, I cringed hearing other children vent about Emily to their parents. It was difficult to explain to Emily and to the other children that her hugs were loving and well-intentioned but not always welcome. I tried to provide children with vocabulary to articulate this to Emily themselves. Instead, I watched, heartbroken, as children increasingly avoided playing with Emily altogether. At drop-off and pick-up time, I chatted with Emily's grandmother, who expressed surprise that Emily cried at all, given her excitement to come to school each day. She agreed that Emily might be adjusting to sharing with peers.

Emily also struggled during transitions. Each morning following circle time, I called on each child to line up along a row of wooden cubbies by the door. In front of the cubbies was a line of circle-shaped stickers labeled with numbers 1–15 in alternating colors, stuck to the floor when I'd inherited the classroom. Each morning, I watched Emily squirm, her face tense, battling tears, clearly aware that she would need to be "called on" quickly to stand on one of the two blue dots. She often rushed to a blue dot before being called on and shoved whichever children were already standing on blue dots into the cubbies. I tried calling Emily back to the carpet to wait. Each time, she crumpled to the floor hysterically and crawled under a table. In a classroom with fourteen children, I found that I alone was unable to manage the transition and console Emily at the same time. The support I had from my assistant teacher at all times was a critical luxury not afforded by many school settings. Each day after pick-up, Jill and I talked about our excitements and challenges. We discussed how we might explain to Emily that getting the blue "thing" was conditional upon waiting, and how we might support Emily in coping with her feelings when she didn't get the blue "thing." We also questioned whether sitting still was an appropriate expectation for three- and four-year-olds, and whether this discipline was at all necessary to meet learning objectives. I found myself unable to name a single legitimate reason we'd had for requiring children to sit still to earn their needs to be met—an expectation that was causing a young child significant, perhaps entirely unwarranted distress. I worried whether it was our expectations of Emily that were the problem and not Emily herself; that our classroom environment was in fact disabling.

Jill shared previous experiences she'd had of reinforcing desirable behaviors with praise. We decided to call on Emily sooner so that she would not need to wait as long, and then acknowledge her for meeting expectations. We expressed excitement to see Emily standing on the blue dot (without tackling another child on the way). For a few days, this "worked," in that Emily followed our explicit expectations. I sat in awe on one occasion when Emily earned a blue dot but ceded her spot to another child. "You go on the blue dot today," she said, "I love blue." In the following weeks, however, Emily's meltdowns returned, and we were forced to reconsider what it was that we wanted to "work." Each morning near the conclusion of choice time, I circulated the classroom to ask each group of children to clean up. In anticipation of the transition, Emily clutched desperately to a blue toy and darted beneath a table. Jill and I reminded Emily that she could join us when she was ready. Emily sometimes joined us if an activity appealed to her. She loved puppet play, dancing to 60's music, and being a "helper" by holding books during read-aloud. Some days, Emily said, "No thank you", and soothed herself as she played under the table. I realized, thinking back to my own childhood when I frequently played in cardboard boxes and blanket forts, that it must feel nice to be tucked away where no one could take her blue toy. Other days, Emily seemed inconsolable, crying with such a forceful retching quality that I worried she might become physically ill.

I winced each day observing Emily's apparent pain and wanted so badly for her to feel happy at school. I found it increasingly difficult to hold back my own tears until the school day ended and I could cry within the privacy of my car. I was also anxious that parents and administrators would think I didn't know how to handle preschoolers and was consumed with the thought (projection) that they may be right. I'd virtuously imagined myself as an emotionally responsive teacher, and it was difficult not to feel as though I were failing. Sharing my experiences with Jill and with my own psychoanalyst helped me explore my sadness and fear. Just as each child has their own subjective experience, adults have conscious and unconscious experiences of working with children that evoke a range of emotions, inevitably shaping how we see each child. While we must not ignore the critical insight afforded by our emotional responses to working with children, it is surely important that we try our best not to map our needs onto children our needs in ways that interfere with our capacity to meet their needs and to teach. A core feature of a psychotherapeutic approach is a continued practice of reflexivity, implicating ourselves in what we "see." Curiosity about children requires curiosity about ourselves with children.

SEEKING MULTIPLE PERSPECTIVES

During October parent-teacher conferences, Emily's parents shared that Emily talks only positively about school. They also shared new insight. At Emily's recent annual pediatrician appointment, they'd learned that sometime in the previous year, Emily's right cochlea had "stopped working." We wondered together whether Emily's hearing change and speech impediment may contribute to daily stress insofar as they affected communication with peers and teachers. I then met with my school director to share my concerns about Emily and what I had learned through the parent-teacher conference and invited her to observe in my classroom. The director urged me to set my feelings aside and be less permissive. She insisted that we cannot allow Emily to have the blue "thing" unless she follows directions and is not violent with her peers; otherwise, Emily's behavior would never change. My school director also suggested that other children too would think they can do whatever they want, and surely, no learning would take place.

In an attempt to gather a range of perspectives, I consulted with field experts, including Dr. Michael O'Loughlin, a professor of early childhood education and child psychotherapist. After sharing my experiences with Emily, I asked, "What should I do?" "Really, Alex?" he responded. "Give her the blue dot. Surely, you know that." Michael validated Emily's desire for the blue "thing". He encouraged me to consider how Emily was experiencing her transition to school. He pointed out that children face many demands throughout their day: getting out of bed, getting dressed, eating, and leaving caregivers to come to school. School brings new challenges, such as needing to share. Children even take bathroom trips at specific times at my school, I realized, in a shared room, no less. "What if," Michael suggested, "having the blue dot, or playing under the table, might make all of those other demands, uncertainties, challenges, more emotionally tolerable for Emily?"

Psychoanalytic theorists such as Anna Freud and Dorothy Burlingham (1944), Clare Winnicott (1955), and Donald Winnicott (1964, 1965) documented the efficacy of providing reliable environments in which children feel safe and assured that their needs will be met. Clare Winnicott (1955) named this function psychological "holding" or the "holding environment."

Recalling my director's concern that other children would believe they can get whatever they want, I considered the possibility that other children might wonder, "what about me?", or "what will happen when I want something?" I realized, listening to Michael, that the ways I respond to Emily might demonstrate for all children that our classroom was a place in which their needs and desires—however seemingly insignificant—would be taken very seriously. Reserving rewards for compliant behavior may send children the message that their desires and needs will be met on the condition that they show us only the parts of themselves we are willing to tolerate, doing little to help them tolerate those parts themselves. Trout (2020) writes similarly of the adult's role: "We *hold* those feelings, even before we know what they are. We don't react; we don't correct; we don't shame; and we don't turn away. We *hold*" (6). "Holding" requires an adult, through their behavior, to demonstrate devotion to the child (Trout 2020). "Holding" felt in line with my commitments as a teacher. In a deeply moving speech, Bill Ayers implored emerging teachers to articulate and continually reflect on their "commitments" in their work with children. "Write these on your mirror," he tells us, before offering the example of his first commitment:

> I will see every child that comes into my classroom as a person of incalculable value. I'm gonna treat that kid not as an object, not as a thing; I'm gonna treat that person as a full human being worthy of my awe, worthy of my reverence, worthy of my respect. (Faculty Academic Center of Excellence at Towson 2014)

I at first felt shame when Michael said to me, "Really, Alex? Give her the blue dot. Surely, you know that." Ayers reminds me that he, like the rest of us, has failed and will at times fail to live up to his teaching commitments, but that we need not discard them (Faculty Academic Center of Excellence at Towson 2014).

Still, Michael cautioned me to not assume what the blue things might mean to Emily, in part because unconscious experiences are never entirely observable. I was reminded of the importance of maintaining a stance of "evenly suspended attention" (Freud 1912). One of my doctoral committee members, another professor of education and child psychotherapist, Dr. Gail Boldt, echoed Michael's wondering, "What if . . . ?" She encouraged me to take up the practice of "hypothesis testing," generating many possible answers to each question I have about a child (i.e., "if . . . , then . . ."). Through a process of hypothesis testing, I might consider how each possibility may differently inform my understanding of, relationship with, and engagement with the child. Gail also insisted that I ought to hold off, in perpetuity, on answering definitively my questions about who a child is, what they are experiencing, and why; and instead dwell in wonder, thinking, and feeling. In contrast to the "therapeutic project," which values "demonstrable positive change in either patient or student," "the emancipatory project cherishes a kind of understanding for understanding's sake, a suspension on the part of the teacher and analyst of immediate judgment to be replaced by curiosity, attunement, analysis, and a focus on creating conditions such that the patient or student can generate material for further elaboration or analysis" (Taubman 2012, 7).

Thinking psychoanalytically about the unconscious mind and the practice of hypothesis testing, we cannot assume the ways in which each child will subjectively experience what we consider a reward, be that praise, opportunities, or objects, nor can we predict what children experience as punishment. We cannot definitively predict how those will be experienced and what either evokes in children. The justification for managing children's behavior and expressions of emotion with rewards, therefore, may be founded on faulty hypotheses entirely. I came to understand multiple ways in which attempts to control children's behavior, even in the interest of supporting their participation in group activities, can be both punitive and disabling. A core tenet of Disability Studies in Education is assuming competence in communication (Danforth and Naraian 2015). Though this typically refers to the range of verbal and nonverbal ways one may forge conscious communication, I see parallels here to the ways psychoanalysis suggests we think about unconscious nonverbal material. O'Loughlin (2013) proposes "recognizing behavioral manifestations and visible psychological dispositions such as anxiety, anger, oppositionality, defensiveness, clinginess, withdrawal, and so forth as mere signifiers of what lies beneath" (38). I found myself wondering, who gets to be competent? Who deserves our willingness to provide objects of desire, to hypothesis test, and to "hold"? I worry that social-emotional competence is assigned to those who make their development known to us in desirable ways, and the frequency with which children with disabilities may not. What if Emily's "undesirable" behaviors were competent communication, and exactly what warranted and demanded of us explicit, loving attention?

Rather than viewing Emily's demand for the blue dot as a result of social, emotional, or behavioral deficits, I began to consider those everyday encounters as part of a natural, productive process: that even those "negative" emotions or behaviors were indicative of Emily's strengths, and ought to be treated as such. Psychoanalysis challenges the idea that compliance indicates development, social-emotional learning, or well-being. Compliance may suggest to an observer that children have learned social norms and expectations, but children's subversion of those expectations inherently reflects equal awareness. Compliance does not indicate that children have overcome whatever fear, anger, and anxieties we suspect may be causing their behavior, but instead may stifle their ability to do so. With reverence to "the utter difficulty of being in the classroom," Bibby (2010) proposed the early childhood classroom as a space where children have the invaluable opportunity to push boundaries, struggle, resist learning, and feel things toward teachers and peers (2). Outbursts and refusal or perceived inability to follow instructions might be understood as meaning-making processes, as development. Compliance may not at all indicate what I believe was most necessary for children to learn, but instead the opposite. Behavioral interventions may dismiss children's needs in ways that needlessly, and quite cruelly, exacerbate the very conditions from which their behaviors and emotions emerge. "If being a certain way produces difficulty for the child," Michael had previously written, "it would seem that a space that values unconstrained being might prove advantageous in promoting the possibility of becoming" (O'Loughlin 2013, 33). Drawing from his experience in clinical practice, he proposed "the provision of a facilitative space with minimal demand is most likely to prove useful in allowing the child the opportunity to articulate desire, or, at a minimum, voice the pressures of external parental or teacher demand" (2013, 33). This shaped my Curriculum Position, recognizing this "facilitative space" (O'Loughlin 2013) as a "standard of experience" (Katz 2007) that children can and ought to be afforded in preschool. Following Michael and Gail's respective advice, I wanted to value what the blue object and the space under the table afforded Emily and to preserve those materials and spaces as tools Emily might use to explore and meet her needs without any demand to verbalize them.

From then on, we saved a blue dot for Emily every day. She was still challenged to wait patiently, which we understood as an opportunity early school experiences afford that may benefit children. We did not always call on Emily to line up first, but we kept an eye on the two blue dots and made sure to call on her while there was still one available to be claimed. We anticipated that Emily might still get upset and run to hide under the table sometimes, and she did. Jill and I began taking turns leading circle time, while the other calmly approached the table where Emily found refuge. "Would you like me to join you?" one of us would ask. Sometimes Emily shouted "NO" as her crying intensified. Other times, Emily welcomed us under the table, often dictating our roles in imaginative play using cars and dinosaurs in a range of colors while she held the blue.

The other children were watching, though none complained or refused to follow expectations. Some children observed casually that Emily was "not with us yet" or "over there playing again." I asked the children questions such as "What do you think Emily is doing over there?" and "Are there spaces in the classroom you want to explore?" Many children remained uninterested; others shared their curiosity and ideas. Several, within just a few weeks and without any direct guidance, proactively engaged with Emily themselves, mirroring Jill's and my approach. One morning, I sat at a table with children painting with watercolors. I felt bumping against my shins and looked under the table to see Emily and two boys playing joyfully with dinosaurs. This continued during circle times, when a child would raise their hand excitedly to offer, "Emily might want to play with me," "I'll go check on Emily!" or "Can I invite Emily to circle?"

I began to observe how the blue things and the table provided a therapeutic space for Emily as an individual, but also for our group. Or really, it was Emily who provided us these opportunities, using the blue things and the table. Naraian (2008) argued that students with and without disabilities benefit from new opportunities to engage with each other in the classroom as those encounters have the potential to generate new narratives about children, disability, and difference. Goodley (2013) explains, "disabled bodies challenge normative ideas of able bodies. This can be productive. Indeed impaired embodiment demands new, inclusive and potentially exciting forms of response from others" (635). Behavior beyond the "norm", such as Emily's meltdowns or her hiding under the table, seemed to do the same. Emily was no longer the child who wouldn't behave; this was no longer a question of whether her behavior—or the underlying mechanisms—could be remediated. When I began to think and respond differently to children's anger, sadness, and physical conflict, children had new opportunities themselves to improvisationally engage with peers' everyday speech and behaviors. Our classroom became more of a "communal commonplace . . . in which individual and group emotional and intellectual work is possible" (O'Loughlin 2013, 38). Danforth and Naraian (2015) defined inclusive education not as "an outcome that must be achieved," but rather, "a process that is always ongoing, continual, and by extension, unfinished" (72), as is too the "emancipatory project" of psychoanalysis (Taubman 2012).

I saw first-hand why Object Relations pioneers Clare and Donald Winnicott prioritized *how* we are *with* children over what we *do to* children (Trout 2020). Koplow (2002, 2008) argues this stance is critical for teachers to become "therapeutic partners" to children; I learned from children that becoming a therapeutic partner also supports children to become therapeutic partners with each other—partners navigating difference. This felt like the real work of supporting development insofar as children led new opportunities for meaning-making. Teachers are not therapists, but we can build environments that better support children to work through rather than repress what had been and had yet to be verbalized. Adopting psychoanalytic practices of reflexivity and not-knowing, listening, holding, and *being with* benefits not only a child deemed in need of intervention but all of us. I believe that all early childhood educators have an ethical obligation to build therapeutic classroom communities in which healing is possible—not just for children with disabilities but for all children and adults, not just for each individual, but for the group.

REFERENCES

Bibby, Tamara. 2010. *Education-an 'Impossible Profession'?: Psychoanalytic Explorations of Learning and Classrooms*. New York: Routledge.

Bloch, Marianne. 2013. "Reconceptualizing Theory/Policy/Curriculum/Pedagogy in Early Child (Care and) Education: Reconceptualizing Early Childhood Education (RECE) 1991–2012." *International Journal of Equity and Innovation in Early Childhood* 11, no. 1: 65–85.

Burman, Erica. 2008. *Deconstructing Developmental Psychology*. New York: Routledge.

Danforth, Scot, and Srikala Naraian. 2015. "This New Field of Inclusive Education: Beginning a Dialogue on Conceptual Foundations." *Intellectual and Developmental Disabilities* 53, no. 1: 70–85.

Faculty Academic Center of Excellence at Towson. 2014. "To Teach. A Talk and Discussion with William Ayers." May 6, 2014. *YouTube*. https://www.youtube.com/watch?v=Pfc5dLWSTZo.

Freud, Anna, and Dorothy T. Burlingham. 1943. *War and Children*. New York: Medical War Books.

Freud, Sigmund. 1912. "Recommendations to Physicians Practicing Psycho-Analysis." In *The Standard Edition of the Complete Psychological Works of Sigmund Freud Volume XII (1911–1913)*, edited by James Strachey, 109–120. London: Hogarth Press and Institute of Psychoanalysis.

Goodley, Dan. 2013. "Dis/entangling Critical Disability Studies." *Disability & Society* 28, no. 5: 631–644.

Katz, Lilian G. 2007. "Standards of Experience." *Young Children* 62, no. 3: 94.

Koplow, Lesley. 2002. *Creating Schools That Heal: Real-life Solutions*. New York: Teachers College Press.

Koplow, Lesley. 2008. *Bears, Bears Everywhere!: Supporting Children's Emotional Health in the Classroom*. New York: Teachers College Press.

MacNaughton, Glenda. 2003. *Shaping Early Childhood: Learners, Curriculum, and Contexts*. Maidenhead: Open University Press.

Naraian, Srikala. 2008. "Institutional Stories and Self-Stories: Investigating Peer Interpretations of Significant Disability." *International Journal of Inclusive Education* 12, nos. 5–6: 525–542.

O'Loughlin, Michael, ed. 2013. *The Uses of Psychoanalysis in Working with Children's Emotional Lives*. Plymouth: Jason Aronson.

O'Loughlin, Michael. 2019. "Engaging Children in Healing Work." In *The Importance of Play in Early Childhood Education*, edited by Marilyn Charles and Jill Bellinson, 213–227. New York: Routledge.

Sapon-Shevin, Mara. 2007. *Widening the Circle: The Power of Inclusive Classrooms*. Boston: Beacon Press.

Taubman, Peter Maas. 2012. *Disavowed Knowledge: Psychoanalysis, Education, and Teaching*. New York: Routledge.

Trout, Michael. 2020. "The Centrality of 'Holding' in Infant Mental Health." Unpublished manuscript.

Ware, Linda. 2011. "Disability Studies in Education." In *Handbook of Research in the Social Foundations of Education*, edited by Steven Tozer, Bernardo P. Gallegos, Annette Henry, Mary Bushnell Freiner, and Paula Groves Price, 244–260. New York: Routledge.

Winnicott, Clare. 1955. "Casework Techniques in the Child Care Services." In *Face to Face with Children: The Life and Work of Clare Winnicott*, edited by Joel Kanter, 145–165. London: Karnac.

Winnicott, Donald Woods. 1964. *The Child, the Family, and the Outside World.* London: Penguin Books.

Winnicott, Donald Woods. 1965. *The Maturational Processes and the Facilitating Environment: Studies in the Theory of Emotional Development.* London: Hogarth Press Ltd.

Chapter 9

The Essential Role of Play in Early Childhood Education

Joanna Fortune

The idea of psychoanalysis in educational environments is certainly not a new or radical consideration. I would like to take a brief look at its origins to then consider how we might apply this learning to the modern classroom and what that might look like.

Sigmund Freud's identification of adult neurosis as having infantile roots sparked a keen interest in the role psychoanalysis could have in early years education. That said, psychoanalysis has never really had a particularly "easy" relationship within educational settings. In the 1920s, Freud wasn't so much speaking about the psychoanalysis *of* younger children as he was about applying psychoanalytic theory to the upbringing of young children. Freud wrote, "none of the applications of psychoanalysis has excited so much interest and aroused so many hopes, and none, consequently, has attracted so many capable workers as its use in the theory and practice of education" (Freud 1925, vii).

But it was Anna Freud, a trained teacher before she was a psychoanalyst, who worked extensively with teachers in classroom environments and was passionate about what a psychoanalytically informed pedagogy might look like. As a result, she was actively involved with the twentieth-century's progressive education movement in Vienna and later the United Kingdom. Anna Freud was heavily influenced by the work of Italian pedagogue Maria Montessori, and her work was very child-centered as a result. But Montessori was never interested in psychoanalysis and so it was people like August Aichhorn, the Austrian educator (in particular with juvenile delinquency) and psychoanalyst, and Siegfried Bernfeld, whose Baumgarten experiment, where he was pioneering a psychoanalytically informed educational environment where children could be "helped" rather than "controlled," and though a flawed and short-lived experiment, it was nonetheless greatly influential in Anna Freud's

173

later work with the Hampstead War Nurseries, who supported her interest in bridging the gap between early years education and psychoanalysis.

In the mid-1920s, Anna Freud was running a weekly reading group on the topic of psychoanalysis and education, and by 1927 she was ready to roll out her own educational experiment, The Matchbox School. Erik Erikson, working as an artist at the time, taught at this school and indeed wrote about this in his 1930 and 1931 publications. The school ran until 1932 but had a maximum number of twenty children, all from privileged society backgrounds. The school was influenced and informed by psychoanalytic thinking and though the teachers did not analyze their students many were in analysis, some with Anna Freud herself.

Anna Freud held the view that

> learning always takes place in the context of an emotional relationship, so that the necessary frustrations of learning are compensated for by the feeling of approval that comes first from others, and later from within in the form of the superego. (Midgely 2008, 38).

Again, we see how she was influenced by August Aichhorn here, as he also strongly asserted that a positive attachment between the young person and the adult seeking to teach or guide them should be fostered so that they could really address their frustration and access the "work." She remained invested in how psychoanalytic theory could support teachers in the classroom setting throughout her career and continued to write and lecture on this topic.

Melanie Klein viewed play as having an important role in child development and in particular in how children learn to communicate. Consider Melanie Klein's "The Psychoanalytic Play-Technique: Its History and Significance" (1955) in which she looks back on her early work with children during the 1920s. In this publication, Klein details how her "play technique" was conceived as a way for children to express their anxieties and unconscious thoughts, feelings, and desires. At this time, Klein viewed the interpretation of children's play akin to the interpretation of an adult's dreams in psychoanalysis because of the way she saw symbolic language saturating every aspect of their toys and games: *the brick, the little figure, the car, not only represent things which interest the child in themselves, but in his play with them, they always have a variety of symbolic meanings as well* (Klein 1955, 137) Play for Klein was a serious form of meaning-making, often compulsive, repetitive, and anxious, with its own syntax, rules, and narrative conventions. She saw it as central to how children learn and develop.

Philip Graham (Graham 2008), in writing about the Malting Schools and Susan Isaacs' role in developing this model between 1924 and 1929 quotes Melanie Klein (Klein 1921) when he refers to her insistence that children needed to be "protected from any over-strong repression of their natural impulses in order to prevent subsequent mental illness or distortion of character development." I understand that Klein was writing about the repression of children's sexuality, but I wonder if we were to take this idea and consider play as the most natural impulse a child has, could we not consider her viewpoint as relevant in advocating for more play-based learning environments in the education of children?

Graham goes on to consider that Klein's 1921 paper on the education of children was heavily influential to Susan Isaacs' establishment of the Maltings School (with the support of Geoffrey Pyke, who was seeking a permissive educational environment for his son). Isaacs was a primary school teacher and also a psychoanalyst, and drawing on the work of not only Klein but also early years education experts like Froebel and Findlay, she was motivated to establish a school rooted in individualized learning. Graham writes of the Maltings School,

> The striking feature of her description of the school is the lack of any mention of classrooms, and in fact there were none. However, there was plenty of space in the garden and an abundance of stimulating equipment whose use the children could explore for themselves. In the garden there was a sandpit with a water tap, a tool-shed, a summer house with roof and open sides, a see-saw (which had detachable weights hung at intervals underneath), sliding boards, movable ladders, and a "Jungle-gym" climbing cage. (Graham 2008, 10)

Graham's paper details the workings of the Maltings School and the pros and cons to it are apparent, notably the critique by James Stratchey. For instance, the school had only twenty students, most of whom came from privileged, professional academic families (as was also the case in Anna Freud's Matchbox School) and taught more boys than girls over its tenure. It also involved separating very young children from their parents for term-time, which can seem shocking given its stated ethos but must bear in mind that the weight we now afford the parent-child connection was not realized at that time by the majority. In reading about this school, I wondered if there was confusion between structure (flexible and adaptable) and what was rigidity (rules with strict consequences) and if the apparent lack of boundaries for such young children might have created a lack of inner-state felt-safety. But I am interested in how the environment was structured. What is described above is an environment geared toward learning through play and Susan Isaacs understood that young children largely learn through play. Her focus on play and spontaneity influenced the work of Piaget, who visited the Maltings School in 1927 to observe the children learning in an unstructured environment. While the school ultimately closed due to lack of funding, Isaacs' influence over early childhood education continued, with her books used in teacher education programs for decades after (Isaac 1933).

Now, one hundred years later, we see that play has a more overt and mainstream place in early years education, but I wonder if we could develop a more integrated way of utilizing play within children's formal learning environments, i.e., schools.

> Learning depends on the capacity for [the growing container] to remain integrated and yet lose rigidity. This is the foundation of the state of mind of the individual who can retain his knowledge and experience and yet be prepared to reconstrue past experiences in a manner that enables him to be receptive of a new idea. (Bion 1962, 93)

In Irish early years education, we have a play-based program embedded within all early years education settings from birth to six years of age. This program is called *Aistear*[1], which is an Irish word for "journey," the idea being that this was a new direction or journey in how we educate young children. The program uses four interconnected themes to describe children's learning and development. These are: wellbeing; identity and belonging; communication; and exploring/thinking.

The aims of the Aistear program are very solid. The child is viewed as being capable and confident, learning best in collaboration with the adult educator. This was a big change when it was first introduced into Irish schools in 2009, shifting thinking and practice from a pure Montessori framework where the adult was the person to initiate and facilitate the child's learning, and the child learned best through structured (albeit fun) tasks. This program advocated a more overt play-based approach to early years education, asserting that play *is* the work of children and it is through play that they learn. It placed the child at the center of their own learning, viewing them as a co-leader in their own learning and development. Now the educator was not the one with all the answers but was the person who would co-construct a playful environment for the child to play and thereby work it out for themselves. This was a move toward child-led play in educational settings. It sounds wonderful, and in theory, it is, but in practice there have been and continue to be inconsistencies. Why would play-based learning end at six years old? Many educational settings have demarcated "Aistear time" or "Aistear room" so that the fully play-based learning is not really integrated into the environment but is apart from it or facilitated within a more adult-led learning environment. It also relies on a playfully minded adult, and that is certainly not an assumption that can be made across all early years educators. Another challenge this program faces in being truly effective is that it is also intended for use at home, but there is very limited interaction between early years education settings (including primary schools) and parents in terms of introducing parents to the program and how to facilitate this kind of play at home.

I am describing this program merely to show that there is a greater awareness of the essential role that play has, or should have, in our children's education. It shows that there is a growing awareness of the interplay between cognitive learning and emotional states of mind. It is no longer a case of designated play-based schools but of play being embedded within all early years education settings. However, what a program cannot prescribe is a playful state of mind. Play is not a corner of a classroom, nor is it an hour of the school day, nor is it a box of toys or props. Play is, moreover, a state of mind and a way of being. This is where I believe that psychoanalysis has a lot to contribute to developing more play-based approaches to formal educational environments.

A playful approach to educating young children starts with the mind of the adult teaching those children. In this way, play cannot be prescribed in a program as it should fill the environment. The words we use, our prosodic vocalizations, our use of pitch, pace, pause, and general musicality of our voices and in our facial expressions and use of humor are all evidence of a playful state of mind.

In other words, *it is play that is universal* and that belongs to health:

> playing facilitates growth and therefore health; playing leads into group relationships; playing can be a form of communication in psychotherapy; and lastly, psychoanalysis has been developed as a highly specialized form of playing in the service of communication with oneself and others. (Winnicott 1971, 41)

Consider how transformative this could be within the classroom setting, in terms of how a more playful approach to learning facilitates children's development and supports group functioning.

> Being in play, being in the state of mind that says, "I wonder what might happen if I tried this" and then not worrying or being afraid of the outcome, is a state of mind that can cope with the unexpected. It can also teach us that we can change the rules. (Rosen 2019, 20)

If we embrace a playful state of mind in terms of how we parent our children (Fortune 2018) but also how we educate them, we are modelling what neuro-psychiatrist Allan Schore (Schore 2003a, 2003b) describes as *affect regulation* and Ed Tronick refers to as *meaning-making* (Tronick and Beeghly 2011). I am referring to the process of modulating the range of the child's emotional experiences so that they contribute to his/her growing sense of self as a person and do not disrupt too much this developing sense of self. Tronick and Beeghly (2011, 107–119) also highlight dyadic meaning-making and reparation between parent and child (I would assert this can also be applied to the relationship and connection between teacher and child though), saying, "the infant-adult meaning-making system is a dyadic, mutually regulated communicative system in which there is an exchange of each individual's meanings, intentions, and relational goals—what we call the mutual regulation model" (Tronick and Beeghly 2011, 111).

Referring back to Bion and his container/contained model (Bion 1962) quoted above for a moment, we can consider how children can experience struggles in learning if they are unable to integrate the function of self-containment. If struggles with learning persist over a period of time, a child can (and will) become anxious and avoidant within the educational setting, which is likely to result in disengagement from the learning environment. When Bion wrote of the function of containment within the parent-infant relationship, he described how the role of the parent is to understand and connect with the infant's emotional state enough to be able to make meaning of their feelings and reflect this meaning back to the infant so that the infant can *begin* to internalize an understanding of their own emotional world.

The infant's life, and later the child's and teenager's life, is made up of moment-to-moment connections and disconnections between the child and those who are with them. This is usually their parents and family members but can also include childminders or teachers. The process of emotional regulation is an ongoing one with mutual regulation of mental/affective states between the child and parent. They can and will each regulate each other's mental states as they move through an emotional regulatory rollercoaster of waves of highs and lows (in synch, out of synch, and getting back into synch) throughout the day together. These moments of disconnection are not harmful; in fact, they bring significant pro-social gains for the child and the relationship between the child and the caregiving adult, as long as they are followed promptly by re-connection. This emotional regulatory rollercoaster helps expand the window of tolerance for both the child and the adult—that is, the state of optimal arousal where we feel calm, confident, and regulated.

When a child is successfully co-regulated by the available caregiving adult (a parent at home, a teacher in school), they feel safe. When they feel safe, they can learn. With his polyvagal theory (that is the science of safety), Stephen Porges (Porges 2017; Porges and Dana 2018) emphasizes the transformative power of feeling safe in our relationships with others and places a high emotional value on emotional connection over behavioral correction. Play is an excellent way to achieve this type of *correction within connection* outcome.

I interpret play as a relational but also as a neural experience. In his polyvagal theory, Porges emphasizes the importance of understanding our own autonomic nervous system (ANS) so that we can travel the ANS pathways in a more fluid and connected way. Without being able to do this, we will get stuck with one ANS state of arousal and rather than travel ANS pathways of connection, we are traveling pathways of protection that do not serve us well, as they disconnect us from the world and people around us. Porges (2011) highlights how our biological health depends on a flexible nervous system, so that survival is not so much of the fittest as it is of the most adaptable amongst us. Play fuels flexibility and adaptability. Play drives connection to self, others, and the world around us. If we want to raise healthy, connected, and flexible young people, we must explore more overt ways to integrate play and playfulness into all aspects of their lives and from the youngest ages.

Play and playfulness are a lovely combination of the ventral state's safety and regulation with the activation/mobilizing energy of our sympathetic state of arousal, with a lovely overlap between the two states. We require ventral energy to connect with others. This is precisely what keeps us connected to ourselves, others, and the world around us. Play calls for sympathovagal balance, which is a blending of both ventral and sympathetic pathways. Polyvagal theory supports a playful state of mind in how playfulness enables us to increase our capacity for vagally mediated Heart Rate Variability (HRV); that is the more variance between the beat/between beats, the greater our degree of flexibility. Polyvagal theory asserts that HRV may serve as a global index of flexibility and adaptability to stressors.

Bion (1967) believed (within his theory of thinking model) that if the infant can integrate their primitive anxieties, then their mind can absorb/integrate new experiences and ideas, resulting in a greater drive toward fresh thinking and new learning. He asserted that the capacity to think arises from being thought about.

We should be encouraging connection between children and their teachers. In an opinion piece published in *The New York Times*, journalist (and retired teacher) David Brooks (Brooks 2019) writes that *students learn from people they love*. In this piece, he refers to the work of cognitive scientist Antonio Damasio, who researched how emotion is essential to learning, and he says that if we want our students to learn, we must give them new things to love. In writing about the relationship between emotion and learning and the neuroscience surrounding this research, he says,

> It reminded us that what teachers really teach is themselves—their contagious passion for their subjects and students. It reminded us that children learn from people they love, and that love in this context means willing the good of another, and offering active care for the whole person.

He goes on to refer to the work of "Suzanne Dikker of New York University who has shown that when classes are going well, the student brain activity synchronizes with the teacher's brain activity. In good times and bad, good teachers and good students co-regulate each other." If people don't care about each other, then nothing will happen. And yet, schools do not have a metric for measuring the emotional quality of the connection between their teachers and students. This is not something that is monitored per se. But play is a great way of gaining insight into this. Play is a relational activity; it fuels connection. Classrooms that are inherently playful, that is to say that play is in the environment and not a designated hour of the day, are spaces where we see connectivity, curiosity, and learning.

Sue Stuart-Smith writes (of gardening but I am relating it to play in this instance as that is how this resonated with me when I read it in her book),

> The past and the present become more or less merged through dwelling on old hurts and the inward turn of the mind means it feels as if "everything" is happening to you. The experience of slow time has an important role to play in counteracting this. Slow time does not mean doing things more slowly . . . slow time is entering into a relationship with the present. (Stuart-Smith 2020, 247)

Now, re-read this sentence replacing the word "slow time" with "play-time." She also writes in this chapter on how finding a safe container for feeling things in nature (again I would substitute the word "play" for "nature" here to feel the crossover relevance) can be the start of a process that eventually helps people move on (Stuart-Smith 2020, 246). Nature nourishes the nervous system because nature is an activator of the ventral vagus nerve, which is where we feel safest and most regulated/connected.

In a broadcast conversation (Freud Museum London, October 13, 2021) between psychoanalysts Lisa Appignanesi and Adam Phillips to promote his book *The Cure for Psychoanalysis* (Phillips 2021), Adam Phillips described himself as very committed to play because it makes anything possible, adding that he viewed play as an extraordinary medium because to be absorbed in play is to forget yourself, to lose yourself in the connection of mutual play and that it is this very experience that is the essence of unconscious communication.

In so many ways, play feels so essential in the education and development of children that it makes me wonder why it is so often an aspect of education that is misunderstood and misused, even dismissed as a nice extra for children to have rather than a core requirement of the education program. I wonder if this comes back to what Winnicott saw as "the enemy of the aliveness that is the potential of development" (Phillips 2021, 27), that is, *compliance.* Referencing Winnicott's specific definitions of both playing and reality, Phillips says, "the reality principle facilitates playing; playing gets us to reality in acceptable ways. Playing and reality collaborate and cooperate . . . makes them mutually enlivening." From here he wonders, "can it [Winnicott's definition of reality] also free you to be more playful and less intimidated, and therefore less intimidating?" (Phillips 2021, 27). Later, in this same chapter, Phillips refers to Winnicott's view that to assume well-brought-up children will be, somehow, less trouble is a glib assumption to make. "trouble here is clearly deemed to be no bad thing. If children are brought up well, in this story, they will become less controllable, less obedient, less predictable, less compliant. Free to restate, reformulate, rediscover" (Phillips 2021, 31).

Josh Cohen in his book *How to Live. What to Do* writes,

This chasm between adult and child is as much a problem for adults as it is for children. The Hungarian psychoanalyst Sándor Ferenczi called it a "confusion of tongues"; adults and children seem to speak the same language but are separated by a cognitive and emotional chasm that mires them in permanent misunderstanding. The child's world is too elastic and excitable, the adult's too rule-bound and repressed. The child doesn't yet know what an adult mind is like, the adult has forgotten what it is to inhabit a child's mind. (Cohen 2021, 5)

Maybe the idea that opening oneself up to emotionally connect with all of one's students and promoting play, curiosity, and wondering on the premise of mutual enlivening results in less compliant children who will not be "less trouble" in the classroom setting gives many early-years educators cause to pause and wonder if a more rigid and rule-based learning environment might not be easier to manage. I can understand that; I don't share the view, but I can appreciate where such a point of view might stem from. I work a lot with parents, and promoting playful parenting at home with just a small number of their own children can be a challenge, so imagine applying this thinking to a crowded classroom of up to thirty young children, all coming from different home environments into your classroom. And so, I wonder if there might be a play protocol that is very suited to the classroom setting, that is child-focused and promotes curiosity, empathy, creativity, and connection through co-regulation that is in fact led by the teacher and, while not at all rigid, is structured (holding in mind that structure here is an approach that embraces flexibility and adaptability; it bends without breaking).

Sunshine Circles is an adaptation of the Theraplay Training Institute's Group Theraplay protocol that is suitable for classroom settings and was launched in 2013. These are teacher-led play groups that last twenty to thirty minutes per session, and a session can be done weekly or more often than that. I view Sunshine Circles as aligned with Winnicott's ideals of playing and reality.

> While Sunshine Circles are teacher-directed play groups, we lead activities in a uniquely playful manner so that everyone in the group will have fun together. We lighten up our teaching style by using playful cue words . . . another way we lighten up is to intentionally avoid teaching academic content or classroom rules during Sunshine Circles. Instead, we focus on helping students feel the joy of personal interactions and playfulness by showing delight in our students as we play with them. When both students *and* adults have fun together, the group is successful because playfulness, itself, has a positive effect on a person's state of mind. (Schieffer 2019, 20)

Sunshine Circles is a right here, right now, way of connecting. No one needs to earn their way into the group play, and no one is excluded from the group. This way of playing is inclusive, intentionally accepting, and positive. And just as Winnicott advocated, "trouble" here is not deemed to be a bad thing.

> When students have difficulty participating or behave in a challenging way during play, we provide guidance in a consciously positive manner to help them to remain engaged. . . . The key is the tone of voice we use and the expression on our face rather than the words we say. . . . While we teachers tend to think in the behavioural methods of reward and consequences, the reward to students for participating in Sunshine Circles is the positive feeling they experience about themselves and the group. . . . Responding in a positive manner to a student's problem behaviours doesn't mean that we don't set firm limits and use clear structure in Sunshine Circles. Let's take a moment to discuss why we think it is so important to use positive methods of guiding students rather than strictly behavioural methods. . . . When teachers offer rewards or institute warning systems into play times, they have to focus on helping children repress impulses as well as teach substitute behaviours. This puts the teacher in the position of judging behaviour and implementing behaviour intervention plans rather than focusing on play. (Schieffer 2019, 21)

In Sunshine Circles, play and, moreover, the connections play enables are the catalyst for behavioral change. This is what Phillips meant when he said we must "relinquish our authority in the name of something more mutual" (Appignanesi and Phillips 2021). In this same conference presentation, Phillips said that the analyst starts explaining when he becomes anxious about his curiosity, emphasizing that explanation can close things. He was making reference to psychoanalysis being an experiment of living and free speech, but it brings to mind Winnicott's statement "when I am tired, I teach." Be it in parenting or teaching children, we can have ideas about what they want and need, but we must create the space for them to lean in and do their own wanting, their own needing. This is how they connect with their own desire as people who are a part of us and apart from us at the same time.

Winnicott described, "psychotherapy takes place in the overlap of two areas of playing, that of the patient and that of the therapist. Psychotherapy has to do with two people playing together" (Winnicott 1971, 38). Phillips picks up on this and adds what Winnicott referred to as "organised nonsense and unorganised nonsense, there are organised games, some of which you can win and lose, and unorganised games, which contain the possibility of inconceivable surprises" (Phillips 2021, 32).

Sunshine Circles, stemming as it does from the Theraplay therapeutic modality, is framed around four key developmental dimensions of Structure (providing inner/outer safety with clear expectations), Engagement (providing opportunities for shared joy, to see ourselves as enjoyable and to enjoy that experience), Nurture (providing opportunities to internalize that we are deserving of good care and to trust that there is someone to take care of us), and Challenge (providing opportunities to stretch ourselves beyond our (dis)comfort zone, build esteem, efficacy, and to explore what we might be capable of). All of the activities are embedded in one or a combination of these four dimensions. Again, it brings to mind what Winnicott said of psychoanalysis: "without rules there can be no improvisation, without norms there can be no surprises" (Phillips 2021, 32).

Another aspect of Sunshine Circles as a suitable play-based structure for the classroom environment is the fact that it has an evidence base and is featured in peer-reviewed studies.

Sunshine Circles is unique in its design and methods of implementation. It is based on attachment theory and is congruent with recent brain research in relation to quality of care, toxic stress, and trauma. Although other interventions are designed to help children manage the impacts of toxic stress and trauma, the authors of this study are not aware of any other interventions that harness the teacher's social engagement system in order to co-regulate with the child, improve the child's felt sense of safety, and open the sensitive neurological gate to learning via play. Emphasizing playful relational engagement in the classroom helps children to build a stronger neuroception of safety (Porges 2011). Sunshine Circles appears to be effective in improving both academic and social-emotional learning due to this focus (Tucker et al. 2021).

Many play-based programs for educational settings focus solely on early years education, the aforementioned Aistear program included. Sunshine Circles is a format that can carry children throughout their education as the activities within the framework can be amended in line with children's growing development and emotional maturity. It embraces the idea that playing has a place and a time. In describing what play is and is not, Winnicott (1971) highlights that "to control what is outside one has to *do* things, not simply to think or to wish, and *doing things* takes time. Playing is doing." It is Winnicott who tells us that play is not, as western society tends to pigeonhole it, a box of toys in the corner or scattered around the floor of a room belonging in the realm of childhood; it is a state of mind and a way of being that carries a myriad of psycho-social and emotional benefits not only for the child nor the adult caregivers in their lives but for our collective society. He writes,

> it is simply a comment on the possibility that in the total theory of the personality the psychoanalyst has been too busy using play content to look at the playing child, and to write about playing as a thing in itself. (Winnicott 1971, 40)

It is Winnicott who reminds us that play is the most basic tenet of the child's life and that to live a full adult life, we must have experienced the joy of imaginary play in childhood, that is, to have known what it is to exist in the blur between the real and imaginary worlds. I believe that Winnicott saw and embraced the relational aspects of playing and saw the connections this fueled as potentially transformative, not only in the lives of children but also in the lives of adults when the analysis was approached with a playful state of mind.

I think this psychoanalytic concept can be carried into the modern classroom both in the guise of structured play-group sessions such as Sunshine Circles, but also in the more holistic approach to teaching and connecting with children. Of course, there needs to be more rigid components to early years education such as learning to read, write, and master arithmetic, but even these more rigid lessons can be approached in a playful state of mind, utilizing prosodic vocalizations (i.e., pitch, pace, pause, and musicality of tone), undulations of voice, and of course, one's sense of humor, using a smile and playful facial expressions to draw the child in and hold their engagement for prolonged periods within this relational playful connection. The imaginative expression play affords us also provides much-needed light relief from the pressures of more stringent cognitive learning. By lowering those stress levels, we integrate what we learn. It is about using imaginative play to process real-life stresses and stretching ourselves to explore our capacity to laugh, question, wonder, imagine, and ultimately learn. Play, especially imaginative play, allows us to take control of a situation that threatens to control us, i.e., lower stress and resistance to learning. It is not enough to provide ring-fenced playtime or areas of the classroom dedicated to free play because this playful approach is most effective when it is embedded into early years education in a more inclusive and pervasive manner. Play is relational, and to be effective in strengthening outcomes in early years education, children need their teachers to embrace a playful state of mind in using play to teach them.

Psychoanalysis has an important role in education because psychoanalysis has an important role in all aspects of life. Psychoanalytic perspectives are evidently present in how early years education is conceptualized, which is not surprising given many early psychoanalysts were also trained teachers who took a special interest in how psychoanalytic theory could be applied to young children's education. From the early writings of Sigmund Freud, psychoanalysis has always emphasized the importance of early years experiences in shaping who we are and how we live.

> Psychoanalytic theory's foremost impact on early childhood education was that it pedagogically legitimized the practice of expressive experiences with young children. Young children's problem solving was essential for their mental health. They could cope and solve difficulties at their personal level through play. (Murphy 1962, quoted in Saracho 2023, 25).

And so, the idea of psychoanalysis in education and children's classroom environments is far from new but perhaps a fresh perspective on *how* this is practically achieved in mainstream classroom settings (rather than the experimental education settings of Anna Freud and Susan Isaacs) is timely. I don't think this requires something entirely new but rather looking at how the play-based modalities that are already developed and peer-reviewed might lend themselves well to the psychoanalytic perspective. In this instance, I am taking two modalities that I am certified in, psychoanalysis and Theraplay (Sunshine Circles), and outlining a clear theoretical overlap between framework and practice and how this approach supports a more play-based and relational approach to early years education that is fully inclusive and accessible in mainstream contemporary education environments.

NOTE

1. The Aistear program is currently being reviewed and updated in Ireland. My observations pertain to the original (and current) 2009 version of the program. I understand that the proposed new program is more inclusive of older ages and calls for more playful approaches to teaching across the syllabus.

REFERENCES

Appignanesi, Lisa and Adam Philips. (2021, October). *The Cure for Psychoanalysis* [Conference Presentation]. Freud Museum, London.

Bion, Wilfred. (1962). *Learning from Experience*. London: Heinemann; reprinted 1984. Karnac.

Bion, Wilfred. (1967). *Second Thoughts*. Heinemann.

Brooks, David. (2019). Students learn from people they love. *New York Times*, January 17, 2019. https://www.nytimes.com/2019/01/17/opinion/learning-emotion -education.html.

Cohen, Josh. (2021). How to live. What to do. Ebury Press UK. https://www.esri.ie /sites/default/files/media/file-uploads/2020-08/SLIDES_Lessons%20from%20the %20pandemic_MCCOY_0.pdf.

Erikson, Erik. (1931). "The fate of the drives in school compositions." In *A Way of Looking at Things: Selected Papers*, ed. E. Erikson. New York: W. W. Norton & Co.

Freud, Anna. (1930). "Four lectures on psychoanalysis for teachers and parents." In *Introduction to Psychoanalysis, Writings, Volume 1*, 73–136. Hogarth.

Fortune, Joanna. (2017a). "The 'iMirror Stage': Not-so-smartphones and the pre-schooler—some clinical observations. In *Lacanian Psychoanalysis with Babies, Children and Adolescents—Further Notes on the Child*, ed. C. Owens and S. Farrelly-Quinn, 225–234. Karnac Books.

Fortune, Joanna. (2017b, June 27). *Social Media—The Ultimate Shame Game?* [Conference Presentation]. TEDx 2017 Ha'Penny Bridge, Dublin, Ireland. https://www .youtube.com/watch?v=ORhwrL71dYc&t=36s.

Fortune, Joanna. (2018). *15-Minute Parenting: The Quick and Easy Way to Connect with Your Child*. Gill Books.

Fortune, Joanna. (2020a). *15-Minute Parenting 0–7 Years: Quick and Easy Ways to Connect with Your Child*. Thread Books.

Fortune, Joanna. (2020b). *15-Minute Parenting 8–12 Years: Stress Free Strategies for Nurturing Your Child's Development*. Thread Books.

Fortune, Joanna. (2020c). *15-Minute Parenting the Teenage Years: Creative Ways to Stay Connected with Your Teenager*. Thread Books.

Freud, Anna. (1931). *Introduction to Psychoanalysis for Teachers*. George Allen and Unwin.

Freud, Anna. (1954). "Psychoanalysis and education." In *The Writings of Anna Freud*, 317–26. International Universities Press.

Graham, Philip. (2008). "Susan Isaacs and The Malting School." *The Journal of Child Psychotherapy* 34 (1): 5–22.

Isaacs, Susan. (1933). *Social Development in Young Children*. Routledge.

Klein, Melanie. (1955). "The psychoanalytic play technique." *American Journal of Orthopsychiatry* 25: 223–237. https://doi.org/10.1111/j.1939-0025.1955.tb00131.x.

Klein, Melanie. (1975). "The development of a child: The influence of sexual enlightenment and relaxation of authority on the intellectual development of children." In *The Writings of Melanie Klein, Volume 1, Love, Guilt, and Reparation and Other Works*, ed. Roger Money-Kyrle, 1921–1945: 1–53. Hogarth.

Mathelin, Cathrine. (1999). *Lacanian Psychotherapy with Children—The Broken Piano*. Other Press.

Midgely, Nick. (2008). "The 'Matchbox School' (1927–1932): Anna Freud and the idea of a 'psychoanalytically informed education'." *The Journal of Child Psychotherapy* 34 (1): 23–42.

Phillips, Adam. (2021). *The Cure for Psychoanalysis*. Confer Books U.K.

Porges, Stephen. (2011). *The Polyvagal Theory: Neurophysiological Foundations of Emotions, Attachments, Communications, Self-Regulation*. Norton.

Porges, Stephen. (2017). *The Pocket Guide to the Polyvagal Theory*. Norton & Co.

Porges, Stephen, and Deb Dana. (2018). *Clinical Applications of the Polyvagal Theory*. Norton & Co.

Rosen, Michael. (2019). *Michael Rosen's Book of Play*. Profile Books Ltd.

Saracho, Olivia. (2023). "Theories of child development and their impact on early childhood." *Education and Care* Early *Childhood Education Journal* 51: 15–30. https://doi.org/10.1007/s10643-021-01271-5.

Schieffer, Kay. (2019). *Sunshine Circles—Nurture Your Classroom with Play*. The Theraplay Training Institute, U.S.A.

Schore, Allan. (2003a). "Early relational trauma, disorganized attachment, and the development of a predisposition to violence." In *Healing Trauma: Attachment, Mind, Body and Brain*, eds. M. F. Solomon and D. J. Siegel, 107–167. W. W. Norton and Company.

Schore, Allan. (2003b). *Affect Regulation and the Repair of the Self*. Norton & Co.

Stuart-Smith, Sue. (2020). *The Well Gardened Mind*. Harper Collins.

Tucker, Catherine, Kay Schieffer, Stephen Lenz, and Sondra Smith. (2021). "Sunshine circles: Randomized controlled trial of an attachment-based play group with preschool students who are at-risk." *Journal of Child and Adolescent Counseling* 7 (4): 1–15. https://doi.org/10.1080/23727810.2021.1940658.

Tronick, Ed, and Marjorie Beeghly. (2011). "Infants' meaning-making and the development of mental health problems." *American Psychologist* 66 (2): 107–119. https://doi.org/10.1037/a0021631.

Winnicott, Donald W. (1971). *Playing and Reality*. Tavistock Publications Ltd.

Part III

PSYCHOANALYTIC APPROACHES TO EARLY CHILDHOOD TEACHER EDUCATION

Chapter 10

A Case for Early Childhood Teacher Education Informed by Psychic Genera

Clio Stearns

Twenty minutes into the observation, I am starting to feel fidgety. So far, I watched Amy lead fifteen children, ages three to five, in a song about snow and guide them through a daily weather report. For ten minutes, Amy asked the children to list acts of kindness they witnessed that day. Each time a child offered a story, Amy affixed a plastic snowflake to a chart up on the wall.

Now, Amy is asking the children to vote on their favorite of three winter activities while she documents their answers on a line plot.

Just like the last time I visited Amy's classroom, Zacky and Quin have left the rug. Zacky is sitting in one of the cubbies off to the side, loudly banging his feet against the floor, intermittently humming the theme song to a popular online video game. Quin is lying on the floor in front of Zacky, and he is crying loudly. His teacher, Marianne, is near him. "Quin," I hear her say, "this is unacceptable. It's okay to have big feelings, but now it's time to join the group." Quin and Zacky get progressively louder, and Amy raises her voice to compete.

I survey the scene on the rug. Emeline has made her way into Amy's lap, where she is dozing off with a thumb in her mouth. Two other kids are rolling around on the floor. At least three have fingers in their noses and ears. Another has her shirt pulled up all the way, and she is inspecting her navel. Amy sees me looking, makes eye contact, and mouths, "sorry." I wonder what she is apologizing for.

This chapter examines what I see as two related dynamics that the opening vignette reflects. First, the sense, perpetuated by a combination of cultural and institutional forces, that even in early childhood classrooms, quality teaching necessarily involves routinized, direct, and whole-group instruction (e.g., Petscher et al. 2020; Solari et al. 2020). Second, the sense among teachers and teacher candidates that children's opposition and resistance are problematic, are outgrowths of trauma, and reflect poorly on the teacher (Egeberg, McConney, and Price 2016). I question these phenomena, which I have observed repeatedly, from a psychoanalytic lens, but with the hope that psychoanalytic thinkers in education can engage more consistently and mutually with teacher educators interested in working within public systems. I want to think seriously about the systemic factors that may lead teachers to apologize for children's playfulness and resistance during an observation, and to consider the ways a more interactive relationship between psychoanalysis and teacher education might open more space for creativity in the early childhood teacher education process.

To unpack these ideas, I discuss my experiences supervising Amy using a state-mandated framework. I am a scholar who frequently applies psychoanalytic theory to work with children and teachers (Stearns 2019, 2022), and for the last several years, I have wrestled with what sometimes feels like the proverbial square peg, round hole problem. There is a practical and increasing urgency in educating and credentialing thoughtful, engaged, loving teachers with staying power in the profession (Darling-Hammond and Hyler 2020). Psychoanalysis—and I use this term broadly, as a catchall for a number of divergent theories and concepts—presents frameworks profoundly different from those used in licensing processes (e.g., Taubman 2012). What does it mean that psychoanalytic thinkers in curriculum theory and teacher education have so little foothold in the logistical processes and frameworks that new teachers have to move through in order to work in schools?

Part of the disjuncture is the force of the rubric the teacher must pass: lessons must be at the center, oppositional and distracting behavior must be minimized, and high expectations must be maintained (Massachusetts Department of Elementary and Secondary Education 2024). This rubric is not unique to Massachusetts, where Amy and I live, nor is Amy uniquely concerned with it (Grissom and Bartanen 2019). It is not a framework that disappears once the teacher achieves a license; the language in these standards is similar to professional standards for teachers, against which teachers are consistently evaluated, in professional associations, unions, and school districts across the country (Nguyen et al. 2020).

Simultaneous to this is the force of increased discourse around trauma-informed practices and trauma itself as it impacts children and schools (Pyscher and Crampton 2020). Attention to trauma as a guiding force in children's lives can be helpful in pulling professional attention to the significance of relationships, but in the context of the other set of forces described above, trauma sometimes becomes an umbrella term for anything getting in the way of pedagogical efficiency and standardization. I rely on Christopher Bollas (1999, 2002), who posits an opposite to trauma that is not healing or recovery, and certainly not compliance, but genera, psychological phenomena that lie in creativity and newness and can never be standardized.

This chapter begins with some information about Amy and the student teaching process she was going through. It proceeds with a discussion of the problematic disjuncture between teacher licensing processes and psychoanalytic approaches to education. Then, it discusses the use and overuse of trauma as a lens for understanding children's difficult behavior in schools. Finally, I explain Bollas' idea of genera in more detail and describe what it might look like to use genera as a guiding concept in understanding and supporting teachers' and children's classroom experiences.

AMY AND THE STUDENT TEACHING PROCESS

The opening vignette comes from one of four formal observations I conducted as Amy's official supervisor during her student teaching semester, as she worked to earn a license in early childhood education. In Massachusetts, every student-teacher is assigned a college supervisor as well as a cooperating teacher: in this case, Marianne, who has been teaching preschool for over twenty years. Amy and Marianne work at a public preschool in a rural area. Their students range in age from just three to almost six years old. Some children come every day, and some come three or four days a week; some stay all day, and a few leave after lunch. Their class is part of an expanding free preschool program in their state.

I met Amy at the beginning of her student teaching semester. Although early childhood educators can work without licenses in Massachusetts, and many choose to because of the time-consuming and costly licensing process, they cannot be head teachers in public preschool or kindergarten classrooms; earning the license is akin to earning pay, protection, and status (Kreisberg 2018). Amy worked as a paraprofessional in a few different preschools for almost a decade prior to returning to complete her bachelor's alongside her teaching license. She told me when we met that she looked forward to the prestige and credibility that came with licensure, but that most of all, she was looking forward to earning "a real salary" for what she does.

The license requirements in Massachusetts have evolved with the professionalization of teaching over the last fifty years, as notions around accreditation and licensing have become increasingly rigorous. In addition to passing several costly tests, Teacher Candidates have to complete something called the CAP, or Candidate Assessment of Performance (MA Department of Elementary and Secondary Education 2024). The CAP is a digital portfolio that compiles specific evidence toward the assertion that, at the end of the semester, the candidate is "ready to teach." The battery breaks teaching down into seven key elements: Subject Matter Knowledge; Well-Structured Lesson; Adjustments to Practice; Meeting Diverse Needs; High Expectations; Safe Classroom Environment; and Reflective Practice.

DESE provides a definition of each of the elements they ask supervisors to look for in observations, but the definitions are often recursive and under-theorized. For example, proficiency in High Expectations according to CAP means that a candidate "consistently reinforces the expectation that all students can meet (high) standards through effective effort, rather than innate ability." There is no clear definition of what "high standards" are. There is no understanding that some students may not be able to meet such standards because, for example, they are struggling with food or housing insecurity. Is a teacher who shows empathy for children in circumstances like those, then, guilty of problematically lowering expectations?

Among other challenges of the CAP is the fact that, except for the impending addition of early literacy standards, it looks the same regardless of what age group a candidate is working with. With its focus on discrete lessons, content delivery, and a particular version of academic rigor, the CAP is notably ill-suited to the well-documented need of young children to explore in free and open-ended ways and come to these things called "academics" on their own terms (Wynberg et al. 2022).

SQUARE PEGS, ROUND HOLES: FITTING YOUNG CHILDREN INTO LICENSING REQUIREMENTS AND FITTING PSYCHOANALYSIS INTO TEACHER EDUCATION

After the children are home for the day, Amy, Marianne, and I sit down to debrief. The first thing Amy does is apologize. I ask her what she is apologizing for, and she gestures to the cubbies where Zacky and Quin had landed. "Those two," she says, "they have a lot of trauma, and I need them to learn the expectations." I look at Marianne, and she nods, "Zacky has been on a lot of different behavior plans already this year," she explains, "and now we've finally got one that seems to be working a little better, but we really have to be consistent with it." I try to explain to Amy and Marianne that whatever the children are bringing to the table on a particular day is fair game. "You don't need to apologize for the children," I say, "I think it's really interesting to watch how the dynamic unfolds in a classroom no matter what is going on." Amy responds, "Well, I'm just sorry the observation got disrupted like that. I'm going to work on it more for next time . . . my classroom management, I mean. I'm sorry the meeting got disrupted."

Psychoanalysis offers teachers the possibility that there is no such thing as a disruption to an educational encounter. A problem with adhering to a predetermined framework for observations is the illusion it creates that the teacher should control the unpredictable in a classroom, instead of allowing it to flourish as part of the educational experience. I do not mean that Zacky and Quin should be allowed to tantrum unfettered in their cubbies; I also don't mean that they shouldn't, or that everyone should turn their attention to Zacky and Quin and their emotional needs. There is no exact "should," and no one needs to apologize for the uncontrollable nature of mutual human experience. As an observer, I might position myself *not* as saying, "Amy didn't get Quin back to the rug," or "Amy did a good job with Zacky's behavior plan." I might ask, "Why did Amy decide to respond to Zacky and Quin the way she did?"

Amy's apologies were not limited to the behavior of students in her classroom. In fact, the thing she apologized for most frequently over the course of the semester was how short her whole group meetings were. Amy and Marianne's goal was to make morning meetings a little bit longer every week or two so that by the end of the year, their oldest students would be "ready for kindergarten," a construct that holds steadfast in early childhood despite numerous critiques (e.g., Tager 2017). When I made my observation schedule with Amy and Marianne, I indicated a wish to come on different days and at different points throughout the day. I enjoy watching children play and thinking with teachers about what is happening during play and choice times. At the same time, I knew that I would be unable to complete the CAP if I did not watch at least one full meeting time, since this was the closest the preschoolers had to a "lesson" block.

Amy and Marianne went to great lengths—often changing the children's whole day around—to ensure that I was only there during structured meetings. After this happened twice, I asked them about it. Amy said, "Well, I want you to see me teaching lessons, to really see me teaching. That way you can give me feedback." I explained to her that just because the children aren't sitting on the rug, listening to direct instruction, this does not mean she is not teaching. "Yeah, but this way, you really see me in action," she insisted. By the end of the semester, Amy grew comfortable dismissing her children from meetings while I was still there, so I could witness the play that happened after the lesson, but she continued to apologize. "I know I should be working on keeping them on the rug longer, but some of them, with their behaviors, they just can't," she said, "that's what we're working on, getting them ready . . . ready for kindergarten and all of that. They won't be able to do this then." By "this," Amy meant playing; when she spoke, she gestured to the rug, where two children sat on Sit'n'Spins, grinning wildly and giggling together as they spun madly round and round. Why should a preschool teacher feel compelled to apologize for children's drive to play? As I mulled this over, I thought about other Teacher Candidates I was supervising, all in older classrooms but similarly inclined to ensure that my observations coincided with direct, whole group instruction, and to apologize and point to "trauma" whenever students behaved in ways outside of the rigid expectations of normative classroom life.

WHAT ABOUT TRAUMA?: THE OVER- AND MISUSE OF TRAUMA AND TRAUMA-INFORMED PRACTICE IN EARLY CHILDHOOD

Amy was quick to name "trauma" as the reason so many of her young students resisted sitting still for long stretches of time or complying with her careful plans. Trauma as a term and concept is ubiquitous in education right now. For the last few years, I have not been able to face my education students or teacher candidates for more than half an hour at a time without the word "trauma" coming into our conversation. New teachers are highly versed in what it means to employ "trauma-informed practice" (Howard 2019) alongside the idea that "this generation" (that they are currently teaching) has so much trauma. I hear teacher candidates referring to "the trauma kids" in their classes, referencing everything from food insecurity to child abuse, from encounters with ongoing systemic racism to divorced parents. Usually, when I hear teachers reference trauma colloquially, they mean a few different things: first, that life is hard for children. This is true! Childhood has never been easy, though arguably there have been long historical stretches where the expectation of ease simply did not exist—for better or for worse (Stearns 2019). Trauma means that life is hard for particular children more than others—also true, for reasons pertaining to systemic injustices as well as intrafamilial and temperamental nuances (Nxumalo and Adair 2019). Trauma seems, for some teachers, to mean that children require a specific type of care, structure, and rigidity, and also that their "behaviors," rather than holding potential as creative outlets, acts of protest, expressions of open-ended pain or joy, are symptoms that the trauma-informed teacher or practitioner can treat. Without trauma, this line of thinking implies, children would be more compliant and the school day would proceed more smoothly. This line of reasoning is not without its truths. Children who are being abused, or who feel exhausted, hungry, or mistreated actually do tend to act more obstinate than well-nourished, well-cared-for children. But it is important to start talking about trauma more cautiously in education, and in fact, this was something curriculum theorists started gesturing toward long ago (Zembylas 2020). The classroom can certainly be a place to bear witness to trauma and to work through trauma. As a number of thinkers have been vociferously pointing out in recent years, the school and classroom can also be places where trauma is incurred: racial trauma, economic trauma, sexual trauma/trauma surrounding sexuality, and more (Dutro and Bien 2014). I have no interest in glossing over the relevance of trauma as a concept in an educational setting. Turning away from what is most difficult or painful has no educational benefit and can exacerbate so many existing injustices (Stearns 2019). But there are flaws in the current overreliance on trauma as a conceptual framework in education. Among them: the lack of a clear, generalized definition of what trauma is, the tendency to use trauma as one more dismissive label, the orientation toward specific programmatic interventions based on that label, and the ways those interventions tend to look past the subjectivity and creativity of the child. I will speak briefly about each of these issues.

First of all, if we are going to talk about trauma in education, we need to have a definition of trauma that people agree on. When my students say that they work with "traumatized children," they sometimes mean that those children come from families who raise them in ways my students (their teachers) find off-putting. If most people can agree that a child who has experienced ongoing physical or sexual abuse has undergone trauma, the term becomes fuzzier when we talk about themes common in childhood like divorce or moving. Some children experience divorce in their families as traumatic; others do not. The reasons include temperament, access to a variety of resources, how and with whom the child has been given the opportunity to process the experience, what kinds of other relationships they have, exactly what the events were, and more. Not every child experiencing trauma will act out in school; the converse is also true.

The problem of lacking a definition for trauma becomes even more acute when we think about the various social injustices that can be interpreted in these terms. For example, systematic, historical, and ongoing racism and racialized violence in the United States can certainly be at the root of trauma. But this does not mean that every BIPOC individual in the United States is traumatized or experiences that trauma in the same way.

There is not a solitary definition of trauma that I want to argue for, but I am concerned that in the absence of such a definition, trauma becomes little besides a label. Labels have always had an ambivalent place in education. They have utility in that they are often at the root of service provision and can generate empathy. The other side of the coin, however, is how much gets dismissed within trauma as a label. What if the child's "oppositional" behavior is communicating or creating something important, something different from the child's pain and need for therapeutic kinds of attention? What if, by kicking, Zacky is not saying, "things are really hard at home," or "my infancy was extremely disorganized," but rather, "this meeting is boring and irrelevant to things I care about?" Or, what if he is saying, "I want to kick right now, it makes a satisfying noise?" At what point does "trauma" become one more oppressive category depriving children of agency?

Related to the complexity of the trauma label is the growing popularity of trauma-informed practices as a way to respond to the many children carrying this label around. The idea that schools should be trauma-informed or trauma sensitive has become increasingly popular (Pyscher and Crampton 2020). As with trauma itself, there are varying definitions of what exactly a trauma-informed or trauma sensitive school is, but the phrases generally refer to schools where teachers understand the different ways trauma can impact the ability to learn, and where there is a focus on helping children feel safe in school (Morton 2019). Trauma-informed schools might focus on building mindfulness and yoga into daily practice, offering children specific and consistent praise, promoting predictability and consistency in school and classroom routines, and emphasizing the significance of relationships throughout the school day. Trauma-informed schools also train teachers about trauma and the many ways it can influence children's lives.

I am, generally speaking, in favor of the pillars that tend to be associated with trauma-informed practice in schools, but I have observed a disconnect in how these pillars are written about in discourse and how they tend to be absorbed and applied in practice. Often, teachers want to have strong relationships with children, but because the behaviors children bring to classrooms can so often be repellent and inconvenient—because of the nature of child development, or because of trauma, or because of the other pressures teachers face, or because children might be legitimately disinterested in those same relationships—these relationships often sound more appealing in theory than they do in practice (Stearns 2022). Further, the task of developing a trauma-informed classroom according to these precepts often works at cross purposes to the seemingly infinite set of other tasks a teacher faces, like getting through a particular curriculum or following a particular timetable.

Finally, there is a way that an excessive focus on trauma looks right past children and what they bring to school. To understand this, we can look back at Zacky. It is so easy to see a child yelling or throwing things and think, "oh, right, that's the trauma. Let's offer him some consistency, let's show him that we understand." But what Zacky is doing when he yells out is, in some ways, less inhibited and repetitive than what anyone else in the class is doing. We can perceive his behavior as a creative act, one that may have roots in something bad he has witnessed or experienced but also one that is moving and changing his current environment into something else. Zacky is not frozen in trauma; he is not foreclosing on the possibility of making an impact on his world. He is doing something else, and the flaw is not in Zacky but in an environment that swoops in with diagnosis and treatment. This raises a question about what, if not trauma, we might use to understand these moments of openness and show teachers how they are useful, not worthy of apology, in classroom life.

WHAT BESIDES TRAUMA?

Psychoanalyst Christopher Bollas (1999) theorized that trauma does have an opposite, but its opposite is not healing or recovery. According to Bollas, the opposite of trauma is something called psychic genera. For Bollas, trauma is an incoherence of psychic experience that leads individuals into rigidity and repetition, with foregone conclusions. "Psychic confusion," he writes, "is part of the full effect of trauma because, unable to narrate the event in the first place, the person now re-experiences isolation" (1999, 67). Genera are the internal and relational structures that emerge newly in and among people who have released some hold on past pain, "psychic freedom of object representation and the liberty of object choice" (1999, 68). Trauma leads us to seek out, again and again, the same systems, thought processes, interpretations, and world views; these both recapitulate our experiences of trauma and keep us safe from the risk that comes with openness to new frameworks and endeavors. Psychic genera are constructs that allow us to think differently from ways we have thought before.

"Think" is only part of the story, though. Psychic genera also allow us to feel and live differently. Bollas describes this in relation to art, for instance, "A subject whose principle of engagement with reality is generative will seek to work unconsciously on specific issues that will enable him to reenvision his reality and in turn sponsor new ways of living and thinking" (1999, 70). They are trauma's opposite because they are open and uninterested in the succor or despair of repetition. For Bollas, genera can be created in a clinical analytic encounter between two people. The patient brings a story to the therapist. Something terrible happened, and the feelings that follow it do not make any sense. The therapist helps establish coherence by listening, retelling, and facilitating further narration. But then the story becomes something new, and the feelings and understandings that go with it change as well. This is a co-created genera and it enables people to live more fully. We can take our most painful stories and play with them, creating something from them. Bollas is careful to explain that "the incubation of genera can be, and usually is, the work of great personal struggle, as any change of one's status quo involves emotional turbulence" (1999, 70).

Psychic genera can emerge in the classroom because of the relational field that inevitably constitutes any consistent educational community. But genera do not come from standards and predetermined schedules, and we cannot plan for them in advance. They are not something to be taught, but rather, noticed and celebrated. Bollas describes the relationship between genera and play, "genera are produced after a period of play work and, once established, transform the subjects' outlook on life, generate new questions and new works, and contribute to the formation of new genera" (1999, 76). The concept of genera is a reminder that something new is always possible in the self, and that stagnation and completion are associations of trauma.

One thing Bollas has to offer is an implicit critique of the idea that compliance with rules and structure, adherence to a predetermined school day or style of teaching with specific learning outcomes or "best practices," is an antidote to trauma. Instead, Bollas might maintain, the opposite of trauma is *in* the play that we can read into a lot of oppositional, allegedly traumatized behavior. He writes of school, "The best moments in any person's formal education are composed of . . . evocative occasions when an object (a theory, another perspective) radically alters one's way of imagining reality" (Bollas 1999, 83). He goes on to speculate that such moments are normally facilitated by significant preceding unconscious work and are not really momentary epiphanies.

The opposite of trauma is not in the reversion to pre-existing norms, wherein a group of children sit quietly on the rug for ever-lengthening stretches of time, but in the generation of new psychic constructs that unfold when one child shows another how to squeeze his small body right into the cubby and sit there kicking mightily. Leaning into that kind of behavior makes a classroom really hard to "manage." It gets louder, sweatier, more chaotic. The teacher suffers, partly because of the sheer sensory experience of existing in the midst of child-directed chaos, but also because of the sense that she is not meeting expectations. The check-boxes cannot be marked to indicate that she is "ready to teach."

This brings up the possibility that teaching as a job is ill-suited to the facilitation of creativity, mutual curiosity, and culture. Do most people assume that children go to school to build something new, or to do a satisfactory job learning what is already there? We hear constantly about the poor work American teachers do at facilitating the latter task, as proven by our children's low test scores, general disaffection, weak knowledge base, and low threshold of readiness for college and careers. What if part of the problem is actually about the first potential task?

THE DAY I GOT THERE LATE

Today, I get to Amy's classroom late. I wrote down the wrong time for our observation, a classic parapraxis. When I get to the preschool classroom, the door is locked, and I have to bang loudly before Marianne lets me in. When she does, she looks irritated. "You were due half an hour ago!" she tells me, "but luckily I've been taking notes. She is almost done. It's been going great—100% participation!"

I see that, indeed, unlike other days I've visited, all of the children in the class are on the rug with Amy, who is showing them pictures of baby birds. Zacky holds a laminated version of his behavior chart on his head like a makeshift umbrella. My entrance has distracted him, and he starts to poke at Willa to his left. "Let's not start that now, Zacky," Amy cautions him, "We've been doing so great."

I apologize to Marianne for my lateness and try to unobtrusively sit down, smiling at the children. Amy waves at me and says, "Dr. Stearns, can you see? We've got 100% participation today! All of our friends have been sitting on the rug for TWENTY MINUTES!" I nod and smile some more. Amy goes on, "but I don't think we can make it much longer, so we're going to have to go to play time. Maybe you can do your observation on a different day."

When the children have moved into centers for choice time, Amy approaches me. "Traffic?" she asks. I apologize again and tell her that I mixed up the time, and she laughs. "Well, you can come back tomorrow or next week," she says. I ask her if she would mind if I stayed, and she says that's fine, "but they're just playing now."

Amy walks over to join the children in the doll corner, and I gravitate toward Willa, who is alone with some farm animals. I sit on the floor a few feet away from her and watch; I'm not sure whether she knows I am right there.

Willa has plastic fencing, and she is building a corral. She sets up a whole ring, then puts three small plastic horses into it. She adds a plastic trough, a small tub, and a plastic bale of hay. Then, she takes a moment to survey the situation. She moves two horses closer to the trough and shakes her head, "not like that," she mutters. She nudges the hay slightly to the left, bends one of the horses' heads down, inches it to the right. She opens the fencing and then closes it again. She takes one horse out of the corral and replaces it with a different one, then picks up the horse she took out and pets it gently with one finger, saying, "You get to ride around." Watching Willa, I am unaware of the passage of time, focusing on trying to figure out what she is thinking and doing. I am lost, too, in memories of my daughter, now a committed equestrian, when she used to play with plastic horses. Where did those horses go? I wonder, wishing I could bring them here for Willa's careful attention.

When I get up, Willa is still engrossed. I find Zacky on a Sit'n'Spin, twirling round and round by himself on the rug. "One, two, THREEEEE!" he chants, then again, "One, two, THREEEEE!" I ask Zacky, "Do you like spinning?" but my question barely registers; he makes eye contact as if to say, obviously, you idiot, then proceeds with the task at hand, "One, two, THREEEE!" I go to sit near Amy, who is at the sensory table now.

At this table, three children are working together to brush sand off of blocks of wood and into a few different cups and pitchers. Amy tells me, "We are talking about which cups are bigger and smaller. The bigger cups hold more sand, right, friends?" One of the children nods, and the other two continue brushing. "This is like a toothbrush," Jaden says idly, "Like the toothbrush got so BIG." The other two children laugh, and Jaden lifts his brush to his mouth. "NO, Jaden," Amy intervenes, "It's not a toothbrush." Jaden laughs and goes back to brushing the wood. "This is like a hairbrush," he amends, but I notice that he does not go to brush his hair. Amy stands, shaking her head and smiling, "You are silly," she tells Jaden, and then she gives the class a two-minute warning before they have to clean up.

"It's really too bad you missed the lesson," Amy told me later when we debriefed, "It was so great how everyone really joined in, we've been working on that." I understand what Amy means. I missed something she had planned for carefully, in accordance with a variety of requirements and curriculum frameworks, and I missed something she felt proud of. I apologized, but it was clear that Amy was sad that I didn't get to see what it looked like for all of her students to be at the meeting for the whole class period. Getting a group of young children to attend to instruction for twenty minutes takes a lot of work, and she accomplished it. Are we building, in Zacky, the stamina he will presumably "need" two years from now in order to make it in kindergarten (e.g., Tager 2017)? What are the right educational moves not just for Zacky, but for a functional democratic society that could potentially reward creativity and social progress rather than compliance and adherence to a status quo?

The problem is not in Amy, but in a system that so deeply privileges a particular definition of teaching and learning, that a preschool teacher whose supervisor gets to witness half an hour of engaged, meaningful play feels that their supervisor has "missed" the observation. During that observation, I was meant to write about Amy's "adjustments to practice." DESE defines this element thus: "Analyzes results from a variety of assessments to determine progress toward intended outcomes and uses these findings to adjust practice and identify and/or implement differentiated interventions and enhancements for students" (MA DESE 2016). If I had seen the meeting, I would have noted Amy's consistent use of behavior plans, her design for seating students, and her use of visuals to facilitate entry into the curriculum. I would have noted her varied use of language, and the modulation of her volume. Even the element called "Safe Learning Environment" is described thus: "(Teacher candidate) uses rituals, routines, and appropriate responses that create and maintain a safe physical and intellectual environment where students take academic risks and most behaviors that interfere with learning are prevented" (MA DESE 2024; Classroom Teacher Rubric 18). When children are playing or working out of the teacher's consistent surveillance, they may or may not be using rituals and routines.

Teachers are meant to calibrate the exact right kind and level of "academic risk" that is never all that risky and then to stay on top of facilitating that at all times. Willa may have made something more interesting and important for both her cognition and internal survival by moving the horses and fencing back and forth, and Zacky from spinning madly, than either of them would have from participating in another ritual or routine. That Willa, Zacky, and their classmates do have times like these during the day is commendable and precious. Each of them made a whole world with their simple toys, a chunk of time, and the absence of close observation and intervention. Each of them gave me hours of things to think and wonder about, and "One, two, THREE-EEE!" prevented me from getting unduly aggravated with the actual traffic I encountered on my way home. Play is for learning, it is true, but what we do not say enough is that play is also for survival. What if we built up *those* capacities, to build little farms and spin and experience unfettered joy, rather than the capacity to sit and listen? How different would schooling be?

I did not observe Amy's adjustments to practice during play because I observed very little of Amy during play and also because of the capacity of children to make the needed adjustments for themselves during the small pockets of time they are granted to do so. I did not observe her prevention of behavior, except for the toothbrush moment, because the situation was not one where wild and noisy behavior was unwelcome. Watching this is not a waste of time; it was the most hopeful I felt in a classroom all semester. We need more of it, children need more of it.

Let us think for a moment about how different the "safe learning environment" is from Bollas' list of "steps in the formation of genera." These steps begin with the formation of devoted inner space in the subject, which is then taken up by increasing chaos and links between ideas and feelings. "Chaos is tolerated, indeed facilitated, as the subject knows it is essential to the process of discovering new concepts about living" (1993, p. 88). Chaos then leads to a provisional sense of coherence, but to sustain vitality, the coherence, too, will eventually yield. Order is not the end goal; it appears from time to time, but overall it is too repetitive and forecloses too much possibility.

The argument that children need more time to play in classrooms is not a new one (e.g., Brooker 2010; Yelland 2011), and it is not one without its flaws. When time in school is devoted to play, it is not devoted to other things: direct literacy or math instruction, for example—and it is these other things that families are counting on to make school more equitable in the future (Brown and Gasko 2012). Psychoanalytic involvement in schools has paid too little attention to this significant set of claims from schools and communities.

My argument about young children and play is this: it does not matter whether or not adults think children should play in school, because children will play in school no matter what. Chaos will ebb and flow. Sometimes, children will play in sanctioned ways: in doll corners or block-building areas. More often, and certainly until they are much older, they will play either in more private ways (in their own minds, for example) or in ways that get them into trouble (2022). These ways are often not going to be called play anymore by adults, but that is exactly what they are.

Some children are privileged or savvy enough that their private ways of playing commute early into what the school thinks of as cultural participation. For example, if a child plays imaginatively in writing, this child might simply get labeled as a good, creative writer. Bollas (2002, 2009) and others pointed out how much cultural participation stems from play, with or without permission from the school. Other children play by yelling, skipping class, poking at their peers, and finding creative if also troubling ways to subvert authority. These children tend to garner ever more punitive, and occasionally therapeutic, but rarely admiring, responses.

My point is not that these kinds of diversions from norms should be celebrated. They can lead to ever-increasing trauma. Instead, I wonder if it is exactly the rigidity of the structures that precede some kinds of rebellion that make ever more violent and urgent deviation particularly appealing. What if we did not rush children quite so quickly out of playtime and toward readiness, toward congratulations for sitting still and listening? Would that afford them a little more time and grace in figuring certain other ideas, ways of being, out?

Amy had taken coursework and read widely about the importance of play in early childhood education and particularly learning, but this did not stop her from seeing her role in play as a timekeeper, inserter of as many "academic" concepts as possible, and guard against even minor physical safety violations. I am increasingly disturbed by the systems that made Amy feel like taking on the role of a teacher means minimizing play and freedom as much as possible, and that teaching only "counts" if it is direct instruction to a whole group, working through a series of routines.

The supervisory frameworks that contribute to that way of thinking simultaneously respond to and create cultural ideas about teaching, what it means to teach, and what should be happening in school. For example, there is an idea that school is for learning and socializing, and learning and socializing are discrete processes that can be identified in specific and predetermined ways (Stearns 2022). There is the newer idea, too, that school is responding to massive social and cultural trauma, and that response should look a particular way.

KILEY PUSHES AMY AROUND

I do end up coming back to observe Amy one more time, mostly because of how badly she wanted me to. This time, Zacky and Quin do not join the group. Zacky sits sulking and kicking at a table, and when his kicks get too loud, Marianne glares in his direction until he stops. Quin is in his cubby again, and this time, Emma, a new and very small three-year-old, also sits in her cubby, tears dripping down her face and thumb in her mouth. Amy tries several times to bring all three of them to the meeting, but they are determined, in different ways, not to come.

Amy proceeds through her usual routines, and when she asks for examples of kindness, Kiley raises her hand. "I was kind outside," she announces, "when I shared the wagon."

"You did share the wagon," Amy agrees and affixes a small plastic flower to the chart. Several other children raise their hands, but Kiley keeps talking, "I have a wagon at my house, and I pushed my brother, my brother pushed me," she says quietly. Amy calls on some other children, and Kiley lies down on her back.

"Kiley, please sit up," Amy says before returning to her flower chart.

Kiley sits up but starts singing a song from a popular cartoon. Her singing gets progressively louder. Amy ignores her at first, but then the singing gets so loud, it is hard to hear anyone else. "Kiley," Amy says, laughing gently, "you used to be so quiet when you first came to our class! Now it really seems like you don't like to follow the rules." Amy is more amused than she is angry. Kiley keeps singing for the rest of the meeting period.

When the children go to play this time, Kiley gets right up and heads to Amy. She puts her hands on Amy's hips and begins shoving. "Kiley!" Amy says, firmly this time, "you can't do that! You used to be so quiet and calm, and lately you like to push me around." Kiley keeps her hands on Amy's hips and starts to shove even harder. Amy removes Kiley's hands and points her toward the sensory table. "Get some of your energy out over there," she tells Kiley.

Amy comes up to me now, shaking her head and smiling. "That Kiley," she says, "she used to be so calm and quiet when she first came, and now she's just pushing me around!" She walks away and joins a different group to play.

The interaction between Amy and Kiley had a different tenor from others I witnessed between Amy and children whose behaviors she found difficult. I noticed how playfully Amy used the phrase "pushing me around," both metaphorical and literal. The interaction with Kiley allowed Amy to relax, play with language, and find surprise. Was it because Kiley was new, or for some reason her infraction seemed less calcified and serious? Was it just that Amy liked Kiley, or that Kiley did not come with a dossier depicting past traumas? The striking part was not in a theory of a cause; instead, it was in the relaxation, amusement, and joy in Amy. She did not apologize for Kiley's disruption; she marveled at it. It was a moment of freedom between them, and though it did not allow for any check marks, it was lovely to behold.

CONCLUSION

One of the reasons classroom observations are so difficult is the sheer stimulus each moment contains. A positive side effect of a particular rubric is the way it focuses observers' energy and attention. At the same time, there is a mismatch between these points of focus and the moments in classroom life that can be most freeing and beautiful. When an observer is only looking for certain things, it removes a sense of import from the aspects of classroom life that do not fit on a checklist. As we have seen with Amy, it contributes to a broader cultural sense that time not spent on academics, on school readiness, and on direct instruction is time wasted. This is a problem across grade levels and subject areas but particularly in early childhood.

Making this argument is an uphill battle, in part because the successes of early childhood programs that result in funding and media attention come from adhering to the models these kinds of frameworks propagate. When we focus on making preschool about getting children "ready for kindergarten," doing pre-literacy and early numeracy activities, and getting them accustomed to direct instruction, we can succeed at doing this, and it can be great for children (Tager 2017), in early childhood curriculum studies, and the pragmatic, daily, sometimes grinding world of teacher education and licensure (Taubman 2012).

But the other piece is true, too: that in doing this kind of work, we filter kids, we sort them, we make determinations about what is acceptable to bring to the classroom, and we foreclose other possibilities. Is this a choice we want to make in the name of more equitable access to economic productivity? Maybe that is exactly what Freud (1930) meant when he said that education is for sublimation, that civilization breeds discontents. But we need to admit that we are making this sacrifice. That admission might help us look less punitively or diagnostically at children who come to school like Zacky does. When we think of play as a waste of time, we are consigning children to do it in subversive ways, and we are showing them that their present needs have to pay deference to a future adults are imagining for them.

Perhaps, though, there is a middle ground where teachers and children can coexist in a more relaxed and mutually agreeable way. Kiley shows us a path toward that middle ground when she "pushes Amy around," and Amy responds by laughing. It is a moment of curiosity about what could possibly be going on with another person, and the curiosity, born from genuine surprise, leads to wonder and joy. These funny, idiosyncratic moments—these are moments where real knowledge gets produced, where ways of relating, thinking, feeling, and living alter. These are moments of genera, and as such, they are education.

REFERENCES

Bollas, Christopher. 1999. *The Mystery of Things*. New York: Routledge.

Bollas, Christopher. 2002. *Free Association*. London: Icon Books.

Bollas, Christopher. 2008. *The Infinite Question*. New York: Routledge.

Bollas, Christopher. 2013. *Being a Character: Psychoanalysis and Self Experience*. New York: Routledge.

Brown, Christopher P., and John W. Gasko. 2012. "Why Should Pre-k Be More Like Elementary School? A Case Study of Pre-k Reform." *Journal of Research in Childhood Education* 26, no. 3: 264–290. https://doi.org/10.1080/02568543.2012 .686471.

Darling-Hammond, Linda, and Maria E. Hyler. 2020. "Preparing Educators for the Time of COVID . . . and Beyond." *European Journal of Teacher Education* 43, no. 4: 457–465. https://doi.org/10.1080/02619768.2020.1816961.

Dutro, Elizabeth, and Andrea C. Bien. 2014. "Listening to the Speaking Wound: A Trauma Studies Perspective on Student Positioning in Schools." *American Educational Research Journal* 51, no. 1: 7–35. https://doi.org/10.1080/02619768.2020 .1816961.

Egeberg, Helen, Andrew McConney, and Anne Price. 2016. "Classroom Management and National Professional Standards for Teachers: A Review of the Literature on Theory and Practice." *Australian Journal of Teacher Education (Online)* 41, no. 7: 1–18.

Freud, Sigmund. 1930. *Civilization and Its Discontents*. London: Hogarth Press and Institute of Psycho-Analysis.

Grissom, Jason A., and Brendan Bartanen. 2019. "Strategic Retention: Principal Effectiveness and Teacher Turnover in Multiple-Measure Teacher Evaluation Systems." *American Educational Research Journal* 56, no. 2: 514–555. https://doi.org /10.3102/0002831218797931.

Howard, Judith A. 2019. "A Systemic Framework for Trauma-Informed Schooling: Complex but Necessary!" *Journal of Aggression, Maltreatment & Trauma* 28, no. 5: 545–565. https://doi.org/10.1080/10926771.2018.1479323.

Interlandi, Jeneen. 2018. "Why Are Our Most Important Teachers Paid the Least?" *The New York Times Magazine*, January 9, 2018.

Kreisberg, Robert. 2018. "Why Are Our Most Important Teachers Paid the Least?" *Eye on Early Education* (blog), January 18, 2018. https://eyeonearlychildhood.org /2018/01/18/why-are-our-most-important-teachers-paid-the-least/.

Massachusetts Department of Elementary and Secondary Education (MADESE). "Home—Massachusetts Department of Elementary and Secondary Education." Accessed May 27, 2024. https://www.doe.mass.edu/.

Modell, Arnold. 2008. "Implicit or Unconscious?: Commentary on Paper by the Boston Change Process Study Group." *Psychoanalytic Dialogues* 18, no. 2: 162–167. https://doi.org/10.1080/10481880801909534.

Nguyen, Tuan D., Lam D. Pham, Michael Crouch, and Matthew G. Springer. 2020. "The Correlates of Teacher Turnover: An Updated and Expanded Meta-analysis of the Literature." *Educational Research Review* 31: 100355. https://doi.org/10.1016/j.edurev.2020.100355.

Nxumalo, Fikile, and Jennifer Keys Adair. 2019. "Social Justice and Equity in Early Childhood Education." *The Wiley Handbook of Early Childhood Care and Education*, edited by Christopher P. Brown, Mary Benson McMullen, and Nancy File, 661–681. Hoboken: John Wiley & Sons. https://doi.org/10.1002/9781119148104.ch29.

Petscher, Yaacov, Sonia Q. Cabell, Hugh W. Catts, Donald L. Compton, Barbara R. Foorman, Sara A. Hart, Christopher J. Lonigan, Beth M. Phillips, Christopher Schatschneider, Laura M. Steacy, Nicole Patton Terry, and Richard K. Wagner. 2020. "How the Science of Reading Informs 21st-Century Education." *Reading Research Quarterly* 55, no. 1: 267–282. https://doi.org/10.1002/rrq.352.

Pyscher, Tracey, and Anne Crampton. 2020. "Possibilities and Problems in Trauma-Based and Social Emotional Learning Programs." *Occasional Paper Series* 43. Bank Street College of Education.

Solari, Emily J., Nicole Patton Terry, Nadine Gaab, Tiffany P. Hogan, Nancy J. Nelson, Jill M. Pentimonti, Yaacov Petscher, and Sarah Sayko. 2020. "Translational Science: A Road Map for the Science of Reading." *Reading Research Quarterly* 55, no. 1: 347–360. https://doi.org/10.1002/rrq.357.

Stearns, Clio. 2019. *Critiquing Social and Emotional Learning: Psychodynamic and Cultural Perspectives*. Lanham: Rowman & Littlefield.

Stearns, Clio. 2022. *Consent in the Childhood Classroom: Centering Student Voices across Early Years and Elementary Education*. New York: Routledge.

Tager, Miriam. 2017. *Challenging the School Readiness Agenda*. New York: Routledge.

Taubman, Peter Maas. 2012. *Disavowed Knowledge: Psychoanalysis, Education and Teaching*. New York: Routledge.

White, Cleonie. 2022. "Psychoanalysis in a Radically Changing World: How Do We Stand?" In *Patriarchy and Its Discontents*, edited by Jean Petrucelli, Sarah Schoen, and Naomi Snider, 205–210. Routledge.

Wynberg, Elizabeth R., Femke van der Wilt, Annerieke Boland, Maartje E. J. Raijmakers, and Chiel van der Veen. 2022. "How Young Children Explore, Follow and Impose Rules During Object-Oriented Play: A Multiple Case Study." *International Journal of Early Years Education* 30, no. 3: 577–594. https://doi.org/10.1080/09669760.2022.2091981.

Work Group Discussions in Teacher Education

Evoking Associative Objects

H. James Garrett

In this chapter, I describe the ways that psychoanalytic theory has influenced a portion of my work as a teacher educator.[1] Specifically, I describe a course that is part of an intensive semester of both university and secondary classroom work that student teachers take before their semester of full-time student teaching. The course is designed with the notion that teaching, one of the impossible professions (Britzman 2009), and learning to teach carry not only intellectual demands but also emotional demands. Given that few initial certification programs (of which I am aware) provide sustained attention to the emotional demands of learning to teach, I have endeavored over the last several years to implement a course that centers on them. My intent is not to offer a set technique as a model. Rather, the purpose of this chapter is to describe the way a particular kind of thinking has come to have consequences for my thinking about pedagogy and illustrations/interpretations of what those consequences have made possible. In my understanding, the dream-work of teacher education has to do with understanding and making explicit the aspects of learning to teach that, like dreams, are ineffable, often confounding, and benefit from interpretations from trusted others for further inquiry, creative exploration, and interpretation.

PSYCHOANALYTIC THINKING IN/WITH PEDAGOGY

While psychoanalysis is productively deployed as a framework for literary and cultural criticism, my understanding of psychoanalysis consistently returns to the idea of it as a theory of the clinic. As a clinical theory, psychoanalysis provides a set of strategies for eliciting and attending to the kinds of emotional vagaries that make for stuck places, dissatisfactions, and frustrations that attend our living with ourselves and others. We go to psychoanalysis to be confronted with the parts of ourselves that are out to get us and consider what we might do with those parts of ourselves other than letting them get us. That we are defended against knowing those things is a process borne of outside (social) and inside (subjective) experiences that become habitual. Our orientations toward knowledge are marked by oscillations between knowing, wanting to know, and turning away from knowing (Felman 1982).

I have found psychoanalysis to be a clinical theory worth considering in the context of the classroom (Britzman and Pitt 2004). In my thinking and practice, though, I do not conflate the work of psychoanalysis with the work of teaching; these are markedly different endeavors. People do not go to classrooms for the same reasons they go to psychoanalysis. People go to classrooms, mostly, either because they are compelled to through laws and practices (through compulsory education and professional training) or because they are employed there (as teachers or professors). Despite these differences between psychoanalysis and education, the classroom can be understood as being home to some similar fundamental dimensions. What happens in the clinic of the classroom, when understood through theories that illuminate the dynamic pushes and pulls of psychical life, is beyond what occurs in the narrow lanes of academic content delivery and its acquisition by students. The classroom is also populated by the psychical lives of the teacher and the student, the social and political discourses of the time, and the histories of all of these that meet in often strange ways in school. Psychoanalysis is as much a way to make sense of what is happening as it is a strategy to foster those happenings.

The notion that people mean more than what we can say and that what we say carries more meanings than we know points to a pedagogical scene rich for inquiry about just what it is we teacher educators are up to when we say we are up to the education of future teachers. Psychoanalytic theories direct us to question ourselves anytime we think we have "the" answer and thus frustrate any desire for the end of inquiry or the settling of a problem. For instance, psychoanalytic theories assist in critiques of the regime of accountability and "value-added" education in elaborating the fantasy of making rigid boundaries around groups of children who are either "on-track" or "behind." However, psychoanalytic inquiry will also point that same critique at rigid boundaries around categories that I happen to like better—racist and anti-racist, for instance (Taubman 2012). In this way, thinking about teaching and learning and learning to teach from a psychoanalytic view urges us to privilege meanings that are unstable and shifting as much as we honor the need for practices as teachers undertake the work of helping students understand their role in the world.

Psychoanalytic ways of thinking provide a vocabulary to acknowledge interior life but maintain a simultaneous acknowledgment that there is no separating that interiority from relations in social and political situations. Psychoanalysis, Frosh (2018) contended, "has what is probably the most developed vocabulary and conceptual armory that offers the required theoretical resources for understanding and interiority that also moves across boundaries" (10). Those boundaries, blurry and questionably helpful as concepts, are troubled because of the necessary sociality of our being alive.

In this view, as Britzman (2015) wrote, education is a place "of affecting content where characters come to lose and make up the mind" (149). As such, she continued, "we might enlarge our view of the favorable human condition" if we allow ourselves to see education as a place where we experiment with the oscillations of the ways in which facing and turning away from knowledge are facilitated (149). Similarly, in group life, as French (1987) wrote, "Simply being with others stimulates primitive, existential anxieties: In what sense will we meet? At what level can we affect each other? Will I be accepted or rejected, liked, loved or hated, ignored or not even noticed?" (484). In classrooms, we are in situations of group life where the above questions are necessarily present and perpetually being asked and answered in a variety of ways. What this means is that, at the same time that students are offering views about one issue or another, whatever the content of the day is, they are also asking those questions or trying to answer them about what significance their words have, how they work once they are part of a social environment, and what happens as a result.

One of the things that Deborah Britzman (2006, 2007) has frequently noted is that education research ought to be careful in considering that students aren't the only people in the classroom who have a psychology. Her critique is that there is a kind of one-sidedness or uni-directionality in much literature on teaching. The students are identified with differentiated abilities, learning styles, issues, problems, skills, and the like. Lately, there has been a push to develop understandings of classroom life that connect those abilities, issues, and skills in relation to culture (as in culturally relevant pedagogies), society, the rules of schooling, and the like. However, much less has been forwarded about the interpretive moves made by teachers when they identify those relationships. That is, the students aren't the only ones in the classroom with a culture, a social situation, a relation to rules and authority, and a relation to their own tendencies toward aggression, rigid thinking, or self-persecution. Teachers have relations, too.

WORK GROUP DISCUSSIONS

Below, I present a course I've developed, informed by psychoanalytic principles and taught in the context of a secondary social studies initial certification program with the intent of creating a space of shared psychological processes. The course centers on the psychodynamic aspects of learning to teach, specifically the confusing nature of returning to schools as teachers and the confounding, frustrating, boring, exhilarating moments that occur therein (Britzman 2003). Before presenting that course, I'll begin the paper by describing the basis for its construction.

The course, what I've called an "observation seminar," is based on my understanding of the Tavistock Model of workgroup discussion seminars (Rustin 2008). These spaces are meant to, depending on the setting, provide groups of people with a structured space to explore the emotional demands of professional life. In contrast to spaces that are focused on problem-solving, the purpose of the workgroup discussion is not to correct mistakes or figure out the solution to a problem. The workgroup discussion model is meant to "sharpen perceptions and to enhance the exercise of imagination so that a richer understanding of the personality interactions described may ensue, based on evidence of motivation springing from internal unconscious sources" (Rustin 2008, n.p.).

Most frequently, workgroup discussions are populated by helping professionals: nurses, teachers, social workers, and the like. The format, as I have learned it, is based on a model of infant observation that is part of psychoanalytic training. In infant observation, the person in training spends a prolonged amount of time observing an infant in their home with their caretaker. The task is to attend not only to what the observer "sees" but to experience that observation as a relation between the observer and the observed. The task is to attend to both what is happening and what that happening provokes in the observer. Then, after the observation is over, one is meant to write a detailed account of that observation—without interpretation and without theorizing. Then, in the workgroup discussion, these written accounts are read out loud and collective conversation about them is undertaken. The task, that is, requires a prolonging of uncertainty and an extension of the time between experience and its interpretation. What that means is that this process is an intervention into the impulse to collapse experience and meaning into the same act. The reason why such an extension of the time between experience and interpretation is needed is because of the tendency to give way to the felt urgency of "needing to know." The idea here is not to abdicate responsibility for being a custodian of some professional and procedural knowledge as teacher educators. Rather, the idea is to make spaces for teachers to confront the idea that procedural knowledge is not going to be a shield against the other kinds of knowledge that are needed to move through classroom spaces in ways that enliven the pedagogical encounter. There, what is needed is an openness to emotional and affective experience—the students' and the teachers'.

THE DIFFERENCE BETWEEN OBSERVATION AND INTERPRETATION

As noted above, the workgroup discussions, while based on the foundational work of infant observation, are attended by people who are helping professionals. The goal is to extend, to the degree possible, the time between what we observe and the settling of the meaning of what we see. It means slowing down and considering a range of possible explanations, where those explanations come from, and which have emotional purchase for us, and why. The widening of our interpretive capacities as teachers is crucial, as it permits a kind of curiosity as opposed to other types of practical certainty. If a student has their head down during a lesson, a collapse of experience and meaning may mean that the teacher quickly assumes the student is being obstinate (or tired, or bored, or sick) and then acts upon that ascribed meaning. In a practice that extends the time between experience and meaning, the teacher would be encouraged to remain curious about the student, to inquire, and proceed cautiously.

While that is a relatively simple illustration, student teachers arrive in their preparation programs with all kinds of ready-made theories about who students are and what they are up to in classrooms. One particularly poignant meaning that student teachers make about students they observe in their classrooms who do not hand in their work regularly is that those students "do not care about their education." The focus of a method that interrupts this sort of meaning-making is on all the kinds of inferences and assumptions that we'd have to make on the road to this final move to closing down inquiry into the settled knowledge that someone doesn't care about their education. The purpose is to notice behaviors and then note as internal reactions (rather than settled meanings) what kinds of thoughts and feelings are enlivened. Put simply, there is a road to knowing other than the road to settled knowledge.

Waddell (2006) has described that during infant observations, the observer is put in proximity to perpetually changing emotions of, for example, peace and disturbance, bliss and terror, anxiety and fulfillment, discomfort and relaxation, whether in parent, baby, sibling, or self. There may be states of intense suffering, of the horror of disintegration, or of "free-fall." By contrast, there may also be states of relief and satisfaction, of the registering of beauty and even of awe, of difficulties overcome and turmoil quelled. Or, indeed, there may be feelings of inadequacy, of competitiveness and envy, or of anger and fear. The immediacy of the realities of life and death, whether literal or psychological, can never be far from the mind (1111).

What Waddell was pointing to here is that when we are attending to scenes of intimate relations, our histories of intimate relations are animated as we attempt to make sense of what is occurring. In connecting this kind of method of paying a particular kind of attention to the clinic of teacher education, I note that not many teacher education programs that I know of attempt to make significance from discomfort, anxiety, disturbance, terror, or disintegration. Yet all teachers know that those experiences are never, as Waddell (2006) said, "far from the mind" (1111). Rather than relegate them to the teachers' lounge or the bar after school on a Friday, this model of workgroup brings those features of classroom life to the center.

DREAM-THOUGHT

While the workgroup discussions do not ask participants to record their dreams, the kind of work is aligned with more common notions of "dream-work." Here, I think with Ogden's (2004) notion (following Bion) that "dreaming occurs both during sleep and waking life" (1355). Ogden explained, "Dream-thought is an unconscious thought generated in response to lived emotional experience and constitutes the impetus for the work of dreaming, that is, the impetus for doing unconscious psychological work with unconscious thought derived from lived emotional experience" (1355). Ogden's idea is that dream-thought is not relegated to what happens when we sleep. Rather, dream-thought is the thinking done in relationship to emotional realities of lived experiences that then put pressure on unconscious processes. Ogden (2007) wrote further that talking-as-dreaming means the "experience of understanding (getting to know) something of the meanings of the emotional situation being faced" (576). What occurs in dream-thought, or in talking-as-dreaming, in other words, is that which instantiates psychological work. I take this view of the workgroup discussion, that it invites a kind of dreamwork through the function of centering what is difficult, often ineffable, and frustrating about the particular experiences of learning to teach.

THE COURSE

The course is embedded in a program and with colleagues with whom I share a broad and shared understanding that teacher education is a fraught and complicated space. We frame teaching as a relational project that requires cultural and historical awareness, community engagement, responsiveness, and critical orientations. We have had a committed and close partnership with the local school district and embed much of our teacher education programs in those clinical spaces, though we now know that these relationships have been disrupted due to the COVID-19 pandemic and the abject failure to contain it on the part of national, state, and university leaders. We acknowledge that students come with their own histories of learning, cultural experiences, and political views. We prompt them to reflect and reflect some more in guided encounters with ever more responsibilities in the classroom. Students take this course during an intense academic semester that carries high-stakes performance assessments like the edTPA that represent a burden on them and on us.

Over the last several years, as the program has been revised in this clinically based setting, I've had the great fortune of designing and teaching a course that I call an "observation seminar." Given the intensity of the experiences (coursework and fieldwork), my colleagues and I thought it would be appropriate to have a class devoted to exploring the emotional demands of learning to teach. Specifically, we acknowledge that the majority (though not all) of our students have always been academically successful—they have, in other words, not had the experience of doing things "not well." We thought it important to create a space where they can be honest about the difficulties of the endeavors of learning to teach. After all, in disposition surveys that are required by our state certification board, students have to profess an increasing warmth and faith in all students. However, no one ever talks to them about what might happen if they don't like a particular student. No one ever engages in a formal way about what happens when their elegant lesson plan, this thing to which they've devoted hours and hours, is met with indifference by their students. There are no official spaces in many teacher education programs where student teachers might engage with how to interpret that frustration. How are they supposed to come to terms with the idea that students didn't care about their beautifully designed jigsaw activity about the Federal Reserve Bank?

The course meets once a week for two hours and is guided by a single prompt and set of activities. Each week, students are to produce a piece of writing that centers on one and only one "moment" in their classroom life for the week. The assignment is as follows:

Once a week, I am asking that you pay particular attention to an instance, situation, student, relationship, tension, frustration, success, failure, embarrassment, confusion, or anything along these lines and then write about it. One way to think about what would be a good "thing" would be to choose a thing that causes you to react strongly in some way or another. *As soon as possible after this happens,* you are to write about the event (or situation, or whatever "it" is). You should include as much detail as possible. What happened? Who was involved? What was said? What did you feel as it was happening? The idea is to write about what is seen *and* felt, and *to do so without interpretation.* The length of such a write-up could vary quite a bit, but we need sufficient material to discuss. We will begin with a minimum of 500 words. This is not meant to be an end-of-the-week "journal." The idea is to write about something that has impressed you, activated you, tripped you up, made you feel great, made you feel terrible, or otherwise stands out as noteworthy. Noteworthy doesn't mean extraordinary. Rather, you may notice something completely ordinary and wonder about it. This is also fine.

Each week, we discuss two students' writing. I choose them both, and while students know that their writing will be the focus at some point, I do not let them know beforehand when their weekly observation will be read. I have that student read their writing out loud while the rest of the students follow along with a pen or pencil in hand. I give directions for students reading along to underline or mark phrases or words that jump out at them.

Associative Objects—Evoking the Dreamwork

The next step I take is to get a list of words that will work as the associative material for us to discuss. Often, the direction I give is for students to "Look at the things you've underlined and then write ten words that come to mind." This is the practice of transforming the students' observations/descriptive writing into an associative object, producing the evocative object for the remainder of that hour. Then, to move the class toward conversation, I ask them to tell me one of those words to write on the board. I get at least one word from each student in the class.

At this point, we have a range of words on the board. Sometimes they are directly related to the explicit content of the observation writing. Other times, though, they are less obvious, having strayed away from the manifest content of the observation. In this way, it mimics dreamwork in that these words foster further psychological work of making sense of felt impressions made available, through language, for exploration. The rest of the workgroup discussion goes like this: I ask, "Who wants to nominate one of the words on the board to talk about?" (It can't be the one they wrote). They nominate it, and I ask them why they chose that one, and then the conversation follows from that student's comments on that word. The manner of my facilitation is mostly for clarification and then asking what else might come to mind when students think about that particular word or phrase. I invite them to think about that word in relationship to the particular writing that was read, their own experiences in classrooms, and any other associations that they have. When the conversation seems to slow, I ask for another word. We talk for an hour about those words and how the students are making sense of them. At the end of the hour, I ask the author of that writing to share about their experience and their thoughts about the discussion. That is all we do, all semester long.

In this way, students are invited to communicate associatively, as they attend to their thoughts and emotions through thinking and talking about these words or phrases. Students are communicating with thoughts and associations as they emerge rather than toward a particular knowledge goal—or argument. The prompts, in this way of thinking, invite me as the facilitator to think of what students then say as a complex nexus of inferences, assumptions, and emotional conditions to be expressed and make "visible" the dream-thought. I'll illustrate this process below.

OBSERVATION SEMINAR—TWO EXAMPLES

At the beginning of the course, students find it very difficult to observe and not interpret. The difficulty is exemplified in a variety of ways. For instance, in one case, a student wrote about a breakthrough they had in relation to their expectations of ninth graders.

In the class, we are broken up into groups of three students in all of our groups. I have felt quite lucky because I can see how much all of the students in my group have a passion to learn and are always questioning things and giving perspectives that is well beyond their ninth-grade years. I especially noticed this in my group with a student by the name of AJ.

In this bit of writing, I notice how much experience and meaning are collapsed. It seems that there is something grandiose about how this student-teacher describes their students. The writing begins with a feeling statement, that of feeling "lucky." The student-teacher reports on why they feel this way, seeing a "passion to learn" in that the students are "giving perspectives" that are "beyond their ninth-grade years."

The intervention that the method of the working group provides comes in the form of the following questions: What are the things that you are observing that make you interpret it as a "passion to learn"? What are your expectations of their ninth-grade years, where do those come from, and what are the perspectives that they are offering? How are they being offered? What are they saying? How are they "beyond"? I ask students these questions slowly in our discussions. I try not to offer the questions as indictments, but rather as curiosities about where our stories about students and who they are come from. We work toward just writing observations that attend to what is observed. It's a process. I get frequent emails in the first parts of semesters asking about whether what they have written is good enough. The students worry: "Is this too much interpretation?" As the semester goes on, the work continues. Some weeks, some students write what I experience as beautiful, poetic writing in their observations that include what they are seeing as well as their noticing of their own emotional reactions to them. Other weeks, that same student will write below the given word minimums in writing that to me feels much more flat. I consider both kinds of writing as part of the same project, trying not to value one as "higher" and the other "lower," trying to recognize that the emotional situation of learning to teach can sometimes feel rather flat and at other times more exhilarating. In both cases, I give them their "points" on the assignment.

In contrast to the above example, I'll present another example from one of the student-teacher's observation papers in which a fleeting interaction is described between the student-teacher, a white male, and a student, an African American female. The student-teacher begins the observation by describing trying out a teaching strategy he had learned from one of his professors: to try standing outside of the door and greeting each student by name as they walk in. While many of the students walk in and ignore him, one student stops.

She looked right at me and said, "I didn't know you wore glasses." This was a fair statement, I responded to her, "I try to use contacts most of the time, but I woke up (Wednesday) this morning with my eyes too sore to put my contacts in."

[The Student] returned, "Oh, that's cool, I broke my glasses last weekend, and I have to wait to go see my grandma to get new ones." I removed my glasses and pointed to the hinge, "I have broken these three different times, but I just keep super gluing them back." She laughed as I showed her the area that had obviously been broken and repaired several times. Her desk is in the front row, and I turned to the board and revealed that I could not read even the biggest letters without my glasses. "Dang, your vision is bad!" We laughed as the teacher entered the class from the hallway to get the starter going.

I see in the above writing an observation that is restrained in its interpretation, as the student-teacher recounts a conversation but provides several associative objects that could be words for further commenting. In this way, the observational writing becomes a grounding element for work that mirrors how dream elements function in psychoanalysis. For instance, I would pick out the words glasses, glue, broken, repair, vision, teacher entered, and hinge as words that I could ask students to associate with their experiences of learning to teach. In this method, there is an invitation to think of their time in classrooms in much more loosely connected and more literary ways than is their typical experience. As Rustin (2008) wrote about observations,

> The details are to be observed, not selected so as to give weight to a particular line of thinking. The aim is to strive for a relatively theory-free and

non-judgmental attitude to everyone involved, including oneself. The apparently meaningless is just as valuable in the record as the probably or obviously significant. The debt to the free-association method within psychoanalysis is an obvious one. (n.p.)

In the above excerpt, I see the observation as following those suggestions, and I see the elements for further free association as being evocative in their own right. The student-teacher's observation writing continues:

I feel like sometimes I try too hard to find the common ground with students. I know it exists, and I want to find it and use it to deepen my connection with the students. But sometimes I get lost in the process of sorting what is common and uncommon, to the point that I'm not practicing presence with the conversation that is going on. It's rude as shit. And it's a weakness that I combat frequently. It is hard for me to connect to people, and yet I felt a connection over a conversation about glasses? As a teacher I feel like I am on guard, always making sure that I am presenting myself in a "teachery-way." And I feel like [the student] cut thru the veil and saw the real me . . . and it was okay.

In the writing above, the student-teacher is representing their experience of getting lost, defensiveness, and vulnerability. What I think is being communicated here is like the reporting of a dream. The student's writing follows an associative path around connections sought, lost, and found. The two physical objects that are present in this writing excerpt are glasses and a veil; both objects revolve around the desire to bring ineffable affective life into focus and then an object that frustrates that desire. It is, in this sense, a kind of dream-thought in that it allows for an emotionally laden working and re-working toward significance. The glasses, the broken glasses, the hinges, the comparison of what each party can see, the humor of what it looks like to see through the teacher's eyes, "dang your vision is bad," and then the student-teacher's writing that he *knows* his vision is bad, he's straining to see something that is right in front of him, and eventually he was "seen" in reality. After class, I suggested something like that to this student. He told me that it hit too close to home.

Ogden (2017) called dream thinking "our richest form of thinking" (3), in which multiple planes of representing experience are occurring simultaneously, ranging in vantage points of perspective, timeframe, fantasy, and reality. It seems as though in the example above, this process could be said to be evident. However, Ogden also cautioned that dream thought is "stifled . . . by the analyst's premature need" to offer interpretations and meanings (3). What this indicates in a pedagogical sense is complicated by the distance and difference between the project of analytic practice and that of the teacher. However, I feel confident that in asking the student further questions about his writing, and taking the liberty of making such literary interpretations of it, I provoked a kind of stifling.

In other words, I had to confront what happens in teaching when a thought goes too far, when an interpretation hits "too close to home." On this occasion, I recall feeling like I needed to wait and see how the student in my class responded. I wanted to follow up outside of class and check in and make sure the student was "ok." However, I did not. I tried my best to resist my own desire for a settled meaning, hoping that the student was not upset. This is to say that my psychical processes are, of course, activated throughout but are most energetically when my statement comes back at me with suspicion. The work of conducting the workgroup seminar in the way that I have been trying it feels risky. It feels as though I constantly fail at "giving" pre-service teachers the education that they ask for, yet a competing excitement arrives when students acknowledge (either through an enlivened class session or through explicit feedback) that their experience of the course was somehow helpful.

THE DREAMWORK OF TEACHER EDUCATION

From the adjacent field of medical training, Marcus (2003) wrote that professional training to be a doctor

> exposes students' feelings about themselves and reveals an inadequacy, perhaps pictured as a defect, which is tender, painful and mortifying. The inadequacy is felt perhaps in comparison to the hero-healer fantasy about power for complete and total cure of even the very ill. (375)

In interpreting the above pieces of writing, I see a similar operation regarding the kinds of things being exposed to this student-teacher and happening in the spaces of teacher education. Rather than the hero-healer fantasy for complete and total cure, we have the fantasy of "authentic connection" with students that will facilitate powerful and transformative pedagogies. It isn't that transformative experiences are unrelated to pedagogy; it is the internalization of the grandiosity of those transformations that I suspect has something to do with the difficulties of learning to teach. And in my view, what the observation does, through writing and discussions like the one I just read above, is provide a leverage point to slow the train of thought and let student teachers sit in the emotional discomfort of learning to teach.

Returning to the psychoanalytic clinic, Ogden (2017) suggested that patient and analyst are "engaged in a process in which the analyst contributes to the patient's development of the capacity to dream (to do unconscious psychological work) his disturbing emotional experiences that the patient is unable to handle on his own" (6). When thinking about learning to teach and in light of the observation seminar, Ogden's writing invites a consideration of progress in terms of the development of a "capacity to dream" difficult emotional material. The purpose here is "not the solution to a puzzle; it is the beginning of a creative act in its own right" (Ogden 2008, 10). My thinking about learning to teach is heavily influenced by this sentiment. There are, to be sure, some kinds of procedural knowledge that can be accessed and studied in the service of the development of the professional practice of being a teacher. However, there are just as many aspects of learning to teach that are in the domain of "creative acts," those that necessitate the recognition of our students' psychical realities and our own (Britzman 2006).

NOTE

1. This chapter is reprinted from the 2020 *Journal of Curriculum Theorizing* volume 36, no. 4.

REFERENCES

Britzman, Deborah P. 2003. *Practice Makes Practice: A Critical Study of Learning to Teach*. Albany: State University of New York Press.

Britzman, Deborah P. 2006. *Novel Education: Psychoanalytic Studies of Learning and Not Learning*. New York: Peter Lang.

Britzman, Deborah P. 2007. "Teacher Education as Uneven Development: Toward a Psychology of Uncertainty." *International Journal of Leadership in Education* 10, no. 1: 1–12. https://doi.org/10.1080/13603120600934079.

Britzman, Deborah P. 2009. *The Very Thought of Education: Psychoanalysis and the Impossible Professions*. Albany: State University of New York Press.

Britzman, Deborah P. 2015. *A Psychoanalyst in the Classroom: On the Human Condition in Education*. Albany: State University of New York Press.

Britzman, Deborah P., and Alice Pitt. 2004. "Pedagogy and Clinical Knowledge: Some Psychoanalytic Observations on Losing and Refinding Significance." *JAC* 24, no. 2: 353–374.

Felman, Shoshana. 1982. "Psychoanalysis and Education: Teaching Terminable and Interminable." *Yale French Studies* 63: 21–44.

French, Robert. 1997. "The Teacher as Container of Anxiety: Psychoanalysis and the Role of Teacher." *Journal of Management Education* 21, no. 4: 483–495. https://doi.org/10.1177/105256299702100404.

Frosh, Stephen. 2018. "Rethinking Psychoanalysis in the Psychosocial." *Psychoanalysis, Culture & Society* 23, no. 1: 5–14.

Garrett, H. James. 2020. "Work Group Discussions in Teacher Education: Evoking Associative Objects." *Journal of Curriculum Theorizing* 35, no. 4: 48–58.

Marcus, Eric. 2003. "Medical Student Dreams about Medical School: The Unconscious Developmental Process of Becoming a Physician." *The International Journal of Psychoanalysis* 84, no. 2: 367–386. https://doi.org/10.1516/PFUF-D9NF-NKHU-9QTH.

Ogden, Thomas. 2004. "On Holding and Containing, Being and Dreaming." *The International Journal of Psychoanalysis* 85, no. 6: 1349–1364. https://doi.org/10.1516/T41H-DGUX-9JY4-GQC7.

Ogden, Thomas. 2007. "On Talking-as-Dreaming." *The International Journal of Psychoanalysis* 88, no. 3: 575–589. https://doi.org/10.1516/PU23-5627-04K0-7502

Ogden, Thomas. 2008. *Rediscovering Psychoanalysis: Thinking and Dreaming, Learning and Forgetting.* New York: Routledge.

Ogden, Thomas. 2017. "Dreaming the Analytic Session: A Clinical Essay." *The Psychoanalytic Quarterly* 86, no. 1: 1–20. https://doi.org/10.1002/psaq.12124.

Rustin, Margaret. 2008. "Work Discussion: Some Historical and Theoretical Observations." In *Work Discussion: Learning from Reflective Practice in Work with Children and Families*, edited by Johnathan Bradley and Margaret Rustin. Kindle ed., n.p. New York: Routledge.

Taubman, Peter. 2012. *Disavowed Knowledge: Psychoanalysis, Education, and Teaching.* New York: Routledge.

Waddell, Margo. 2006. "Education Section: Infant Observation in Britain: The Tavistock Approach." *The International Journal of Psychoanalysis* 87, no. 4: 1103–1120. https://doi.org/10.1516/195B-8VW0-7287-JVR7.

Chapter 12

Our First Foray into Work Discussion Groups with a University Laboratory School

Alex Collopy, Kailey Price, Lydia Bingham, and Carley Rader

During the fall 2023 semester, Alex taught a new Child Observation Seminar for a class of undergraduate and graduate students at Weber State University. Seminar participants included several mentor teachers in the Melba S. Lehner Children's School, Weber State's on-campus early childhood laboratory program. This chapter, co-written by Alex with seminar participants and mentor teachers Kailey, Lydia, and Carley, is the product of a self-study on our experience of the course. Following Alex's introduction to the pedagogical method, we explore a few key themes and moments that we identified as especially profound and enduring from our teaching and learning that semester. The examples in this chapter illustrate how psychoanalytic Work Discussion is a valuable addition to graduate and undergraduate teacher education programs, including those with lab schools.

"Work Discussion Groups," as we and others are calling them (Jackson 2005, 2018; Jackson and Berkeley 2020; Jackson and Klauber 2018), are also referred to as "work study groups" (Jackson 2005) and "Work Group Discussions" (Garrett 2020), though each are really "applications of work discussion" (Lisman-Pieczanski and Blessing 2011), at least loosely derived and owing credit to the approach to infant observation pioneered by Esther Bick (1964) and her later students at The Tavistock Clinic in London (Bradley and Rustin 2018). In Bick's approach, psychotherapists in training were responsible for conducting weekly home visits to observe an infant over two years' time; they brought these observations to the accompanying Work Discussion seminar, where they engaged in a deliberate practice of noticing very specific details about the infant with their caregiver(s) and the psychotherapist's own emotional experience of observation (Bradley and Rustin 2018; Alperovitz 2018).

Though already widely proliferated in psychoanalysis and other care professions around the world, Alex first became aware of Bick's approach in the United States as it was employed at the now-defunct Washington School of Psychiatry's (WSP) Infant and Young Child Observation training program. Faculty at the still-active Washington Baltimore Center for Psychoanalysis (WBCP), some of whom participated in both institutions, have been engaged since 2008 in a partnership with a local Community-Based Organization preschool called Jubilee JumpStart (JJS) (Alperovitz 2018). Joining efforts, analysts from WSP and WBCP brought Work Discussion to JJS in 2011, where they have facilitated groups with teachers on and off since. After completing her first fellowship at the Washington Baltimore Center for Psychoanalysis in 2016, Alex became greatly interested in the ways WBCP and WSP faculty and their trainees engaged with staff and children at Jubilee JumpStart. It was for this reason that she conducted her dissertation research at JJS, first intending to observe Work Discussion Groups, which were then unfortunately paused for that year. Though the analysts were not present at JJS during her study, Sharon Alperovitz facilitated her entrée to the school, and several of the prior Work Discussion facilitators served as informants in her study, providing context for the relationship between psychoanalysis and the preschool. It was these analysts whose work inspired Alex to develop a psychoanalytic Child Observation Seminar at Weber State, and the semester we enjoyed and this publication for which we will be named would not exist without them. Our seminar differs significantly from the unique JJS model and should not be considered an offshoot of theirs, especially given that the WBCP analysts did not train Alex to do this nor were any involved in this course. This chapter notes specific features of our WSU seminar that were taken from the JJS model as it was told to Alex during her (2019) research and explains why those tools were useful in this new context.

Work Discussion has long been adapted for developing the observational skills of teachers and school staff in the United Kingdom. By supporting group participants to notice and unpack their ways of seeing (and not seeing) the children with whom they work, facilitators documented educators' increased self-awareness and resulting changes in their classroom practices (Jackson 2005, 2018; Jackson and Berkeley 2020). The approach has been adapted at universities in places such as Vienna (Datler, Datler, and Wininger 2018) and Athens (Antypa and Anagnostaki 2024) yet remains hardly visible in the United States. Beyond those in D.C., there are rare locatable examples of psychoanalytic Work Discussion conducted in U.S. schools, only through partnerships with psychiatric institutions (Snyder and Berman 1960). We are not aware of anyone other than Jim Garrett, whose 2020 work was republished as the previous chapter in this volume, currently using a variation of this approach in a university teacher preparation program in the United States. There are no locatable publications on Work Discussion adapted for National Association for the Education of Young Children (NAEYC)-accredited teacher education programs, early childhood Laboratory School programs, or public early childhood (birth age 8) educator licensure programs in the United States. There are no publications on the use of any psychoanalytic pedagogy in early childhood education or teacher education in Utah, where Weber State is located. Still, there are always critical limitations to any academic literature review of clinical or pedagogical practice. There may exist many teacher educators, administrators, teachers, clinicians, and Reflective Supervisors/Consultants, for example, whose observation procedures mirror aspects of Work Discussion and have yet to be featured in academic publications or who use different terms to describe their approach. Many of those outside of academia do not have the time, capacity, or incentive to pursue academic publication. Moreover, mainstream scholarly publication in the United States remains largely inaccessible to those without the academic and linguistic capital and professional networks to which the authors of this chapter are privileged.

The qualifications and orientations of facilitators of Work Discussion, or those who claim to be Work Discussion-informed today, vary widely. In psychoanalytic training programs, facilitators are analysts. In educational settings, facilitators may be analysts, psychologists, social workers, psychiatrists, professors, or education consultants. Those professors and education consultants may or may not have undertaken formal study of psychoanalysis but are likely to have found value in Work Discussion enough to practice and write about it through intensive engagement with psychoanalytic literature and/or communities. Increased attention to Work Discussion, as with any clinical tool in education, will provide and require opportunities to discuss across disciplines the ways in which educators can be most prepared to undertake this task, if at all. Emil Jackson and Trudy Klauber (2018) run five-day training courses for those interested in becoming Work Discussion facilitators. We have not been able to participate in such training, but as with Jackson and colleagues' other work we cite in this chapter, we found it well worth reading about what they learned through that pilot project and may pursue such training in the future.

The ways in which those professionals facilitate seminars vary, but not neatly by their field, as educators implementing Work Discussion are always using some of the tools of the clinicians from whom we have learned about this approach. There are significant differences, of course, between Bick's approach and the ways in which we in education have come to apply it. First, the location of observation varies. The Infant Mental Health field, which includes psychoanalysts, social workers, early interventionists, and other care providers, focuses on work with caregivers and children together, which many argue necessitates observation in home environments, even for those trainees who may go on to do predominantly clinic, school, or other community-based work outside of the home. Participants in Work Discussion as part of an infant observation psychotherapy program would each visit a child weekly over two years' time, but then come together with peers who do not directly engage with each other's observed children. Pre-service teachers could be assigned a child study that would require frequent observations in a child's home and then come together in seminar with peers who observe different children, but that would in most cases need to be confined to the one semester in which a teacher is enrolled in a given professor's course. A longer child study may be undertaken as a capstone, thesis, or dissertation project, but it would likely be the project of an individual student without an accompanying group seminar. Though many early childhood educators, including the mentor teachers at our Weber State laboratory school, conduct home visits, teachers' home visits are typically far rarer and may occur just once or twice per year. At some schools, teachers conduct home visits for each child just once upon intake. Teachers within a given school may be engaged in Work Discussion for as long as Bick's original students, but they would be observing a child or children in their own classrooms. Sometimes preschools are set up in ways such that teachers would be familiar with children in each other's classrooms; other times they would be less or not at all familiar. Each of these factors will tremendously influence observation and discussion.

Of equal importance, psychoanalysis teaches us, is the relationship between the facilitator and group participants. In some cases, such as Garrett's (2020), the group participants in a higher education setting are each engaged in student teaching at other schools. At Weber State, the laboratory school where our mentor teachers work is housed in the same department as Alex's faculty appointment. The relationship between faculty and laboratory school teachers is distinct from a typical university instructor-student relationship. Alex, Lydia, Carley, and Kailey had known each other for a few years in relationships more collegial than instructor-student or the oft compared analyst-analysand relationship, with inherently different power dynamics. Though this was the first time that Lydia, Carley, or Kailey had participated in one of Alex's classes, all of the authors, as faculty and staff of Weber State, had participated in department and college meetings and events. As a supervisor of undergraduate practicum students in the laboratory school, Alex had worked amicably with Kailey, a mentor teacher to whose classroom Alex's students were assigned. One might use psychoanalytic theory to argue that this interferes with the process of observation, and that a Work Discussion facilitator should have greater separation from the participants. Such collegial relationships might also unintentionally steer the project of Work Discussion from observation too far toward consultation or supervision. The role of faculty members in laboratory schools varies by university but also between professors within departments. Unlike others, Alex does not have any supervisory role at the laboratory school and could not have any effect on the employment of the mentor teachers. Though Alex held the power of assigning a grade to each student registered for the course, students generally understood that if they were to submit their observations, attend and participate in discussion, they would pass this course. She attempted to make this seminar, in contrast to others of her courses, one with as few demands as possible, while required to grade their work for the university and for NAEYC accreditation. Our relationships are inseparable from the ongoing outcomes of our Work Discussion, and though, as in any education or clinical encounter, we advocate for attention to such relational dynamics, they need not (nor could they) be replicated for learning and change to happen. Attention to what are always uniquely complex facilitator-participant dynamics should propel self-inquiry into pedagogical practice rather than dismiss the applicability of a given approach. Our intention is not to dictate a model of Work Discussion but to show with full transparency how we thought through ours. As in ethnographic research, psychotherapy, and all classrooms, building rapport between instructor and students, and among students, proved critical. Our preexisting relationships made more accessible and shareable personal feelings and experiences that we noticed in-the-moment and in our later analysis and discussion of transcripts.

Methods in which participants are expected to document observations and later present them in group (e.g., through writing, verbally, or videos) further vary, and each carries great unique potential. The method of producing and sharing observations may best be determined by the purposes of the setting in which the participants work and the setting in which the participants are engaged in Work Discussion. In the chapter preceding ours, Jim Garrett very thoughtfully explores, using both theory and examples from his students, the ways in which his course design facilitated the "dreamwork" he sought. His students met once a week for two hours each time, during which students' written observations would be discussed, but Jim took a creative approach to both the writing prompt he provided to students and how he chose which and what of those observations the class would discuss each week. Rather than sitting for a scheduled observation, students were prompted to write about a particular (likely emotionally loaded) moment they experienced in their own classrooms that week. Instead of the students then reporting their writing to the group exactly, everyone in the class would identify words or phrases in their peers' writing that jumped out to them; those became what he conceptualized as the "evocative objects" during class discussion.

Some facilitators of Work Discussion in schools seek to adhere as much as possible to Bick's approach in the observational method, the questions they ask participants, the order in which they ask those questions, and, crucially, the ways in which they expect participants will make use of their observations. The WBCP analysts' initial approach was to require teachers to bring a written description from a thirty- to sixty-minute classroom observation to be read aloud to the group. Soon recognizing the barrier to participation and the tremendous frustration that writing posed for many of the teachers who were non-native English speakers and limited on free time, the WBCP facilitators, including bilingual social workers, shifted to an approach where teachers would communicate observations verbally during Work Discussion meetings. Later, responding to ongoing discussions with school administrators reflecting on the utility of Work Discussion at JJS, the analysts shifted again, this time to a video discussion model. Teacher participants were now responsible for recording a brief video clip of a child in their classroom to bring to Work Discussion. During groups, after viewing a recording, the WBCP analyst would ask each group participant, "What did you see?" and then, "How did that make you feel?" In interviews from Alex's dissertation research, two psychoanalysts from WBCP described this adapted approach to Work Discussion as transformational and empowering to teachers. Analysts described teachers' changing perspectives, made possible by welcoming new and mutable orientations to teachers' own emotional experiences. In another example, a psychoanalyst explained, "as the teacher separated her feelings from her observations with the child, it didn't mean that the teacher's feelings or concern for the child subsided, but rather that she could make use of them" (Collopy 2019, 41).

Though not communicated by the WBCP analysts in such specific terms, their shift from requiring written observations to facilitating video discussions reflects a more Universally Designed approach (CAST 2018), providing participants increased access to learning by varying methods of representing information and methods for participants to demonstrate what they know, indeed, to demonstrate themselves. Moreover, Work Discussion Groups "provide multiple means of engagement" insofar as the method may "foster collaboration and community," "facilitate personal coping skills and strategies," and uniquely support students to "develop self-assessment and reflection" (CAST 2018). Alex therefore thought this approach would be especially valuable for the largely non-traditional student body of Weber State University, an open-access, dual-mission institution that prides itself on access to degree achievement regardless of students' personal, professional, and educational backgrounds. Like many students at Weber State, Carley, Lydia, and Kailey work full time, take other courses, and would have little time to produce weekly written observations for this seminar. The JJS video model provided a foundation for inclusive pedagogy. Work Discussion may provide teachers access to knowledge (e.g., knowledge of diversity in child development, emotions, and behavior) as well as access to skills (e.g., observation, documentation, and professional, emotional communication). Inclusive, psychoanalytic pedagogy for practitioners working with young children may similarly be conceptualized as multiple modes of access to learning *as change*—therapeutic change—and demonstrating change, not only cognitive, behavioral, or seemingly intra-psychic but also interpersonal. Work Discussion both facilitates and provides insight into change; as Garrett (2020) notes, "psychoanalysis is as much a way to make sense of what is happening as it is a strategy to foster those happenings" (49). Alex feels, as Jim does, a great responsibility to teach in ways that hold true to the ways in which she understands the work of teaching and learning, that is, through a psychoanalytic lens.

Researchers, clinicians, and educators alike have long been advised to leave their feelings, effectively their selves, "at the door," as if such sever-ance were either possible or desirable, despite over a century of scholarship in psychoanalysis and anthropology vehemently suggesting otherwise. In contrast, contemporary psychoanalytically oriented professionals primarily operate under the assumption that the analysand's or participant's (in this case, the teacher's) transference and feelings are an ever present and emerg-ing dynamic space, a tool through which we may (or even may only) begin to understand a child's emotional experience and desires inaccessible to us through purportedly "objective" observation alone. Though contempo-rary psychotherapists remain empirically curious about clients' earliest life experiences, it is for this reason, among others, that practitioners emphasize active, multimodal attendance to what is "in the room": the client's verbal and non-verbal language that emerges within that specific therapeutic alliance, in that specific time, in that specific space. Collective, explicit exploration into what emerges "in the room" may provide a client insight into patterns of experience in their everyday life.

Over the last several decades, multimodal approaches to psychotherapy have gained greater visibility, integrating perspectives from neuroscience and from somatic psychotherapy with more classically conceived psycho-analysis. Renewed calls to critically examine the limits of verbalization, and talk as "cure," have appropriately done less logically to reject the psycho-analytic value of attention to the verbal and not-yet-verbal (which we shall not abandon, nor should you) than to importantly validate the necessity of simultaneously decentering verbal communication. Such creative approaches highlight the inseparability of conscious and unconscious thought from physi-cal development and present embodied experience. We do not have expertise in any of this work. However, if we hold even theoretically possible that observation and interpretation are not only psychic, cognitive, and emotional but are inseparably physiological processes and products, educators would be remiss to overlook in modality what is rather easily imminent access to identified physical sensations. Alex also came to value the question "What are you feeling in your body?" from her own experience as a client in psychotherapy. Though she still holds great respect for psychoanalysis that does not explicitly engage the body, this approach allowed Alex to get unstuck from the trap of intellectualizing. Very different stories emerged. Her physical sensations then became an observational tool more accessible to her in everyday life and work. Her students were provided this additional tool to take away from the course.

When we ask students (or anyone) "What did you feel?," they may not identify having an emotional reaction: "I don't know," "I felt fine," or "I liked it," and leave it at that. When we ask students "What did you feel?," they often do not attend to their physical sensations, even though the question does technically invite this. They may not have practice in noticing physical sensations or may not think of those sensations as valuable information to share. They may knowingly or not suppress physical sensations—something teachers are widely known to excel at. Even students able to identify and articulate to the group both emotional and physical sensations may find themselves surprised by perceived inconsistencies between them, which provides a valuable provocation for self-observation. For example, we know that anxieties emerge during child observation, but the felt sense of whatever feelings those anxieties evoke may be taken for granted and disconnected from an emotion to which those are consciously assigned during the moment of watching the video, and then while telling their peers and professor about it. All of this is insight. Alex's idea was to use Work Discussion to expand access to all that her students might observe. The questions that facilitators ask are provocations we afford material to become accessible to participants. This additional provocation, and in turn, material with which to associate, proved valuable especially because our Work Discussion was limited to fourteen, 50-minute class meetings within one semester, far more limited time to engage in self-observation than typical for Work Discussion. Alex therefore took a semi-structured approach, asking students "What did you see?", "What did you feel?," and "What are you feeling in your body right now?"

The WBCP analysts argued that the use of video in Work Discussion at Jubilee Jumpstart also provided "space for the child to tell the story" for group consideration, alongside that of the original observer and videographer (Collopy 2019, 41). Providing space and learning from multiple stories is a methodological goal similarly shared by researchers in early childhood education. Though very different projects, we may see parallels between ethnographic inquiry and psychoanalytic observation that support us in crafting approaches to Work Discussion. In the "Preschool in Three Cultures" method (Tobin, Wu, and Davidson 1989; Tobin, Hsueh, and Karasawa 2009), researchers filmed a typical day in a preschool and shared this video with teachers to solicit their insider perspectives on everyday life in their classrooms, which gave way to greater understanding of what might otherwise be tacit and unspoken cultural values and practices. When the videos were re-watched, informants' responses to the video were not understood as correcting or more accurate than their prior comments, but instead as an opportunity for the interviewees to keep making meaning. In the "Preschool in Three Cultures" method, the research data was not the video footage but the interviewees' perspectives on the video verbalized in the context of the interview. The researchers were not trying to determine with as much detail as possible what was happening in the videos, but to understand as much as possible what the informants thought about what they were seeing. Alex, Lydia, Kailey, and Carley conceptualized "data" in this vein; the "data" in this self-study are not the video clips that students brought to class, but instead the dialogue that emerged after viewing the video, featuring the voices of the authors of this chapter.

It is for both this reason and for confidentiality that the content of the video clips viewed during class meetings is not detailed in this chapter. The children in the videos are not research participants, nor are other students who were enrolled in Alex's course. We are, appropriately in line with our theoretical orientation, most interested in what the videos evoked for the student authors. We also recognized that it would not be possible to maintain the confidentiality of the children in the laboratory school were we to describe what happened in the videos, given that our university affiliation is public and that there are a low number of children in each of the mentor teacher's classrooms, who remain their students at the time of this writing. University faculty, administrators, and school staff are (for the better!) intimately familiar with each of the children in these videos, as is an ever-rotating group of practicum students. Were we to describe the content of the video clips, it would be impossible that these children would not be recognized from their identified mentor teacher, the children's age, developmental and behavioral characteristics, and other contextual anecdotes the student authors provided during Work Discussion. Successful Work Discussion depends on teachers' ability to speak openly. Sharing the content of the video clips would make it such that the student authors' unfiltered feelings about specific children still enrolled in their classrooms would be made public. We agreed that even any of the most stringent Institutional Review Board-approved protections would not be sufficient to include the children as research participants in this unique case. We strongly suggest that others who may experiment with Work Discussion in such settings take similar precautions. The extent of information about participants that we reveal in this work mirrors the valuable information provided in others' (e.g., Alperovitz 2018, Garrett 2020).

CHILD OBSERVATION SEMINAR

Alex's syllabus includes the course description from the university course catalog:

> The Child Observation Seminar is a small group reflective practice seminar. Students meet weekly to view and discuss video clips from work with young children in school, home, or community settings. Groups are facilitated to support early childhood professionals in feeling and awareness in their subjective emotional present, toward new experiences of themselves with children, families, and fellow early childhood professionals that may transform their work. This course is designed and offered in face-to-face format.

There was required "attendance in weekly meetings, held on Tuesdays from 4:30 to 5:20 pm." The syllabus explains:

> Each student will be required twice during the semester to submit a short video clip of a child or children they regularly engage with. Each class meeting will be focused on watching and discussing one clip. The instructor will assign these dates during the first week of class. You will submit the clips on Canvas by 11:59 pm on the Monday prior to each of your assigned class dates. . . . Students are required to submit reflective journal entries 7 times throughout the semester.

Course learning outcomes in the syllabus are aligned with selected NAEYC Professional Preparation Standards for Early Childhood Educators (National Association for the Education of Young Children) to meet our program's accreditation requirements, and Competencies for Culturally Sensitive, Relationship-Focused Practice (Michigan Association for Infant Mental Health), which would support students in seeking Infant Mental Health Endorsement® if they wish.

We began each weekly fifty-minute class meeting seated in a semicircle in front of a large projector screen where we watched a video clip provided by the student assigned to submit footage that week. Alex then began the discussion by asking a student, "What did you see?" Students then proceeded to answer that question clockwise. Sometimes Alex asked follow-up questions to prompt students to provide greater detail, or more often, to ask students to "back up" when they had unintentionally provided what appeared closer to an interpretation than an observation. For example, instead of saying "the child is curious," students were encouraged to identify what suggested to them that the child was curious, by attending to details such as the child's eye gaze. After discussing "plainly" what each student "saw," Alex asked students, "What did you feel while watching the clip?" Students reflected not only on what the content of the video made them feel but what it felt like to watch and discuss the video clip in their particular present being(s), in this particular class environment, increasingly explicitly recognizing too the professional and interpersonal dynamics between faculty, mentor teachers, and students. Alex then asked, "What are you feeling right now?" and to those students who did not include both emotions and physical sensations, followed with, "What are you feeling in your body right now?" We then rewatched the clip and repeated this process. We then rewatched the clip without sound and repeated the process. Finally, Alex asked, "What are you wondering about?" Alex then provided students the opportunity to add any thoughts or feelings that emerged for them while listening to others. Sometimes, discussion really accelerated just as class was ending. Students were not only warming up but had ample material provided by their peers to associate with and respond to. For this reason, Alex began asking if there were any video clips that students wanted to re-watch. We shifted our weekly schedule to accommodate those.

"THAT WAS TOTALLY UNACCEPTABLE IN MY HOUSE GROWING UP"

After watching a video clip for the first time during our third class meeting, Carley spoke first: "I see a child stabbing markers down on the page, making dot-like marks," using her hand to imitate the child's arm and hand motion.

After each student had shared initial observations, Alex asked, "What do you feel?", prompting Carley to again speak first.

"Even though I'm excited seeing the child engaging creatively with materials," she responded, "and I really value the way he's doing this given what I know about development, I am feeling like I have this urge . . . like fighting an urge to intervene."

"Why?" Alex asked.

"Someone might see them as ruining the markers, stabbing them into the paper like that. I feel protective of the child because I'm anticipating someone stopping him. If I had done that as a child, I would've been in trouble."

"Why's that?" Alex asked.

"You just didn't do that. Ruining markers like that was totally unacceptable in my house growing up," Carley explained.

Alex asked, "What would have happened?"

"Oh . . . ," Carley responded, looking surprised. "I'm not sure, but I feel anxiety about it."

Alex asked, "What do you feel in your body right now?"

"I feel like a knot, right here," Carley said, bringing her fist against the lowest point of her sternum.

Lydia: I think back on the first class when Carley just opened up about life. I was like, "Carley, that's stuff that you haven't even shared in your therapy sessions."

Carley: I shared that I had conflicting feelings of both anxiety that the markers would break, but also a feeling of protectiveness over the child. This was a very personal thing for me to share with anyone, let alone my professor and classmates.

Lydia: I wondered what made her feel so comfortable, where it took her like the whole semester to be able to share some of that at work.

Alex: Was it comfortable? You might have said it, and it didn't necessarily feel comfortable. What was it like to share?

Carley: I felt comfortable . . . it wasn't like an unsafe feeling or push to do it. It didn't feel like, "you have to answer this right now, tell me exactly," but it made me think. And it was direct enough that I was like, "oh, okay. This is what I'm feeling right now. This is where it's coming from." I wouldn't say that I was just like, "let's just share my life," because I don't do that.

Lydia: Just asking more about that, but not diving into like, "now tell me about your childhood!" you know . . . it followed a train of thought where it was easier for us to slowly make the connections.

Carley: Being asked a couple of direct questions on how I felt . . . Why do I think I felt that way? Have I experienced that feeling before? Where do I feel that in my body?

Alex: It seemed like one question that really pushed you was when I asked what would have happened.

Carley: Yeah. And I think I felt comfortable answering that because I wasn't focused so much anymore on the people in the room, as I was focused on figuring that out within myself. I really was trying to figure out like, "what would have happened? I don't know . . . let me think about that. Where am I feeling this anxiety in my body?" I was focused on myself, inward. Because of that I wasn't focused on the people around me or what they would be thinking . . . which you brought up, Lydia, these are things I haven't shared with my therapist.

Alex: What allowed you to do that in our class?

Carley: I'm not always focused inward when I'm with my therapist, which is kind of weird and different . . . I'm not getting such direct questions about what

I'm physically feeling and where. It's a lot of me talking, and maybe getting a couple of questions along the way.

Kailey: That's a good point. I like that the discussion is open, but I think sometimes the questions help you see it in a different light. It makes me wonder about what would happen if we all just did it at work, and we didn't have Alex asking those questions . . . would it provoke the deeper thinking if there isn't an outsider there? If it's just our colleagues that already know the environment and the kids in the video, would we ask each other that and think to provide that perspective?

Carley: It was this curious environment. When you asked questions, it didn't feel like, "tell me all the woes of your childhood." It was just curious. It really felt like "I think what you said is really interesting, tell me about your experience. Sometimes people ask questions, and it feels like they want to have a specific answer. Or they want to know what's wrong with you, like "why on earth would you do that or think that way?" Instead, this was like "I wanna know more and I want to understand."

Lydia: That's interesting you put it that way. In therapy sometimes we choose to do that, because we know that we can talk it through and help ourselves, and that somebody's there to help us. But if it's not that someone's there to help you, it's just you processing those things.

Carley: And I go to therapy with a goal, right? Every week I go and I'm like, "we're going to talk about this, and we're going to do this," right? And so, in class, there wasn't a goal that day, it was a more natural occurrence, per se.

Lydia: Space for you to be able to process it and not like, "By the end, you're gonna know how your childhood has affected you, and what you should do differently in the classroom because of that."

Kailey: I loved listening to the discussions with Carley that were attached to this video. Not only has the child learned a lot in the past weeks, but so have the teachers. It was amazing how she had said this doesn't cause as much anxiety as it did before, or at least it wasn't her first instinctive feeling.

"WILL WE EVER FULLY UNDERSTAND WHAT CHILDREN ARE THINKING?"

At the start of a class midsemester, we watched a minute-long video clip where the frame was limited to one child on an outdoor playground. Though they were visibly engaged with the video, the student authors had fewer comments in response to this clip than those we watched in previous weeks. Their brief comments primarily focused on their genuine excitement that the child was enjoying the outdoor playground and demonstrating gross motor skills, and that the child's behavior was "cute." On this day, conversation seemed to stall out, as if everyone had already said all that could be observed and felt about the clip, which reflected a rather mundane event in their everyday teaching experiences.

A purpose of child observation is surely tuning into just that: what we might otherwise see as mundane or disinteresting and stop there in our inquiry. Alex wondered, pleased at the prospect, whether students were engaging with the video, professor, and classmates authentically, without pressure to say more as a performance of what others might like to hear. Still, Alex wondered about ways to keep in-class conversation moving. She started to wonder whether a better approach in these situations might be to ask the student who provided the video clip that week why it was that they had brought the video to class for our consideration; what the student might be wondering about the child. Thinking about both the original and longstanding variations of the Tavistock approach, and the approach to ethnographic interviewing in which she was trained, Alex was equally concerned about adapting the model in ways that might influence the observations and reflections of the other students.

In the moment, Alex improvised by offering an observation to the students during class: "I noticed that all of your comments have been very positive."

Each of the student authors' faces reflected surprise at Alex's statement, followed by nods of agreement.

In this example, Alex found that the student authors expressed far more in their reflective journal entries following the class meeting and in our later self-inquiry discussions among authors. Our seemingly stalled in-class discussion that day might have suggested that the students felt they had understood all that one needed to or could about the child in the video clip, but their writing and our discussions suggested differently.

Alex: Kailey, you wrote this in your journal:

> Why does she enjoy climbing? What feelings does she have when she completes a cycle? What is her body telling her? I know when I was a kid it just felt good to stand somewhere tall. To climb and try to get high places on the playground. Even now as an adult, it is fun to climb and balance on the materials. Is she thinking the same way I did? Is there more to her play . . . Will we ever fully understand what children are thinking?

I think a piece that Kailey talked about a few times in class throughout the semester was really about delighting in the child. In class, she talked about this being fueled by what I interpreted as a sort of nostalgia of her own, but Kailey also seemed to find new curiosity about the child and an understanding of their individuality through that. What are your thoughts about that? Is there anything else you'd like to share with us?

> *Kailey:* I know in the way that we plan and the way we use "the inquiry cycle," sometimes we have to make assumptions about a child's intent in order to help us provide new experiences and new materials that they might need, however I realize that sometimes in thinking of their intentions and assuming their intentions . . . that's when you miss the mark or you put those assumptions in, you may be stifling their creativity and what their true intentions were. You may be changing the direction of their play entirely based on your own assumptions. I think there's a fine line between interpreting their intentions and acting on it. I want to try observing deeper for longer periods of time and practice taking out the idea of intention.

> *Alex:* I have found it so interesting to learn about your joy and positivity and delighting in, that's happening, while knowing you've all been moving through these real challenges that teachers face. What allows you to feel joy when you observe?

> *Kailey:* I forget the negative interactions almost as quickly as they happen. As I listen to others discussing what they saw during class, I notice that I don't exactly remember what they had observed, if it comes to a behavior like throwing something or something that would typically elicit a negative response. I observed mostly through a positive lens. It made me think about other times I might have done this, and I realized I do it all the time. I do it when watching the children and their interactions with each other, I do it when discussing a child's day with parents, and I do it when coaching the preservice teachers I work with. I don't necessarily think this is a bad thing. (Each of the authors nodded in agreement.)

> *Alex:* Knowing that the positivity is genuine, for what reasons do you think that students seemingly had less to say on some days?

> *Lydia:* In class, sometimes I feared saying things, unsure of how other people felt about it. Or like . . . maybe I'm the one who's thinking about this wrong. And I was not wanting to offend other students. In other video clips, I was a little worried about some of the situations, but I realized that I might be the one who is lacking knowledge . . . so I allowed for some of my thoughts to not be shared at that time . . . even if there were things in clips or in discussion that are somewhat against my philosophy when it comes to working with children.

> *Alex:* I remember one week in class we watched a video clip that a student brought in from a very different setting than our laboratory school. Is that what you're referring to?

Lydia: Yes. I realize that this may have been my thinking, and I wasn't sure how to bring it up in a way that would not offend that classroom teacher.

Alex: I was thinking about how the three of you are coming to class not only as preschool teachers and as my students, but also as mentor teachers.

Lydia: I really wanted to do some quick educating. I am wondering if this is simply because this is a part of what I do as I mentor college students in my classroom or am I a bit narrow minded and think that all children need the environment and teaching style that I provide.

In some approaches to Work Discussion, it is only the facilitator who asks questions. After a few meetings in which students had seen and experienced the kinds of open-ended, follow-up questions that Alex was asking, she encouraged them to ask each other follow-up questions if they became curious about something. She hoped this would provide them another tool to take away from the course. Students asking questions gained practice in using specific wondering language and could experience and model not-knowing as part of their professional competence. Lydia's stance here of wondering whether she might be wrong is interesting. It is not uncommon for teachers' worries about their professional competence to emerge during Work Discussion. Here, Lydia was intentionally adopting a stance of not-knowing where she remained competent but curious, an observer of her peer. Given that mentor teachers are uniquely in a position of needing to know what to do and model it for others, her willingness to question her own approach to teaching here was impressive. This may be an opportunity uniquely provided by Work Discussion. It is not the role of the facilitator or the participants in Work Discussion to educate, and needing to resist this evokes thoughts and feelings in each of us that may provide insight into our work.

Planning for individuals and groups is the purpose of most observation in preschools and therefore teacher education. Teachers are expected to translate observation into practice. Their abilities are often judged by the educational outcomes of those practices. It is no surprise that teachers often feel pressure to interpret their observations in the "right" way and know exactly what to do differently when they return to the classroom. Sharon Alperovitz told Alex that the JJS teachers were often anxious or frustrated that Work Discussion was not this goal-oriented. Alex was surprised that the student authors did not, at any point during seminar discussion throughout the entire semester, push for answers from her or their peers about what to do in the classroom. It would have been natural, perhaps even easier, for them to do so. This difference between observation and observation for planning is evident in the distinction between Work Discussion and other forms of staff group discussion in schools. Others, such as Louis (2020), have developed "new" models of supervision in response to perceived limitations of existing psychoanalytic models of "group consultation," in which she includes Work Discussion. Teacher education, Supervision, and Work Discussion are very different tasks. It is worth noting here, however, something of Louis' "Work Group Supervision," which in contrast helps us see what is unique about Work Discussion. Louis (2020) uses "Work Group Supervision" as a space for educators to examine the theories about child development and learning implicit in what they observe and conclude about children, helping them to be intentional about their instructional planning. In "Work Group Supervision," the facilitator is told to ask: "How much, and how well, do you think the child is learning?", "How much do you think a change in the learning environment would support and extend learning?", and "How could your interaction support and extend learning?" (Louis 2020, 75). Alex knew that her students were already adept at making classroom observations as part of their curriculum planning cycle. They are already prepared to do this in their other courses as required by our NAEYC accreditation, and in their work as preschool teachers. Alex created this course having noticed an opportunity missing in-between, one that Kailey suggested in the dialogue above. This was a reminder of our need to maintain Work Discussion (in whichever forms educators may claim to).

"WHAT ALLOWS SOMEONE TO TALK IS THAT THE GROUP COULD HOLD IT"

During the third week of the semester, Lydia wrote in her reflective journal:

> I realized I felt a little unsure about the experience I had videoed. I tried to explain my reasoning for taking the video . . . as well as to protect the children, as I know a 1-5-minute video only gives a small glimpse into the world I live each day. I truly care for these children and want some insight into what others see and feel while watching them, but I have spent a lot of time with them and may know or understand more than others do.

Each of the student authors later shared with Alex during our self-study meetings that they hesitated about showing certain videos to the class because they worried that their peers would focus on particular things about the child. Students watching the videos might be bothered by a child's behavior and have a desire to intervene because they are already studying and might wish to demonstrate their ability to identify developmental differences. The student authors worried that peers would say negative things about the children in their classroom. Though this ultimately was not the case, this urge to pro-tect the children in their classrooms frequently came up during Work Discus-sion. During the last few minutes of class one week, Lydia shared something that a caregiver had said about their child, who had been in a few videos we watched this semester. The whole group fell silent.

> *Lydia:* I'm realizing the parts that are sticking out to me from this class are all things that had a bigger emotional response, and you can feel the shift in the room or in a person . . . the marker video, it elicited such an emotional reaction. The day we talked about the child in my classroom, you could *feel it* in the room. That elicited deep conversation.

> *Kailey:* Yes. The more and more people talked about these emotions and then brought up these harder things.

> *Alex:* I'm really struck by this piece about the shift in the room. I think that was the only day Kailey and Carley weren't there. If you were to tell them about the shift in the room, what would you say?

> *Lydia:* Saying it, I realized how much that I'd been carrying . . . I could feel myself smiling like "oh, it's gonna be fine" but inside I was like oh no, this is hard. Like "I'm still smiling it's fine," but you could see everybody in the room just all of a sudden lean back and just tense. It felt like nobody knew what to say or how to respond. Then finally you jumped in, and your voice was shaky . . . and you just said you could see my face and body's response to having said it.

> *Alex:* Yeah.

> *Lydia:* I wanted to stop myself from saying it because it felt like it was too much for people to handle. When I said it, everyone was like dang, wow, speechless. They didn't know how to respond. Everybody was walking out, and you could just feel this like . . . somber. . .I don't know. It was heavy. It was heavy. It was like, all right class is up and everybody's like, I don't know if I'm ready to leave. I feel like we need to process this more before we leave.

The following class meeting, Alex did not want to start with our typical rou-tine before providing Lydia and the group time to process how our last semi-nar had ended. Alex also did not want to force discussion in one direction, but she realized that more time in which students could bring up what they wished, before the last few minutes of class, would provide opportunities to say what may have been left unsaid. She began class by asking "How's your work?" and proactively began one subsequent class later in the semester with the same question.

> *Alex:* I was a little worried about . . . I didn't ever want it to seem like I was really over handling, like let's steer it back to this thing that I thought was

interesting because it was emotionally charged. But I did then share like, that felt heavy last week. I was struck by what you said.

Lydia: Like, are we really getting up right now?

Alex: Yeah, I was also left feeling that way. Everybody left really slowly.

Lydia: It felt like people couldn't handle it. The idea with a group would be that like . . . what allows someone to talk is that the group could hold it, I guess. I felt like I overwhelmed them. I was like, never mind. I'll take it back. I was holding it fine myself. It's cool, just ignore that comment.

Alex: It was a moment where I was reminded of why I originally created the class, like how I wanted to teach, and what my role was supposed to be as the facilitator. I'm telling you guys to tune in to yourselves and the person facilitating has to be able to tune in to themselves, but really to be able to hold it all for the group participants. And I was caught off guard in that moment thinking holy shit, I don't know if I'm going to be good at this, because I'm supposed to be the person who can hold this without starting to cry in front of everybody. I was like I gotta go home and process this myself so that next week I can come back and be what I need to be. And I needed to think like, to what extent am I drawn to talking about this again next week because of my own feelings about what you said, and my anxiety about not doing it right?

Lydia: Maybe something for the future is, because sometimes I did later think about something after class . . . maybe there's just space in the beginning like, "did anything sit heavier with you, or did you think about anything since last week?"

Alex: Asking the students, "What things did you reflect on throughout the week?" Okay.

Lydia: Just leave that space to see. And make the classes longer. Because so many people wrote things in their journals they didn't bring up in group. To me, it felt like this general theme of like, protectiveness of what we do. Protectiveness of our children, right? And then I think that protectiveness of ourselves, like, do I dare share this? Do I want to put this on them? I can hold this feeling. I'm holding it. I'm doing great . . . I was trying to protect the peers in that classroom as well. I could see protectiveness going in every direction.

Alex: So, you were taking protective measures?

Lydia: Yeah, but when you watch videos in class, it's like, it's right there. You can't hide from it. And then you're able to talk about it.

REFERENCES

Alperovitz, Sharon. 2018. "Fostering Psychic Transformation through the Discipline of Infant Observation: The Eyes—and Mind's Eyes—Have It." *Psychiatry* 81, no. 1: 96–99. https://doi.org/10.1080/00332747.2018.1440120.

Antypa, Theofania, and Lida Anagnostaki. 2024. "The Functioning of a Work Discussion Group as a Peer Group in Preschool Education: a Reflective Account." *Journal of Child Psychotherapy* 50, no. 1: 132–144. https://doi.org/10.1080/0075417X.2023.2236706.

Bick, E. 1964. "Notes on Infant Observation in Psychoanalytic Training." *International Journal of Psycho-Analysis* 45: 558–566.

Bradley, Jonathan, and Margaret Rustin. 2018. *Work Discussion: Learning From Reflective Practice in Work with Children and Families*. New York: Routledge.

CAST. 2018. "The Universal Design for Learning Guidelines." Accessed April 1, 2024. https://udlguidelines.cast.org/binaries/content/assets/udlguidelines/udlg-v2-2/udlg_graphicorganizer_v2-2_numbers-yes.pdf.

Collopy, Alex. 2019. *Jumpin' with Jubilee: An Ethnographic Case Study of Inclusion and the Emotional Lives of a Bilingual Pre-kindergarten Classroom in Washington, DC*. Pennsylvania: The Pennsylvania State University.

Datler, Wilfried, Margit Datler, and Michael Wininger. 2018. "Evaluating the Impact of Work Discussion Techniques on the Formation of Psychoanalytic Skills and Attitudes: Research Designs and First Results." *Infant Observation* 21, no. 2: 204–219. https://doi.org/10.1080/13698036.2019.1566015.

Garrett, H. James. 2020. "Work Group Discussions in Teacher Education: Evoking Associative Objects." *Journal of Curriculum Theorizing* 35, no. 4: 48–58.

Jackson, Emil. 2005. "Developing Observation Skills in School Settings: The Importance and Impact of 'Work Discussion Groups' for Staff." *Infant Observation* 8, no. 1: 5–17. https://doi.org/10.1080/13698030500062044.

Jackson, Emil. 2018. "Work Discussion Groups at Work: Applying the Method." In *Work Discussion: Learning from Reflective Practice in Work with Children and Families*, edited by Margaret Rustin and Johnathan Bradley, 51–72. New York: Routledge.

Jackson, Emil, and Andrea Berkeley. 2020. "On the Leading Edge of Learning: Work Discussion Groups for Headteachers." In *Sustaining Depth and Meaning in School Leadership*, edited by Emil Jackson and Andrea Berkeley, 132–150. New York: Routledge.

Jackson, Emil, and Trudy Klauber. 2018. "New Developments: Training in the Facilitation of Work Discussion Groups." *Infant Observation* 21, no. 2: 241–260. https://doi.org/10.1080/13698036.2018.1559075.

Lisman-Pieczanski, Nydia, and Deborah Blessing. 2011. "News from Washington DC: Infant and Young Child Observation Program." *Infant Observation* 14, no. 2: 224–226. https://doi.org/10.1080/13698036.2011.583442.

Louis, Stella. 2020. *How to Use Work Group Supervision to Improve Early Years Practice*. New York: Routledge.

Michigan Association for Infant Mental Health. n.d. "Endorsement for Culturally Sensitive, Relationship-Focused Practice Promoting Infant and Early Childhood Mental Health®." *Alliance for the Advancement of Infant Mental Health*. Accessed April 10, 2024. https://www.allianceaimh.org/endorsement-licensing.

National Association for the Education of Young Children. n.d. "Professional Standards and Competencies for Early Childhood Educators." *National Association for the Education of Young Children*. Last modified November 2019. Accessed April 11, 2024. https://www.naeyc.org/sites/default/files/globally-shared/downloads/PDFs/resources/position-statements/standards_and_competencies_ps.pdf.

Appendix

Trauma-Informed Healing-Centered Practice: Teddy Bears in Traumatic Times (Fall 2021)

The Center for Emotionally Responsive Practice at Bank Street

Lesley Koplow

LIST OF THEMES BY MONTH

September: A Safe Place for Bears
October: When Teddy Bears Remember
November: Some Things Change; Some Things Stay the Same
December: Together and Apart
January: Teddy Bears Come Back: Discoveries and Artifacts from a Visit Home
February: Imaginary Friends
March: Losing and Finding
April: A World for Teddy Bears: Teddy Bear Town
May: Transformations (Growing and Changing)
June: A Good Good-bye for Teddy Bears

RATIONALE FOR SEPTEMBER–DECEMBER THEMES AND PROCESS

These themes coupled with transitional object use are designed to:

1. Create a welcoming and comforting school climate.
2. Promote the capacity to self-comfort and have empathy for others.

3. Make a bridge between the 2020 school experience and the current school year experience (re-entering the larger, in-person school community).
4. Offer remote learners and in-person learners invitations for self-expression and social/emotional connection.
5. Give the big feelings that come from disruption and loss a voice in school-friendly ways.
6. Decrease social and emotional isolation in children and teachers.
7. Reduce the risks of unresolved grief and post-traumatic stress in children and teachers.

STAFF BOOK GROUP RESOURCES

Koplow, L. (2009). *Bears, Bears Everywhere*: Chapters 2, 3 and 9. New York: Teachers College Press.

Koplow, L. (2002). *Creating Schools That Heal*: Chapter 12. New York: Teachers College Press.

Koplow, L. (2020). *Emotionally Responsive Practice*: *A Path for Schools That Heal*: Chapters 6 and 7. New York: Teachers College Press.

Video Resource: (2015) *Bringing ERP to Life*: Transitional Objects Section.

PRE-IMPLEMENTATION ORIENTATION MEETING FOR STAFF

Before beginning the teddy bear work, plan to meet with the colleagues in your building who are also following the Teddy Bears in Traumatic Times Curriculum.

Meeting Agenda

- One colleague reads aloud to the others the book *Outside, Inside* by LeUyen Pham. Take time to study the pictures.
- After the read-aloud, take five minutes for quiet writing and/or drawing in response to the prompt, "What did this book make you think about?"
- Share with the group (not necessary to read what is written, but tell about it!)
- Ask, "What was it like to have time to think about our pandemic stories and to hear each other's stories?" Discuss.
- Ask, "how can we support the different feelings that children and parents will have when school begins?" Discuss.
- Ask, "How do we hope the teddy bears might support all the feelings that are coming to school with the kids?" Discuss and brainstorm.
- Look together at the September theme and activities, and share initial ideas.

- Make a plan for everyone to check in regularly over the school year as you implement the Teddy Bears in Traumatic Times curriculum.

EXAMPLE MONTH: SEPTEMBER

Theme: "A Safe Place for Bears"

Orientation and Rationale for This Month's Theme: This theme invites children to identify with their Teddy Bears, who will need to feel safe at school in order to be emotionally stable, socially connected, and engaged in their learning. The activities invite children to create their bear's identity, as well as representing important things that they want peers to know about their own identities. When bears and children represent what they need to feel safe at school, they become connected within the community in authentic ways.

Sub-Themes and Inquiry:

- How can our classroom become a safe place for Teddy Bears?
- Routines: How and when can Teddy Bears be part of classroom life?
- Who is who? Our Teddy Bears all look the same. What makes your bear unique? How will we recognize your Teddy Bear?
- Some of us speak different languages at home. What languages does your teddy bear speak?

Index

academic functioning, 94
Adjustments to Practice, 194, 202, 203
Adler, Alfred, 54
adolescence, 50, 51, 54
adult heterosexual identity, 54
Aichhorn, August, 173–74
Aistear program, 176, 184, 185
Akhtar, Salman, 142, 154
Alvarez, Anne, 83, 84
American Psychoanalytic Association's (APsA), 3
Anna Freud Foundation, 4
anti-bias, 60, 64
Apgar, Amanda, 36, 37
Appignanesi, Lisa, 180, 183
Asikainen, Helka, 31, 36
Association for Child Psychoanalysis, 4
associative objects, 216–18
attachment theory, 183
autonomic nervous system (ANS), 179

Baader, Meike Sophia, 144
Baker, Bernadette, 145
Barthes, Roland, 29
behavior problems, 109
Bernfeld, Siegfried, 173
Bettelheim, Bruno, 151
Bibby, Tamara, 27, 160, 167
Bick, Esther, 5, 17, 223–24, 226, 228

Bion, Wilfred R., 176, 178, 179
Birksted-Breen, Dana, 24–29
Bleiberg, Efrain, 77, 78
Bollas, Christopher, 16, 192, 199–200, 204
Bowlby, John, 112
brain development, 150
Britzman, Deborah, 24, 28, 211
Brooks, David, 179
Burlingham, Dorothy, 2, 3, 165
Burman, Erica, 23, 24, 31
Butler, Judith, 52

Candidate Assessment of Performance, 192
care settings, 65–66
care workers, 61
chaos, 77, 110, 119, 200, 203, 204
Child Observation Seminar, 223, 224, 232–233
Child Protective Services, 134
children: behavioral interventions, 168; cognitive development, 150; cognitive processes, 150; conscious and unconscious experiences, 164; creativity, 192; curiosity about, 165; emotion, 167; emotional response, 151; gender-diverse children, 61; helplessness, 61; licensing

requirements, psychoanalysis into teacher education, 194–96; need, 110; opposition and resistance, 191; playfulness and resistance, 192;; psychosexual development, 52; therapeutic setting, 61; trauma, 192; unconscious reality, 62

children, learning difficulties: anxieties and impulsive acts, 76; disorganized households, 77, 79; ethnic, racial, and socioeconomic backgrounds, 75; insecure patterns of attachment, 76; meaningful exchanges, 83; neuropsychological evaluation, 81–82; phonological-deficit reading disability, 75; physical impairments and language delay, 83; statements and drawings, 80

child well-being, 137

chronology and hierarchy: developmentalism, 38–39; playing, doing of. *see* playing; possibility and uncertainty, 24; psychoanalytic temporality, 25–27

classroom, psychoanalytic theory in: attachment figure, 111–12; behavioral challenges, 110; behavioral programs, 115; child behavior, 118–23; "evidence-based" methods, 110; internal working models, 115, 120; mental health, 118; misbehaviors/taunts of child, 118; preschool teacher's problem, 111; teacher self-confidence, 111

clinical counseling, 46

clinical psychoanalysis, 8, 24, 32

clinical services, 3

cognitive constructs, 58

cognitive deficits, 10

cognitive functioning, 89, 92, 93, 101

cognitive process, 150, 151

communication, 9, 11, 16, 29, 31–32, 75, 79, 84, 95, 96, 99, 116, 133, 136; with peers and teachers, 165

Community-Based Organization, 224

compulsory education, 144–45, 210

compulsory heterosexuality, 47

concept knowledge, 92

countertransference, 10, 95, 97, 100–102, 154, 155

COVID-19 pandemic, 3, 13, 133, 135, 215

cross-gender identifications, 60

cross-gender play, 48, 49

curriculum: IQ tests, 147; selection of, 145; social philosophy, 143: theory, 192

developmentalism, 8, 23–24, 37–39, 46

developmental theories, 6, 53, 58, 59, 109, 160

Disability Studies in Education, 8, 167

Draw-A-Person Test, 31, 78

Duckworth, Eleanor, 152

dyslexia, 74, 75, 81

education: "fosterage" system, in ancient Ireland, 143; German education, 146; in Japan, 146; psychoanalytic thinkers in, 192; in society, 143; in United States, 145

educators: capabilities and characteristics of, 110; children's psychosexual development, 52; and policymakers, 9

emotion, 98, 167, 178–79, 230, 250, 253

Emotional Intelligence, 148

Emotionally Responsive Practices, 132

emotional well-being, 62, 127

enculturation, 143, 144

Erikson, Erik, 6, 92, 112, 174

feminism(s), 47

Ferenczi, Sándor, 2, 181

formal curriculum, 159

Freud, Anna, 2, 3, 10, 53, 92, 128, 165, 173, 174

Freud, Sigmund, 2, 6, 95, 96, 185, 206

Freudian theory: adult neurosis, 173; gender, and sexuality, 46, 51–57; human behavior, changes of, 47;

releasing of emotions, 50; sexual expressions and identities, 54
Froebel, 144, 175
Frosh, Stephen, 211
full-scale intelligence quotient (FSIQ), 91, 93, 101

gender, 65–66; bias, 48; care workers, 59–60; in classroom, 51; conforming, 64; diversity, 45; expression, 64; interpretations and enactments of, 49; and sexuality, 47, 49
gender binary, 54,55, 56, 58, 62, 63, 64, 66
gender-diverse children, 6, 7, 49, 54, 57, 59, 61, 64
gender dysphoria, 50, 66
gender fluid, 48, 49, 64
gender identities, 47, 49, 59, 60, 62, 64
gender nonconforming, 50, 58, 65, 66
Gesell, Arnold, 10, 89–93
Gesell Developmental Observation-Revised (GDO-R) assessment, 10, 89–93
Gill-Peterson, Jules, 23, 49, 50, 55
Goldsmith, Douglas, 119
Goleman, Daniel, 148
Goodley, Dan, 31–32, 160, 169
Graham, Philip, 60, 174, 175
gross motor behavior, 90, 91
gross motor skills, 90, 236
group pressure, in school, 147

Heart Rate Variability (HRV), 179
Herzog, James, 142
heterosexuality, 47, 48, 51–56, 62, 63
heterosexual matrices, 48
Histories of the Transgender Child, 55
Hitschmann, Eduard, 2
Hoffman, Stuart D., 146
human rights, 47, 56
hypothesis testing, 166, 167

Illich, Ivan, 149
"improvisational teaching" approach, 153, 169
inductive reasoning, 103
Infant and Young Child Observation training program, 224
institutional practices, 47
internal working models, 11, 109, 111, 115, 119, 120
International Psychotherapy Institute, 5
intersectionality, 23, 47
intersex conditions, 55–56, 59
IQ tests, 148

Jackson, Emil, 58, 223, 224, 225
joint attention, 90
Joseph, Betty, 97
Jubilee JumpStart (JJS), 224, 230

Kanter, Joel, 3, 5
Karabon, Anne Elizabeth, 152–54
Katz, Lillian, 14, 15, 18, 168
Kernberg, Otto, 10, 95
Kitchenham, Andrew, 152, 155
Klauber, Trudy, 223, 225
Klein, Melanie, 10, 53, 54, 96–98, 174
Kohlberg, L. A., 7, 46, 57–59, 61, 66
Kohut, Heinz, 147, 155
Kristeva, Julia, 26, 37

language behavior, 91
learning: and behavior outcomes, 11; child's feelings, 151; cognitive learning, 177; difficulties. *see* children, learning difficulties; emotional demands of, 209; Montessori and adult-structured learning, 14; Safe Learning Environment, 202
Lesbian, Gay, Bisexual, and Transgender (LGBT), 65
LGBTQI issues, 49
Likierman, Meira, 77
listening, 16; empathic attunement, 142; enculturation, 144; fosterage and

apprenticeship, 144; mental activity, 142; narcissism, 142–43

MacNaughton, Glenda, 159, 160
Malin, Heather, 29
Malinowski, Bronislaw, 51
Mang, Pamela, 143
Marcus, Eric, 220
Marsden, William, 145, 146
Mathelin, Cathrine, 78, 81
Maturational Theory of Child Development, 91
Mead, Margaret, 51
Meeting Diverse Needs, 194
memory, 10, 93, 94, 98–102, 109
mental health care, 2–4, 13
Merchant, Almas, 28
Merleau-Ponty, Maurice, 91
Montessori: and adult-structured learning, 14; in psychoanalysis, 173
Montgomery, M. R., 142
Motta, Robert W., 79

narcissism, 15, 17, 142–43, 148
nconscious negative feelings, 154
negative feelings, 128, 154
neurodevelopmental disability, 76, 77
non-heterosexual sexuality, 55
nonverbal (performance) intelligence, 92

observational writing, 218
Oedipus complex, 46, 53, 54
Ogden, Thomas, 27, 28, 96, 214, 219, 220, 221
O'Loughlin, Michael, 5–7, 12, 15, 28, 160, 161, 165, 167, 168, 169
overt behaviors, 91

Pajak, Edward, 142, 148
paranoid-schizoid position, 97, 98
Pearson, Karl, 93
pedagogical methods, 223. *see also* work group discussions
peer conflicts, 163

Pervasive Developmental Disorder NOS, 130
Pestalozzi, 144
Phillips, Adam, 3, 180–83
physical sensations, 230, 233
Piaget, Jean, 7, 46, 57–59, 91, 150, 151, 175
Piagetian theory, 47, 57–59, 66
Picture Concepts subtest of WPPSI-IV, 99
playing, 204; aliveness, experience of, 28; anticipation over participation, 27; anxieties and unconscious thoughts, 174; classrooms, 180; cognitive learning, 177; curiosity, 181; emotional states of mind, 177; feelings, and desires, 174; holding back and waiting, pleasure of, 27; Irish early years education, 176; mental illness, 175; Montessori framework, 176; nature, 180; normative childhoods, 28; parent-child connection, 175; presumptions and performances, 28; primitive anxieties, 179; and reality, 181; scribbles, 29; Squiggle Game, 30; squiggle method, 32, 38; structured play-group sessions, 184; unconscious communication, 181
Poland, Warren, 100
political agendas, 23
political movement, 145
Porges, Stephen, 179, 183
Post Traumatic Stress Disorder, 130, 246
problem-solving ability, 90, 91
projective identification, 96–98; in clinical situation, 96; concordant countertransference, 99; countertransference, 97; emotion, 98; intolerable feeling, 96; nonverbal communicating feeling, 96; paranoid-schizoid position, 97, 98; Picture Concepts subtest of WPPSI-IV, 99; unwanted/split-off feeling, 96

pro-social behavior, 129
psychic confusion, 199
psychic genera, 16, 199
psychic reality, 25
psychoanalysis, to early childhood education, 1, 46, 62; behavior and learning outcomes, 11; chronology and hierarchy. *see* chronology and hierarchy; clinical method, 2; comfort and empathy, 13; community and school settings, 3; developmentalism, 8, 9, 23–24; early childhood education, 5; emancipatory project, 169; financial and time constraints, 5; foundational knowledge of, 12; in geographic areas, 3; internal working models, 11; master's and doctoral programs, 6; non-clinical practitioners and researchers, 5; quantitative assessment, 10; structural inequality, 3; trauma and trauma-informed practice in, 196–99
psychoanalytic institutions, 3, 4
psychoanalytic psychotherapy, 1
psychoeducational evaluation, 73, 75
psychological assessments, 89, 94, 98, 102
The Psychological Bulletin, 93
psychological dispositions, 167
psychological "holding," 165–66
psychotherapeutic practices: identified disabilities, 160; misconceptions, 160
public-school system, 131

Quantz, Richard, 144, 147, 148
queer feminisms, 62–65

Reactive Attachment Disorder, 130
reasoning, 50, 57, 59, 93, 98, 99, 101–3, 145, 150, 196
Reconceptualizing Early Childhood Education (RECE), 8, 160–61
Reflective Practice, 194, 232
Reich, Wilhelm, 2

Reik, Theodor, 115
religious movements, 145
Rijke, Victoria, 29
Rogers, Carl, 148
Rorschach, Hermann, 93
Rorschach Inkblot Test, 31, 94
Rosenfeld, Herbert, 96
Rustin, Margaret, 17, 218, 223, 224

Safe Classroom Environment, 194
Safe Learning Environment, 202, 203
Salomonsson, Björn, 76, 80, 84
Sapon-Shevin, Mara, 160
Schore, Allan, 178
Schwaber, Albright, 142
Sentence Completion test, 74
sex characteristics, 55
sexual abuse, 109, 197
sexuality, 6, 45, 46, 48, 51–56, 61–66, 109, 175, 197
sexual orientation, 49, 65
Sherry, John, 154, 155
social behavior, 48, 129
social implications, 55
social justice, 3
social norms, 24, 167
social reasoning, 57
social structures, 32
social support systems, 59
Spearman, Charles, 93
Squiggle Game, 8, 24, 29–31; drawing of duck's foot, 33; drawing of hand, 34
Stolorow, Robert D., 142
Stuart-Smith, Sue, 180
Subject Matter Knowledge, 194
Sunshine Circles, 182–85
supplemental funds, 4

Tavistock, 5, 212, 223, 236
teacher licensing processes, 194–96
teacher-pupil relationship, 149
teachers' narcissism, 15
Teddy Bears in Traumatic Times Curriculum, 133, 245–47

teletherapy, 3
Thematic Apperception Test (T.A.T.), 31
therapeutic classroom communities,
130, 137, 169
therapeutic consultations, 30, 32
trans childhoods, 50
trans-disciplinary field, 124
transference, 10, 53, 95, 100, 103,
153–55, 229
transgender development, 49, 50
transgender theory, 56
trans identities, 55–56, 66
transition, 13, 101, 163–65
transitional objects, in classroom life,
245–46; emotional integration, 128;
emotional integration and healing,
129; teacher-child relationships,
129; Teddy Bear use in, 133–36;
therapeutic nursery, 130–31; in
twenty-first century, 132–33; uses of,
131–32
trauma, 192–93, 196–99, 204
Tronick, Ed, 178
Tustin, Frances, 78

United Kingdom, 173, 224
United States, 4, 5, 83, 110, 144–45,
153, 197, 224, 225

verbal comprehension, 92, 93, 101, 102
violence, 23, 56, 132, 154, 197
visual-spatial skills, 10, 101, 102
Voneche, Jacques, 150
von Freund, Anton, 2
Vygotsky, Lev, 92

Waddell, Margo, 213–14
Warner, Leslie, 93, 152, 154, 155
Washington Baltimore Center for
Psychoanalysis (WBCP), 3, 19, 224
Washington School of Psychiatry
(WSP), 5, 224

Wechsler, David, 92, 93
Wechsler Adult Intelligence Scale
(WAIS), 93
Wechsler-Bellevue Intelligence Scale for
adults (WBIS), 92, 93
Wechsler Intelligence Scale for Children
(WISC), 93
Wechsler Preschool and Primary Scale
of Intelligence (WPPSI), 93
Wechsler Preschool and Primary
Scale of Intelligence—4th Edition
(WPPSI-IV), 91–95, 99–101
Wechsler Preschool and Primary Scale
of Intelligence—Fifth Edition
(WPPSI-V), 92
Well-Structured Lesson, 194
Whyte, Kristin Lyn, 152
Winnicott, C., 165
Winnicott, D. W., 8, 24, 27, 30, 32–36,
77, 78, 80, 81, 83, 127–38, 165, 184
Work Discussion Groups, 17, 223,
224, 228; course, 214–17; dream-
thought, 214; experience and
interpretation, 212–14; facilitators'
qualifications and orientations, 225;
infant observation psychotherapy
program, 226; observation seminar,
217–20; partnerships with psychiatric
institutions, 224; personal coping
skills and strategies, 228; personality
interactions, 212; psychoanalysis
and preschool, 224; skill access,
229; Tavistock Model, 212; teacher
education, 220–21
World Health Organization (WHO), 32,
56
World War I, 2, 145
World War II, 2, 3, 30, 146

young children, 5, 12, 47–48, 65, 66,
121, 129, 132, 141–42, 175–77

About the Editor and Contributors

EDITOR

Alex Collopy, Ph.D., IECMH-E®, is the president of the Utah Association for Infant Mental Health. After nine years of research and teaching at Penn State and Weber State universities, Alex sought joy and purpose in returning to direct work with children. Alex is in practicum training for play therapy as a Master of Social Work student at the University of Utah, where she is also an associate instructor of Infant and Early Childhood Mental Health and holds a fellowship in Interprofessional Infant Mental Health. She has completed three fellowships in psychoanalysis, at the Washington Baltimore Center for Psychoanalysis and the Contemporary Freudian Society. Alex was the recipient of the 2021 American Educational Research Association's Critical Perspectives in Early Childhood Education Dissertation Award.

CONTRIBUTORS

Lydia Bingham is a mentor teacher at the Melba S. Lehner Children's School, an early childhood education laboratory school in the Department of Child and Family Studies at Weber State University. She is currently a Master of Education student in the Weber State University Graduate Studies of Education program.

Greta Carlson, Psy.D., ABPP, is a board-certified licensed clinical psychologist who works with children, adolescents, and adults. Dr. Carlson is nationally certified in Trauma-Focused CBT and trained psychodynamically at George Washington University. She completed her postdoctoral training in trauma, dissociation, and stressor-related disorders at Sheppard Pratt's Trauma Disorders program and a residency in child and adolescent psychotherapy and assessment at the Center for Cognitive Therapy and Assessment. She is currently a staff psychologist at Kennedy Krieger Institute, a Johns Hopkins University affiliate teaching hospital, in the Center for Child and Family Traumatic Stress, and a clinician in private practice in Montgomery County, Maryland.

Lisa Farley, Ph.D., is a professor of education at York University. Her research considers the uses of psychoanalysis in conceptualizing the meaning of childhood and education. Her book *Childhood Beyond Pathology* (2018) examines how psychoanalytic concepts can inform ongoing challenges of representing development, interiority, and relationality. Within teacher education, Farley has explored teachers' memories of childhood and schooling as key parts of becoming a teacher, and her most recent work examines the meaning and challenges of museum programming and practices that represent difficult knowledge with children.

Dr. Joanna Fortune is a psychoanalytic psychotherapist who specializes in the parent-child relationship and the role of play across the trajectory of our lives. She is the author of four books (a three-book play-based parenting series called 15-Minute Parenting 0–7 years; 8–12 years; the teenage years) and *Why We Play*. She has published a chapter in *Lacanian Psychoanalysis with Babies, Children, and Adolescents* and in *Theraplay—Innovations and Integration*. She has published an article in the British Psychoanalytic Council's *New Associations* and other journal articles. She writes a weekly column in a national newspaper in Ireland and presents the parenting slot on a national radio show each week, as well as hosting her own podcast and regularly guesting on others. She holds a doctorate in psychotherapy from Middlesex University. She is a recognized conference speaker and has presented to educators on the important role of play in education and the lives of children.

H. James Garrett is a professor of social studies education in the Mary Frances Early College of Education at the University of Georgia. Jim's research centers on the emotional demands of learning and teaching about the social world, particularly when that learning has to do with trauma, crisis, or vulnerability. His latest research project involved studying the circulation of affect and emotion during classroom discussions of current sociopolitical issues such as gun violence, anti-Black racism, and immigration. Currently, he is interested in what social studies teachers can learn from the methods of civil rights activists of the past and present. His book *Learning to be in* *the World with Others: Difficult Knowledge & Social Studies Education* was published in 2017 by Peter Lang. Prior to pursuing his career in academia, Jim taught high school courses in world studies, economics, psychology, and media studies. He received his Ph.D. in curriculum, instruction, and teacher education from Michigan State University.

Alexandra C. Gunn, Ed.D., is a professor of education at the University of Otago College of Education | Te Kura Ākau Taitoka, Dunedin | Ōtepoti, Aotearoa New Zealand. An early childhood teacher by profession, Alex teaches and conducts research into many aspects of early childhood education and teacher education, curriculum, inclusion, and issues of gender and sexuality.

Eileen Johnson, M.S., is the director of Little Missionary's Day Nursery in New York, New York, and a member of the Alliance for Psychoanalytic Schools, where her expressed mission is to teach children to understand their feelings and the feelings of others, and to help parents value the healthy expression of emotions in the family. Eileen is the author of *The Children's Bill of Emotional Rights*, *What Happens When You Die* (The Wound of Mortality), *Emotional Education*, and *Ten Steps to an Emotionally Healthy Child*. These books have been used in undergraduate early childhood teacher preparation programs and Master of Education programs across the nation at institutions including Pennsylvania State University and Weber State University. Eileen has a Master of Science Liberal Studies degree from Excelsior College in Educational Leadership, an undergraduate diploma and National Teacher Certification from University College Dublin, and an undergraduate diploma in Anglo-Irish Literature from Trinity College Dublin.

Christopher Konieczko has experience working in the community assisting individuals with disabilities to achieve their employment goals and independent living. Christopher is earning his Ed.S. in counselor education and supervision from Kent State University. His professional accomplishments include invitations to present at the state level. Christopher is a member of state and national counseling associations, including executive board membership (president-elect) with the Ohio Rehabilitation Association.

Lesley Koplow is a clinical social worker, teacher, and author who lives in New York City. She is the founding director emeritus of the Center for Emotionally Responsive Practice at Bank Street College. She is also the founder of the Schools That Heal Network. Lesley is the author of several books including *Unsmiling Faces: How Preschools Can Heal*; *Creating Schools That Heal*; *Bears, Bears Everywhere: Supporting Children's Emotional*

Health in the Classroom; *Politics Aside: Our Children and Their Teachers in Score-Driven Times*; *Emotionally Responsive Practice: A Path for Schools That Heal*, and several books for children.

Janice Kroeger, Ph.D., is a professor of curriculum and instruction and early childhood education at Kent State University in Kent, Ohio. As a qualitative researcher and early childhood educator, Janice supports reconceptualizing practice. She conducts research and teaches inclusive forms of inquiry in social sciences and education. Kroeger utilizes an eclectic blend of philosophical, discursive, ethnomethodology, and mixed-methods research, advancing social justice and inclusive practices.

Dana Oleskiewicz has thirty years of experience in scientific collaborations and community-based engagement toward effective public policy. Dana is earning a Ph.D. in cultural foundations at Kent State University with a concentration in gender studies and health disparities for vulnerable populations. Career accomplishments include publications, invitations to present nationally, successful fundraising, and professional awards.

Kailey Price is a mentor teacher at the Melba S. Lehner Children's School, an early childhood education laboratory school in the Department of Child and Family Studies at Weber State University. She is currently a Master of Education student in the Weber State University Graduate Studies of Education program. She has been teaching children from ages one to six for the last thirteen years. She thoroughly enjoys teaching children and is always looking for new learning opportunities to better help her support children at every level of development and through all different needs and interests.

Carley Rader is a mentor teacher at the Melba S. Lehner Children's School, an early childhood education laboratory school in the Department of Child and Family Studies at Weber State University.

Andrea Sanchez has been an early childhood educator for over fifteen years. Andrea is currently earning a Ph.D. in curriculum and instruction from Kent State University with an emphasis on early childhood education. Prior to beginning her doctoral studies, she taught kindergarten, using her work to examine how play supports children in the general education curriculum and working toward building community with parents and families. She is currently a graduate assistant at Kent State teaching courses for pre-service teachers.

Ionas Sapountzis, Ph.D., is an associate professor at the Derner School of Psychology of Adelphi University and the director of the School Psychology programs. He is a faculty member and supervisor in the Psychoanalytic Psychotherapy Program and in the Child, Adolescent, and Family Psychotherapy Program of the Derner School of Psychology. His articles have been published in the journals of *Psychoanalytic Psychology*, *Psychoanalytic Review*, *Psychoanalytic Perspectives*, *Psychoanalysis, Culture and Society*, and in the *Journal of Infant, Child, and Adolescent Psychotherapy* (*JICAP*). He works with children and adolescents with emotional and learning disabilities and also with children and adolescents on the spectrum. He maintains a private practice in Garden City, New York.

Clio Stearns, Ph.D., is an assistant professor of education at Massachusetts College of Liberal Arts in North Adams, MA. She teaches classroom management and other foundational elementary education courses and supervises student teachers. Her scholarship focuses on affect in classroom life, the relationship between emotion and behavior in childhood, and on how some psychoanalytic theory can help us understand children's and teachers' experiences in school. She is interested in exploring ways to move education away from narrow visions of learning. Her writing has critiqued codified social and emotional learning, and in general, she is an advocate both for public education and for a vision of children as whole and complex beings. Clio is the author of *Critiquing Social and Emotional Learning: Psychodynamic and Cultural Perspectives*, published in 2019 by Lexington Books and *Consent in the Childhood Classroom* (2022).

Michael Trout, M.A., has worked in the mental health field since 1968 and in private practice since 1979. Since 1986, he has directed the Infant-Parent Institute, which engages in research, clinical practice, and clinical training related to problems of attachment. Michael was the founding president of both the Michigan and International Associations for Infant Mental Health. He did his specialized training in infant psychiatry at the Child Development Project, University of Michigan Department of Psychiatry, under Professor Selma Fraiberg. He is the co-author (with foster/adoptive mother Lori Thomas) of *The Jonathon Letters*; the author of *Baby Verses: The Narrative Poetry of Infants and Toddlers*; the producer of two meditation CDs, including *See Me as a Person: Meditations for Sustaining Relationship-Based Care* and *The Hope-Filled Parent: Meditations for Parents of Children Who Have Been Harmed*; and co-author (with Mary Koloroutis) of the 2012 textbook for healthcare providers, *See Me as a Person*. His final book *This Hallowed Ground: Four Decades in Infant Mental Health* was published by Cambridge Scholars in 2021.